"Teachers are always looking for a fresh way to introduce beginners to a complex field. With this book, Judith Caron offers an introductory text on ethics that merits the consideration of teachers and undergraduate students in ethics. In readable prose, and with discussion questions at the end of the chapters and case studies integrated in the chapters, she provides an attractive educational resource. The bibliographical references in the footnotes make for a brief 'Who's Who' in contemporary ethics.

"Caron's work shows that good ethics must be interdisciplinary. Her approach to ethics is sensitive not only to the developments of biblical studies and theology, but it also draws on advances in the behavioral and social sciences and feminist ethics to give a holistic, relational, and person-centered character to moral analysis and decision making. Anyone who wants to be a more informed, critical discerner of the complexity of moral decision making will benefit from this book."

Richard M. Gula, S.S.
St. Patrick's Seminary
Menlo Park, California

"Today we hear a lot about replacing an ethics of rules, principles, or abstract philosophical analysis with an ethics of relationships and character-building. Caron draws on the insights of psychology and pastoral counseling to show how identity and moral character are formed, thus giving these new proposals concrete substance and nuance. Her case studies are realistic and provocative, challenging us to think through the ways moral responsibilities can be fulfilled consistently. This book would be an excellent discussion starter for classroom or study-group use."

Lisa Sowle Cahill
Professor of Christian Ethics
Boston College

"Judith Caron offers the student of ethics a wide range of materials to chew on, inviting her reader to consider how moral development theory, psychology, ethical theory, and sociology mutually inform the moral agent. Particularly delightful are her engaging case studies. Working from her own Christian tradition, but sensitive to other traditions as well, she offers an illuminating discussion of the nature and limits of freedom in the 21st century as she challenges each reader to become a morally mature decision maker. Teachers and students will appreciate the questions for reflection at the end of each chapter, as well as the dialectic between practical and theoretical work."

Karen Lebacqz, Ph.D.
Professor of Social Ethics
McGill University, Montreal

CHRISTIAN ETHICS

Shaping Values, Vision, Decisions

JUDITH CARON

TWENTY-THIRD PUBLICATIONS
Mystic, CT 06355

Acknowledgments

Besides the family and friends who encouraged me in this endeavor, I wish to specially acknowledge a debt of appreciation to the following, without whom the fabric of my life and this text would be less rich: to Dr. Kathleen Oliver, Tom Artz, and Dan Connors for their continued personal support and editorial wisdom; to the administration, faculty, and students, especially the Classes of '97 and '98, St. Bonaventure High School, Ventura, California, for their interest, encouragement, and the opportunity to share experiences about life and ethics in and outside the classroom; to the 1994-95 Period 1 prep group whose camaraderie made it possible to continue during long days and dry writing spells; to the faculty and peers at the Graduate Theological Union, Berkeley, California, whose academic and research challenges inspired many of the personal and experiential goals of this text; and to the faculty and peers in the doctoral studies program at the Graduate Theological Foundation, Donaldson, Indiana, whose personal and academic support enabled me to broaden my understanding of the continued impact that ethics has upon my educational and ministerial professions.

Twenty-Third Publications
185 Willow Street
P.O. Box 180
Mystic, CT 06355
(203) 536-2611
800-321-0411

ISBN 0-89622-658-1
Library of Congress Catalog Card Number 95-60625
Printed in the U.S.A.

CONTENTS

INTRODUCTION

I. Acquiring an Ethical Vision

Many years ago while I was pursuing graduate studies in theology, my route to the university library took me through the building that housed the art studios. Having failed art throughout elementary and secondary school, I held in awe anyone who could use a maze of paints and colors to transform a piece of canvas into some semblance of beauty. As I hurried through the warm building on cold winter mornings, I glanced into studios where the student artists worked silently on their canvases. Sometimes I paused a few seconds at a doorway to admire a particularly striking canvas, and then hurried on as if afraid to disturb a future Rembrandt of the world.

As the weeks passed, one young painter caught my attention. Each morning as I paused to look into her studio to see what new wonders she had wrought, I found her always gazing out the studio's large glass windows. Her body stood motionless while her eyes intently scrutinized the distant horizon. Yet in the evenings as I came back on my way home, there she stood before her canvas, her body and fingers alive and creating works of beauty whose simple vibrancy tore a gasp of wonder and admiration from me. After the third such incident, Brianna turned from her canvas and invited me in to inspect her work more closely. Thus began a lifelong friendship.

Over the next months, I often stopped at Brianna's studio. Over many cups of coffee, I shared with Brianna the complexities of moral theology while she shared with me the nuances of her work. Her sharings instilled in me a growing appreciation for oils and acrylics and varied art forms. For the first time in my life art seemed fun, and eventually I began to dream of trying my hand at painting. Of course, I knew that nothing I might paint would ever compare to Brianna's work, but I felt compelled to give painting a try. Gradually overcoming my fears of embarrassment and rejection, I asked Brianna for help in painting my favorite refuge, the duck pond at the far end of campus. Brianna enthusiastically gave me one of her blank canvases, a set of brushes, acrylic paints, and some simple instructions on how to mix the paints. Beyond that she offered no more help and merely encouraged me to "do my thing."

Surrounded by a forest of trees that were then in their first spring bloom, the duck pond was more than a habitat for a variety of ducks. It was actually a miniature lake that served as the focal point for interspersed nature trails and winding bike paths. Wildflowers grew everywhere, making the scene a riot of color, an artist's dream landscape. After watching Brianna, I felt that it would not be too hard to get all this down on canvas.

Seven days and many frustrating hours later, I threw down my brushes in disgust, packed up my things, and stormed into Brianna's studio to vent my feelings. She listened in silence to my ranting of frustration, to my descriptions of how I followed her method of sketching out a preliminary scene, mixing my paints, and working on one section of the canvas at a time. Then, while I waited in embarrassed silence, she examined my canvas. Her only comment was a gentle request for me to meet her at the duck pond at mid-morning the next day.

As I approached the duck pond I saw Brianna in her characteristic pose of utter stillness, her eyes scrutinizing every detail of the scene before her. Finally, she turned to me and quietly said, "The problem is that you have lost a sense of the larger vista for that individual stand of trees, the larger picture for the smaller scene that captured your interest. In so doing, you have no sense of the larger vision of the grandeur before you, of the larger picture that you need to guide the smaller scene you are trying to depict."

Uncomprehendingly, I stared at her and at my canvas, which she had set up before her. All I knew was that something was wrong—my green blobs of paint did not resemble the forest before me, and so far her answer had failed to enlighten me.

Grabbing my arm, Brianna dragged me back about one hundred yards to the small rise above the duck pond. Sweeping her hand across the scene before us she asked me to *really* look at the trees. "Your canvas conveys only one shade of green for a whole panoply of multicolored shades of green. Look closely at the treetops and how each tree is a different shade. No two trees are the same color green. Look at the pond. Your pond is one shade of deep blue. But if you look closely, you can see that along the edge it is a light blue green that changes as the currents of the lake and movements of the ducks cause little eddies of blue, green, and white." And so it continued for twenty minutes, as an entirely different scene came to life through her more discerning eyes.

What had been monochromatic blobs and a narrow view of just the duck pond suddenly burst into a panoramic vision of colors and shades that Nature had cleverly combined.

That hour with Brianna changed my life in many ways. I did finish my painting and felt for once the thrill that Brianna must have felt many times in capturing some small part of the breadth and depth of creation's beauty. Although I no longer paint, I always continue to look for the rich and varied hues and shades of nature in the world around me. In so doing, I have been impressed by the larger strokes and more breathtaking beauty of our environment. Now, as I work in the area of ethics in general and biomedical ethics in particular, Brianna's words remain with me. Her admonition to keep the particular scene always within the context of the larger picture or greater vision, and to note carefully its various shades and hues, are crucial insights not only in painting but in ethical formation and decision making as well.

The Broader Canvas of Ethics

Traditionally, the field of ethics in general, and morality textbooks in particular, have tended to focus more narrowly on one or both of two important and interrelated ethical questions. First: "What is the morally correct choice, the right decision that one must make in a concrete situation?" The emphasis here is on the motives of the actor and the rightness of an act in a particular situation, on a consideration of the "oughts and shoulds," the rules and doctrines of civil society and religious tradition. Second: "What kind of person do I become if I perform this action? What kind of character do I display by the choices I make?" Here the emphasis is on either the degree of inherent goodness of an act, or the consequences of the act and their effects upon individuals and society.

There is, however, a third important and related question that seems to be often forgotten but nevertheless impacts the broader canvas of our ethical lives: "What kind of character do I bring to each situation that requires a choice or decision?" To answer this question we need more than an objective understanding of a person's motives or decision-making processes. This question can be broken into two parts. Part one asks: What is the context and my unique understanding of the nuances and changes possible in every situation within which I am called to make a decision? Part two asks: How do I understand and handle the ongoing interrelationship of "being transformer and being transformed"—of being called to interact with and to transform a world that has already exerted and continues to exert upon me a variety of complex social, environmental, personal, physical, mental, spiritual, emotional, and intellectual forces?

In other words, I need to be aware that I may be the author of each *Summary* ethical decision I make, but each of these decisions in turn impacts and transforms me, others, and the world.

Therefore, the quality of one's ethical decisions is dependent not only upon an understanding of motives and objective rules, but also upon an understanding of oneself and of one's gifts and limitations in each situation. This requires a knowledge of the interplay of human psychology, faith, and ethics within one's life.

 However, knowledge of and response to these three important questions form only the smaller picture. In any given ethical dilemma the smaller picture enables a person to arrive at a possibly correct moral decision. What is missing, and what is needed, is the awareness of the larger social moral vision or attitude that should be evolving within oneself and should be brought to bear on personal and social situations. The canvas of moral dilemmas and choices is broader than individual acts, motives, consequences, and rules.

At the level of this larger, broader moral vision, a person is challenged, individually and socially, to understand and demonstrate the broader moral vision of life that permeates each ethical act. For some *Norm* persons, their broader vision of the good has been influenced by a Judeo-Christian vision of being born in the image and likeness of the creator. For Muslims, the good life is envisioned by the Qur'an's dual beliefs in the unity of God and righteous living. For the Buddhist, good comes from wisdom achieved through ascendancy in right thinking and acting. For still others, the vision is more eclectic and less traditional. Whatever the source of this broader vision, it serves to provide the person and also the entire society with an ethical sense or vision of what is right and good.

II. Understanding the Human and Ethical Context

Certain factors influence each person's development. Every person is born into a particular time, geographical place, race, and culture. Each person is an evolving entity shaped by relationships and a complex process of physical, psychosocial, moral, and faith stages of growth and development that evolve over an entire lifespan. A variety of needs, concerns, and goals characterize the human lifespan, and these are constantly changing according to where the person is in life.

Persons are also relational beings. Who we become is influenced a great deal by, and dependent upon, the myriad relationships that surround us from before birth until death. It is within this relational context that humankind learns to consider more than the individual self; we are also challenged continually to explore and decide exactly how we should act as individuals and as a community if we are to achieve our fullest potential as human beings.

As individuals and as members of a community, human beings experience life as a constant process of change, growth, and development on many levels. This process is continually shaping and being shaped by human decisions regarding goals that will achieve the greatest amount of human fulfillment, happiness, or good. Throughout the history of civilization, individuals and communities have articulated and taught an ethical code as part of their socialization process. Ethics is understood as the historically and culturally bound code of right or good behavior believed best to achieve what individuals or a society have defined as bringing about the greatest human good, happiness, or fulfillment. Each person is taught and challenged to be ethical, that is, to incorporate into personal and communal decisions the code of right behavior that has been articulated by society as bringing about the greatest human potential or good.

Implied in this call to be ethical is an understanding of ethics as both attitude and action. An ethical attitude is a way of being in the world, an inner disposition toward seeking the esteemed values or virtues needed to achieve the desired highest human fulfillment or good. Ethical action is a way of behaving in the world that enables persons to procure the esteemed values and virtues necessary to secure the highest good or fulfillment.

III. Distinguishing Between Ethics and Morality

"Ethics" refers to the broader philosophical and academic study of the good, of right situations, motives, and actions upon which to base good and appropriate human decisions. "Morality," while often informed by philosophy and ethics, refers to what is actually lived as shaped and influenced by a particular religious tradition, creed, or theological background. Although the human challenge is always to be ethical, individual and communal decisions are often (though not always) colored by a religiously or theologically based system of morality. The terms "ethics" and "morality" are used interchangeably in this text. I do not assume, however, that a person's attitudes and actions are automatically influenced by a particular religious or theological tradition.

The ethical and moral systems that influence human relations tend to differ according to historical times, cultures, and religious traditions. Therefore, it is important to remember that what is morally or ethically appropriate—or morally or ethically inappropriate—in one historical period or for one culture or community, may differ in another historical time or culture or community. The differences occur because of the ever-evolving understanding of human beings and what is most appropriate for the fulfillment of human destiny. Many times these time- and culture-bound understandings are guided by revered core values and principles, but they are always expressed in a particular way by each particular culture, religious tradition, and society. For example, the Netherlands legally and ethically permits physician-assisted deaths under certain specified conditions. In other countries, however, this action is viewed as morally wrong and is considered theologically to be a strong impediment to human good and fulfillment.

In summary, each person exists within an ever-changing and evolving moral context. Within that context, each person is continually challenged to live morally and to make sound moral decisions. Simultaneously, each person lives in an ever-changing social context that inculcates the person with a broader ethical vision. This broader ethical vision summons the person to make choices and decisions that are based on individual moral codes of right and wrong, but that also reflect a wider ethical vision. As times change, human beings will need to reevaluate and to articulate anew the broader ethical vision that underlies their individual ethical or moral codes. The response to this challenge will call for personal and social transformations that, in the words of Robert Bellah,

> ...have to happen at a number of levels...Personal transformation among large numbers is essential, and it must not only be a transformation of consciousness but must also involve individual action. But individuals need the nurture of groups that carry a moral tradition reinforcing their own aspirations (*Habits of the Heart*, 286).[1]

IV. Goals and Format of the Text

This text differs from others in that its primary focus is on the relational context of ethics rather than on philosophical theory or theological doctrine. Because of this, I intend to engage and challenge the reader in practical ways to consider and broaden his or her own ethical vision, which is fundamentally relational with self, all of creation, and God or some higher power or good. In order to do this, I will interweave psychological, moral, and spiritual threads throughout each chapter. Although the basic approach will be Judeo-Christian, I will incorporate other Western and Eastern traditions so as to encourage the reader to compare and contrast his or her own traditions with those of others.

There are two goals within this relational context. *The first goal is to help the reader become more aware of the complex and interrelated processes involved in the particular psychosocial, moral, and spiritual development of the self as a decision maker.*

To this end, Chapter I considers the emerging psychosocial and moral individual and the factors influencing an individual's development in these areas.

Chapter II explores two areas: what it means to be a social being whose fullest development occurs only in community, and how human relationality is expressed through the four interrelated dimensions of covenant, the search for meaning, values, and principles. To illustrate the first dimension, a covenant vision of relationality is considered.

Chapter III examines the remaining three dimensions of human relationality: the search for meaning, values, and principles.

Using the broader insights of the individual as an ethical being (as discussed in Chapters I through III), Chapters IV and V examine the particular components of an ethical decision: the development of a sound conscience, the types and acquisition of ethical knowledge, and the various influences affecting a particular decision. Chapter V also details an Ethical Guidewheel, one practical method for decision making.

The second goal of this text is to help the reader to become aware of and to examine a broader ethical vision of the good, and to consider the ways in which this vision can be transformed and deepened on both individual and societal levels. To this end, Chapter VI examines the issue of human sexuality while Chapter VII focuses on other ethical issues. Using the concepts and method introduced in the first five chapters, Chapters VI and VII also model the ways in which a relational vision of ethics involves both an awareness of the person's own individual ethical code and a broader ethical vision that moves the person to decision making based on the context, on an awareness of self as an emerging multidimensional unity, and on the lived experiences and teachings of society and varied religious traditions.

The format of each chapter addresses the two above stated goals by placing them in a relational context. Each chapter begins with an exploration of general psychosocial concepts as they affect personal and relational development. For example, we will consider ideas about personality development, sound conscience formation, and the social, gender, and recreational influences on moral and personality development. We will also look at the effects these ideas have on the dual development of relationships and on an ethical vision. Next follows an exploration of specific ethical topics in terms of actions and their potential consequences. Each chapter contains a variety of learning resources, including discussion questions, case studies, and limited suggestions for additional research projects/activities.

Each chapter features a particular type of ethics—e.g., environmental, business, biomedical, sexual—and a contemporary ethical dilemma in that field. While highlighting the chapter's contents, the ethical dilemma challenges the reader to integrate the chapter's information and the concepts of the previous chapters in order to arrive at a personal or class response to the dilemma.

It is my hope that as you work through this text you will develop a better understanding of the complex, multidimensional factors that affect the actions and decisions of individuals and of society as a whole. I also hope that the information and resources provided by the text will enable you to take an active part in contributing to the fashioning of a broader ethical vision within whatever community or nation you live.

Chapter I

The Emerging Psychosocial and Ethical Individual

Overview

I. The Emerging Psychosocial Individual
A. The Development of Self-Concept: Erik Erikson
B. The Origins of Self-Concept
C. The Unfolding of the Unique Personality
D. Attitudes and Lifestyles

II. The Development of the Ethical Self
A. Values
B. Ethics
C. Religion
D. The Centrality of Relationships
E. Development of Moral Character: Kohlberg's Theory
F. Other Views About Moral Development

III. Feature: Understanding Other Ethical Codes
Questions for Research, Reflection, and Discussion

IV. Case Study
"A Universal Religion's Hope in America"

Case Study Discussion Questions

Overview

Traditional approaches to ethics and morality are usually concerned with the complex interrelation among motives, actions, and consequences, and the ways this interrelation affects moral decision making. In contrast, a relational ethical approach begins with the awareness that, if life is a process of change and decision making, then, as a decision maker, each person must have a sound understanding of the "me" that is making the decisions. This understanding requires an understanding of self in what Paul Tillich calls a "multidimensional unity"[1] that is composed of biological, chemical, physical, spiritual, emotional, intellectual, sexual, psychological, and moral dimensions. Central to this multidimensional unity is an emerging sense of self as an individual—an individual continually affected by a complex interplay of personal, psychosocial, and spiritual forces. These forces affect both individual and societal ethical decision making. This chapter will focus on two dimensions of the emerging individual: psychosocial development and moral development.

I. The Emerging Psychosocial Individual

Personality is the exterior self that each individual presents to the world. Wrapped within this exterior self are dynamic processes of psychosocial development: self-concept, self-esteem, perceptual field, attitudes, values, morality, religion, and life philosophies. All of these in turn are constantly being bombarded with, and changed by, a variety of interrelated personal, social, environmental, and cultural factors. Part of the human vocation is to strive toward the good and to achieve a certain ethical potential for ourselves and our world; such a response cannot be given without first understanding the nature and role of personality.

A. The Development of Self-Concept: Erik Erikson

As a newborn moves from infancy to childhood, one of the most striking developments to watch is the emergence of a sense of self. The view of self as an individual "I," how the child feels and thinks about itself, is called "self-concept." "Self-esteem" is the sense of worth, value, and love that the individual has about the self. The more positive the self-concept and the greater the self-esteem, the more healthy the child's growth and development.

Erik Erikson's classic theory of psychosocial development[2] offers insights into the shaping of a positive versus negative self-concept. Erikson delineates eight sequential stages of human development, each characterized by a particular pattern of positive or negative psychosocial traits:

Stage One   (approximately birth to one and a half years), trust versus mistrust;

Stage Two   (approximately one and a half to three years), autonomy versus shame, doubt;

Stage Three (approximately three to six years), initiative versus guilt;

Stage Four (approximately six to eleven years), industry versus inferiority;

Stage Five (adolescence), identity versus role confusion;

Stage Six   (young adulthood), intimacy versus isolation;

Stage Seven (adulthood), generativity versus stagnation;

Stage Eight (old age), ego integrity versus despair.

Erikson believes that if the child experiences the fulfillment of the basic needs necessary for healthy growth and development in each particular stage, then he or she develops the positive traits associated with that particular developmental stage. If the child is deprived of this fulfillment, however, then negative traits develop. For example, at the first stage, the young child's early positive experiences with parental and other significant figures generally lead to a trustful attitude. If, on the other hand, the child's experiences with parents and other adults are not so positive, then he or she will be more likely to develop a basically mistrustful attitude.

As Erikson sees it, this first stage, involving trust versus mistrust, has an enormous influence on the child's future. For example, as the child moves to Stage Two (autonomy versus shame, doubt), its ability to begin making a choice for self (autonomy), or its fixation with traits of shame and doubt, will be influenced greatly by how trustful or mistrustful the child feels toward the world. As Salvatore R. Maddi points out in *Personality Theories*,[3] "for Erikson, each new stage inherits the legacy of past stages. Weak points in character contributed by earlier fixations will influence—indeed jeopardize—successful development in the current stage" (297).

One way to observe Erikson's view of self-concept development is indirectly, through the child's actions in play or its behaviors toward self and others. A child who tends to be outgoing and happy probably has had a strong experience of itself as esteemed, loved, trusted, and creative. Such a case is Jacqueline:

> Forgotten by her mother, Jacqueline stood before the mirror in the Ladies' Wear Department, all thirty-five inches of her drawn to rapt attention as she gazed excitedly into the mirror. Around her neck was a long neon pink feathered boa, and long black silk gloves covered her hands and arms right up to her armpits. At her feet lay a stack of women's formal hats. As Jacqueline chose one large green hat and placed it wondrously on her head, she could be heard murmuring at the garish vision in the mirror: "Mirra, mirra on da wall, who's da fairest one of all?" And in her three-year-old, high-piped child's voice came the delighted response: "ME!"

Jacqueline's action—unabashedly trying on hats in the midst of an adult environment—reveals a developing healthy self-concept. Her parents, along with other influences in her life, have helped her to develop the basic psychosocial traits of trust and autonomy; Erikson's Third Stage positive trait of initiative and his Fourth Stage trait of industry are also clearly evident in her behavior.

In contrast to Jacqueline's story is that of Timmy and his mother:

> She was expensively dressed in a white two-piece suit with matching red accessories. The hurried staccato of her high heels and the frown of displeasure on her face indicated to a casual observer that she was either in a hurry or not happy to be there. As

she moved down the school hallway, a little boy burst out of the kindergarten classroom, his shirt spattered with paints and his hand clutching a still wet sheet of paper. Spying his mother, he rushed up to her and grabbed her about the knees while crying out with pride, "Mommy, look what I did!" She angrily pushed the little boy back from her now paint-smudged skirt. "Now look what you have done to my white skirt!" she said. "And that has to be the ugliest thing I have ever seen. You didn't even keep in the lines!" Eyes downcast, the little boy dropped the painting, purposefully stomped on it, and slowly followed his irate mother out to the car.

Over the next three months, Timmy became sullen and combative; he also refused to participate in creative art activities or, if he did, would only color by keeping within well-defined shapes.

In contrast to Jacqueline, Timmy's self-concept has received a severe blow. His mother's criticism and rejection of his art work, combined with other negative experiences, have provided an environment not conducive to trust, autonomy, and initiative. If viewed through Erikson's psychosocial developmental lens, Timmy's early life experiences of mistrust (Stage One), shame and doubt (Stage Two), and guilt and failure (Stage Three) have now combined with a sense of inadequacy and inferiority (Stage Four) that is masked by his overt negative behaviors of sullenness, combativeness, and lack of cooperation. Within a short amount of time, Timmy has become a withdrawn, fearful child who now remains locked into a set, ritualistic style of play. Creativity and spontaneity have been crushed by experiences that represent mistrust and non-support in Timmy's life.

Failure and frustration are a necessary part of growth. Jacqueline's generally positive psychosocial environment will enable her to learn from her moments of pain, failure, and frustration. Timmy, in contrast, has experienced a home environment that seems to have left him ill-equipped to handle difficult experiences of pain, frustration, and rejection. As Maddi points out,

If the child's parents have loved and helped him or her enough, however, the child will learn by failure...The basis for adult initiative and responsibility will have been achieved. But if the fail-

ure is exaggerated by unnecessary punitiveness, the child will experience considerable resignation and guilt, experiences that will
form the basis in later life for acquiescence, feelings of un-
worthiness, and even irresponsibility (296).

B. *The Origins of Self-Concept*

The psychosocial environment of the person provides the initial context for the development of self-concept. The family is the first significant influence. The age of the parents when the child is born, the
child's place within the family (first-born, second-born, etc.), the socioeconomic status of the family—these and more all contribute to the
family's influence upon a child's developing self-concept and self-
esteem. Subtle influences, like how welcome the child feels within the
family, ethnic and cultural background, and the parent's views of education and recreation, also affect the budding self-concept. Again, had
Jacqueline, the child in the first example above, been constrained always to act in a socially correct way or constantly admonished with
"little girls do not act this way in public," or, as happened to Timmy,
been publicly embarrassed with comments like "how terrible that
looks," she would never have been able to enact so unselfconsciously in
public what she has undoubtedly done many times in private—dress
up in her vision of "being grown up like mommy"—nor would she
have been able to take such delight in what she considered a beautiful
costume, something that the adult world would never have supported.

Significant adults, sibling and peer relationships, and school play experiences also help shape the individual's self-concept. Messages received during these experiences remain long after time and further
experiences have dimmed the details. "Smart," "genius," "cute," "creative," "dumb," "fat," "lazy," and "uncooperative" are words that the
child may have heard and unconsciously, uncritically applied to self
and others. Those for whom the words have shaped a negative self-
concept spend much of their future lives overcoming this early negative shaping.

Other factors that influence self-concept are the messages the child
receives about its name, body image, talents, and abilities. From an early age, a child learns whether his or her name is special or the result of
indifference or token adherence to the family custom of naming the

first child after a distant or revered relative. Body image, how the person perceives his or her body, is often measured by the standards found in television and magazine advertisements. Talents and abilities esteemed by society are also filtered through the lens of what our culture considers age-appropriate and gender-appropriate abilities. For instance, thirty years ago female children were not allowed in traditionally male sports like Little League baseball. Today, mixed gender soccer and T-ball teams are considered the norm.

It is a myth that people see things "purely objectively." What people see and experience has been and is constantly being colored by feelings, emotions, learned responses, prejudices, fears, and wishful thinking—all of which go into forming the "perceptual field," which is the lens through which an individual sees and reacts to the world, the unique way each individual has of looking at life. The perceptual field is another dimension of self-concept. Therefore, the understanding of self or another cannot be fully grasped until one is able to understand the particular perceptual field involved.

C. The Unfolding of the Unique Personality

Taken together, the dimensions of self-concept and the factors that influence its development come together and are usually referred to as one's personality. "Personality" is that dynamic collection of behavioral, temperamental, emotional, and mental traits that characterize every individual in a unique way. Personality is also affected by heredity, environment, and their interplay. Science still debates the degree to which heredity and environment each contribute to the overall development of the person. It is known that one inherits certain physical traits, like gender, height, and a certain amount of native intellectual ability. It is also known that environment exerts its own type of influence through both physical factors (e.g., the amount and types of foods eaten) and intellectual factors (e.g., parental and social attitudes about the types of education a "well rounded or successful" person should obtain). As the examples of Jacqueline and Timmy illustrate, and as Erikson's theory points out, environment also influences personality through the psychosocial climate that surrounds the developing person.

Personality traits characterizing each individual are sometimes learned through direct teaching of what the family or school considers

the desired or admired traits. Other traits are imitated or copied from
the people that a child identifies with and wants to be like, or from
what society considers acceptable and unacceptable. One only has to
look at one night of prime-time television shows and advertisements to
discern the traits conveyed as most admired by current society.

Theories of how personality is developed differ according to a variety of theoretical schools. For example, Sigmund Freud[4] belongs to
what has been characterized by Maddi (184-186) as the Conflict Model,
which sees personality emerging as the result of dealing with the intrapsychic forces within a person. Freud theorized that the healthy personality emerges as the individual learns to deal with the conflicts
among the intrapsychic forces of ego, id, and superego. In contrast, the
Fulfillment Model (Maddi 187-189), as exemplified by Abraham
Maslow,[5] emphasizes the development of personality through the fulfillment of inherent capabilities. According to Maslow, these inherent
capabilities cannot be actualized until there is first a satisfaction of
physical and psychological needs (25-26). Once these needs are met, the
unique personality moves toward self-actualization, which is its
unique, healthy fulfillment (97).

D. Attitudes and Lifestyles

Attitudes are also part of personality. "Attitude" can be characterized as the person's enduring emotional responses to perceptions and
beliefs about life in general and relationships in particular. As Milton
Rokeach explains in *Beliefs, Attitudes and Values*,[6] an attitude is an organization of beliefs, which are "predispositions to action" (113). As
Rokeach's studies have indicated (114-116), every attitude is composed
of three very closely interrelated components: knowledge (beliefs),
emotions, and behaviors.

As persons mature and proceed through various developmental
stages, they develop attitudes toward life, learning, relationships, ca-
reers, conflict, religion, sexuality, family, politics, and death. Life philosophies are the incorporation of these attitudes into ways of living
that reflect attitudes toward self, others, and the world. In *Moral
Realism and the Foundation of Ethics*, David Brink[7] discusses some of the
more classic life philosophies. The conventionalist, for example, accepts
authority, values good manners, does not "rock the boat," and tends to

do whatever is socially appropriate. The idealist is keenly sensitive to injustice, wants to change society, and so becomes very active in local and national movements. The hedonist, isolated from self and others by the single-minded quest for pleasure, lives only for the present and makes the quest for pleasure and the avoidance of pain the whole motto in life. The pragmatist sees practicality as the primary purpose of all things. The nihilist sees life, people, and existence as having no meaning. Although one lifestyle is dominant at any one time, traces of the other life philosophies can be found within each person.

When a person is faced with the need for attitudinal change, it is important to clarify which component of the attitude—knowledge, emotions, or behaviors—is problematic. Adults are often heard saying to a recalcitrant adolescent, "I don't like your attitude! Change it!" Often the adolescent's response is either a blank stare or a negative, defensive retort. The conflict is probably due to a lack of understanding about the three components of attitudes. The adult and adolescent, or any two people for that matter, need to discuss and negotiate what specific change(s) in the beliefs, emotions, and behaviors would be acceptable before the process of attitudinal change can begin.

II. The Development of the Ethical Self

Accompanying psychosocial development is the interrelated process of ethical or moral development. This process is often influenced by the same personal and societal relationships that affect personality development. It is through these relationships that a person first learns about values, ethics, and religion—three major influences in ethical living and decision making.

Family and school inculcate in a child a system of values, ethics, and religion that usually is blindly accepted. As a person moves into adolescence, one's images of God, spiritual and devotional practices, core doctrinal beliefs, moral values, and the degree of denominational participation all begin to change. Adolescence often marks a point at which many persons begin a lifelong process of reevaluating these dimensions so as to appropriate for themselves a religious tradition and a system of values and ethics.

A. Values

Values are those things that the culture considers as good and essential for ethical living. As such, values form the basic social and moral foundations of society. Values are learned and cultivated through much the same experiences and influences that affect the child's development of self-concept. However, there are two aspects to values: an internal attitude of being in the world, and an external disposition toward a certain way of right or "good" acting. As William Frankena[8] emphasizes in "Moral Value and Responsibility," values are personality or character traits that dispose people "to do certain kinds of actions in certain kinds of situations, not just to think or feel in certain ways" (49). A life based on values must exemplify more than right or good action; it must also involve an internal integration within the person so that a value awareness perspective permeates the way people view life.

Throughout history, various values, sometimes referred to as virtues, have been promoted as primary or cardinal by a culture. Frankena explains that cardinal virtues are those "which all other moral virtues can be derived from or shown to be forms of" (50). The Greeks, for example, esteemed wisdom, courage, justice, and temperance (moderation or self-control). Faith, hope, love, prudence (foresight to see difficulties and consequences of one's actions), fortitude (courage), temperance, and justice (fair dealings) are the primary virtues traditionally taught by Christianity. Other virtues, such as equality, moral integrity (commitment to take a stand for dignity, justice and equality of humanity), honesty, and stewardship (right management of resources of creation) have also emerged as important values in contemporary Western ethical living. If taken together and taken seriously, values affirm not only a particular individual or society's vision of the good, but also a way of being in the world that actively moves individuals and societies toward developing an inner and external awareness of a larger world ethical vision of life.

B. Ethics

Ethics is the code of behavior that is considered acceptable by a society and culture. An ethical code is built first upon esteemed values, which are then translated into specific rules and principles. Like values, ethics is a two-sided phenomenon. On the one hand, ethics contains a culture's view of the "ideal" good, of what a person "ought or should do" to be good. On the other hand, the ideal is taken one step further and is embedded in very specific principles that translate the ideals into obligations and expectations to be carried out by the members of the society. Ethics expresses a certain "way of being" and "way of doing" that a particular culture or society esteems at a specific time in history. Like all other time-bound things, what a society values and encodes in an ethical system is continually affected by human growth and development and by particular, as well as larger, visions of ethical living.

C. Religion

"Religion" refers to the moral and spiritual traditions to which a community adheres because they provide for this community the best answers to life's ultimate questions: Who or what is a higher power or good? What is the meaning of life? What is death? Is there an afterlife? Traditionally for Western cultures, "religion" has been expressed in the context of Judaism and Christianity.

Recent studies in the field of sociology of religion by Meredith McGuire, Robert Wuthnow, and Wade Roof and William McKinney[9] have noted that, since World War II, religion as a social phenomenon has been in a state of constant flux. There have been major changes in the meaning and role of religion, religious life, and religious movements in the United States as well as in other Western countries. Their research has indicated that complex upheavals are underway in the traditional ways of defining religion and of viewing such aspects of religion as belief, ritual, community, and denominational membership. For example, there now seems to be an increasing trend for people to move in and out of traditional religious denominations and belief systems, and to be willing to experiment with membership in different types of religious communities.

In addition, researchers like Bryan Wilson, and Rodney Stark and William Bainbridge[10] have noted the increasing influence of Eastern philosophies and religions in the Western world. They have also documented the growth of a variety of sects and cults and observed how these groups are affecting mainline denominations. For example, within the last five years, there has been a marked increase in Muslim membership among black Americans in the United States. Such growth comes amid increasing controversy about the exact character of Islam's mission in the United States; media portrayals of Muslim terrorists bombing cultural centers conflict with the peace-loving and service-oriented lifestyles of Muslim citizens in many urban areas.

The result of these changes has been a transformation in the traditional views of religion in general and ethical systems in particular. The implications of all this must be taken into account when fashioning a particular and a larger ethical vision of life.

D. The Centrality of Relationships

Another major contributor to the development of the ethical self is relationships. Values, ethics, and religion have little meaning outside a relational context. In *The Eternal Message of Muhammad*,[11] Abd al-Rahman Azzam quotes the second major tenet of the Qur'an:

> And the believers, men and women, are protecting friends one of another; they enjoin the right and forbid the wrong. And there may spring from you a nation who invite to goodness, and enjoin right conduct and forbid indecency. Such are they who are successful (Qur'an 9:71; 3:104).

Likewise, the Judeo-Christian Scriptures express an idea similar to that in the Qur 'an. From that first primeval demand of "Where is your brother Abel?" (Genesis 4:9), through the Jewish reminder that "each one helps the other" (Isaiah 41:6), and finally to the Christian challenge that "in one Spirit we are all baptized into one body...and we are all made to drink of one Spirit" (1 Corinthians 12:13), the Judeo-Christian Scriptures continually echo the interdependence of relationality, ethics, and morality.

E. Development of Moral Character: Kohlberg's Theory

Humans are not born with an individual moral code or broad ethical vision. Both the varied content and methods of acquisition of ethical knowledge are learned. Over the past thirty years, there have been numerous studies of ethical and moral development. Lawrence

Kohlberg[12] and his classic study of cognitive moral development pioneered the way.

Kohlberg's work tends to focus on the concept that moral judgment is determined by the quality of reasoning about moral dilemmas. This moral reasoning begins early in life and proceeds through six sequential stages. Movement to the next step does not occur until the previous steps have been mastered. Although all six steps are possible to attain, Kohlberg maintains that most people never reach Stages Five and Six.

In Kohlberg's Stages One and Two, approximately ages four to ten, children make moral decisions based on their own needs and wants. In Stage One the desire to gain rewards and avoid punishments forms the primary basis of the child's decisions. Stage Two's primary moral impetus is the pleasing of oneself, even at the expense of pain to another.

Stages Three and Four, approximately ages ten to thirteen, find moral value in maintaining what is traditionally considered as appropriate, and in pleasing others. The person at Stage Three seeks mainly to be known as "a good girl/boy" and will do that which pleases others or gains their approval. Stage Four finds the same moral value being achieved by obedience to laws and rules through the respect for authority and the prevailing social order.

Stages Five and Six, ranging from adolescence to adulthood, require a moral maturity that enables the person to value more abstract motives. In Stage Five the standards and ideals of a society are seen as socially and morally binding. At this level one is motivated by the good of society. Taking part in civil rights movements or supporting causes for the homeless might be logical expressions of a person at this level of moral maturity. In Stage Six the following of one's conscience, which has been oriented to universally agreed upon ethical principles, becomes the guiding criterion for moral conduct. Therefore, a willingness to take a stand based on individual conscience or a moral principle (such as justice or equality) takes precedence, even though such a stand can pit one against family, friends, and society. Some conscientious objectors who protested or fled to Canada during the Vietnam War era are examples of people at this stage.

F. Other Views About Moral Development

Using Kohlberg's work as a springboard, the works of Carol Gilligan and others[13] have implemented a variety of related research areas to broaden our understanding of the nature, role, and function of such formative influences as gender and play orientation upon a person's ethical or moral development.

Because Kohlberg's research involved only boys, his results failed to consider what subsequent studies have brought to light about the differences in the ways girls and boys may acquire ethical knowledge or how they make moral judgments (Gilligan 18). Gilligan's work presents a contemporary theory of gender development that takes into account some real differences between genders. Her work indicates, for example, that girls tend to value Kohlberg's Stage Three (pleasing others). This preference suggests that girls have a primary focus on establishing and nurturing relationships. Boys, on the other hand, tend to value Stage Four (law and duty), indicating a primary focus that says the maintenance of a relationship or ironing out of a conflict should first conform to preestablished rules. Gilligan's study further indicates that because persons are androgynous, a blend of male and female qualities, there are some boys who will value Stage Three above Stage Four, and vice versa.

A second observation that has been made about Kohlberg's stages is that they are strictly cognitive (intellectually based). Therefore, Kohlberg's research does not reflect what the later studies of Gilligan, Nancy Chodorow, Janet Lever, and others discover—the influence of such non-cognitive factors as gender formation, play, social orientation, emotions, values, and religion on decision making. For example, Gilligan contrasts the research of Janet Lever and Jean Piaget (9), who both note that differences in styles of play for boys and girls have a direct impact upon their personality development.[14] Boys at play are more interested in following the rules of the game, in fair procedures for settling disputes, and in dealing directly with competition and conflict. Girls at play, on the other hand, primarily value relationship and the maintaining of solidarity and positive feelings. Girls engage in more solitary or pair-orientated play activities, and disputes will result in the ending of the game rather than in hurting the feelings of the playmate. Girls are more tolerant of rule innovations and exceptions.

Thus, the stress for girls is on relationships, empathy, and sensitivity toward others (22). Because the boys tend to be more concerned about the team and fair play, the stress for them is on learning the organizational skills necessary for group activity and for future leadership in the corporate world. By adolescence, the male developmental goals accent identity and separateness and a more defined "legal" sense that prepares them for the corporate world. The adolescent girl, on the other hand, is driven less by a legal sense than by a sense of identity informed by a more developed empathic and relational sense. Her preference may not be a stagnation in growth but a product of socialization for her gender.

If Gilligan, Chodorow, and the others are correct, then play, gender, and social orientation have extremely important implications for the development of moral character. For the male moral character, the foundation for ethical decision making tends to include an ethical vision that stresses the rights of the individual, a Stage Four following of the rules, and a Stage Six view of impartial justice. In general, males tend to be more concerned with adherence to formal abstract rights and a morality that is equated with a just and fair non-interference with individual rights. The female's moral character orientation seems to be very different. She has been trained to focus on the relational context and the narrative, on the multiple facets of being responsible and maintaining good and caring relations, and on a morality that defines good as being caring, helping, and being responsible for the overt and covert ties that bind people to one another.

A recent nationally publicized criminal trial provides an example of how gender differences may have had a significant effect on the outcome of a criminal case. It may also reflect something of an emerging ethical vision in the United States. Two brothers admitted to killing their wealthy parents. Many people saw this as a clear-cut case of greed that led to first-degree murder. Mirroring popular sentiment, the male-led prosecution based its strategy upon a violation of the rules prohibiting murder, and justice in the form of punishment for violation of the rules. The defense attorneys, predominantly female, took a surprisingly different tack. They based their case on an alleged history of abuse by the parents, which drove the brothers to kill their parents because the brothers feared for their lives. Yes, the defense lawyers admitted, the rules against murder were broken, but in this case the relational context provided enough justification that the strict, objective injunction against murder should be waived. Much to the surprise of many, some jurors for each brother concurred with the defense, and both juries failed to reach unanimous verdicts, resulting in mistrials. One jury was found to have split along gender lines; the male jurors refused to consider anything but the clear-cut breaking of the rules against murder, while the female jurors seemed to give more credence to the relational situation that could have caused the brothers to murder their parents.

In summary, just as there are many factors influencing the unique character development of each individual, so too there are factors influencing the moral development of males and females. It is important to be aware of these differences when trying to understand an individual or community's moral code of behavior and general ethical vision. At this time in history and in United States culture, when morality and ethical decisions are no longer as clear as they perhaps were in the past, more awareness must be given to gender and to cultural and ethical factors, as well as to socioeconomic and a host of other differences that might affect the molding of the ethical character of an individual and a society.

III. Feature:
Understanding Other Ethical Codes

The Western world has long been familiar with the Ten Commandments or the Golden Rule as bases for an ethical vision and theological moral code. It has only been within the last thirty years, however, that there has been increased interest in exploring the ethical codes of the cultures of the Middle and Far East. With the current growing tendency to tolerate a more eclectic and less traditional ethical code, individuals and communities are experimenting with integrating Eastern ethical visions into more traditional Western moral thought.

Buddhism
Around 530 B.C.E., a young man named Siddharta Gautama came

forth to challenge the prevailing ideas of the Brahmin priests of India. Called the Buddha or "Enlightened One," Gautama sought to reform the then present religious system by introducing a novel concept: The endless cycle of death and rebirth (reincarnation) can be broken. The key is the attainment of wisdom: If a person attains enough wisdom in one lifetime, the endless cycle of reincarnation can be broken. Based on a deep reverence and respect for all human beings as well as all other living beings, Buddha's main ideas are captured in The Four Noble Truths, which seek to explain the source of suffering in the world and to offer a possible cure. According to Ward Fellows in *Religions East and West*,[15] Buddha characterizes life as endless suffering that is caused by humankind's selfish cravings and desires. Therefore, Buddha reasons, if one eliminates the selfish cravings and desires, then suffering will no longer exist (155-156). The attainment of wisdom is the key to ridding humankind of its selfish desires and the world of suffering. Buddha then elaborates what has been called the Eightfold Path to wisdom. By successfully ascending the spiritual steps in the Eightfold Path, a person can achieve what Buddha calls "Nirvana" or the release from endless pain and selfishness (160-161).

Islam

After Muhammad's death in 632 C.E., the prayers and preachings of the prophet were written down in what was to become the Qur'an, Islam's sacred book. In contemporary renditions of Muhammad's essential message, scholars such as Abd al-Rahman Azzam (*The Eternal Message of Muhammad*) delineate two essential tenets to the Islamic message: a deep abiding belief in the unity of God, and the ethical commitment to right-doing or acts of righteousness. From these two tenets spring the other earmarks of the Islamic faith and ethical vision. From the belief in Allah, the supreme being or God, come the exhortations to pray five times a day and to fast during the month of Ramadan, and the command to make a once in a lifetime pilgrimage to Mecca, Islam's holiest city. For Islam, the ultimate goal of all human endeavors and the path to human perfection lie in the belief that there is one God. Echoing the Judeo-Christian concept of "covenant," Islam also proclaims that Allah and humankind are linked by indissoluble bonds of relationship that cause the individual and the community to be linked

COMPARING THREE ETHICAL VISIONS

BUDDHISM[16]	ISLAM[17]
FOURFOLD WAY	*FIRST TENET OF THE MESSAGE OF THE PROPHET*
First Noble Truth: Everything in life is suffering and sorrow.	Worship none but Allah, the unassisted author of Creation. (3:11).
Second Noble Truth: The source of human pain and suffering is selfish cravings.	-the opening of the hearts of all peoples leads eventually to the perfection of Creation.
Third Noble Truth: Relief from pain comes from ridding oneself of selfish desires and cravings.	the perfect society whose ultimate good is achieved through human intelligence and a conscience based in faith.
Fourth Noble Truth: The way to attain wisdom and relief from selfish desires is following the Eightfold Path.	-mercy & charity are the marks of this society of faith. (9:58–61, 71–72).
	SECOND TENET OF THE MESSAGE OF THE PROPHET Faith, mercy, and charity lead to acts of righteousness which in turn are expressed through the following:
The Eightfold Path Right knowledge Right purpose Right speech Right action Right living Right effort Right mindfulness Right meditation	1. Universal brotherhood of all humankind (9:71): -war and aggression are only for religious freedom. 2. Life of virtue: truthfulness, courage, sociableness, sincerity, and unselfishness. 3. Solidarity: the individual is responsible to the community and the community is always responsible for the individual (21:92,59:9). 4. Trustee over creation: Humanity is Allah's earthly representative and is entrusted with the care and conservation of creation's resources.

CHRISTIANITY	
TENET I:	*TENET II:*
Love the Lord your God, with all your heart, with all your soul, and with all your mind (Mt. 22:37). - Worship of one God. I am the way, and the truth and the life. No one comes to the Father except through me (Jn. 14:7). Know that I am in my Father, and you in me, and I in you (Jn. 14:20). - belief that all life is sacred because of the indwelling of God and Jesus through the Holy Spirit.	Love one another as I have loved you. No one has greater love than this, to lay down one's life for one's friends. You are my friends if you do what I command you (Jn. 15:12–14). You shall love your neighbor as yourself (Mt. 22:39). Go into the whole world and proclaim the good news to the whole creation (Mk. 16:15). For in one Spirit we are all baptized into one body (1 Cor. 12:13). - True happiness on earth and in eternity comes from internal belief in and external following of Jesus' life and way. The fruit of the Spirit is love, joy, peace, patience, kindness, generosity, faithfulness, gentleness and self-control (Gal. 5:22–23). - Belief in Jesus involves a sense of solidarity and a lifestyle that actively promotes certain virtues as a way of being and acting in the world.

to each other as well as to Allah. The genuineness of this faith is testified to by an ethical lifestyle based on individual and communal right-doing, the solidarity and equality of all human beings, justice, and support of the poor.

On pages 28 and 29 is a brief outline of three of the more familiar ethical visions: those of Christianity, Buddhism, and Islam. Although the outline in chart form is in no way intended to be comprehensive, it does provide a basis for comparison and contrast. The chart shows striking similarities between the two sets of teachings and the Ten Commandments and the teachings of Jesus Christ and the Apostle Paul.

Questions for Research, Reflection, and Discussion

1. Delineate and explain four positive and negative factors influencing the development of self-concept. Explain how these factors have worked in your own life.

2. Explain how differences in socioeconomic status, ethnic and cultural backgrounds, and parental views on acceptable public behaviors have surfaced in people in conflict situations involving gangs, city weeknight curfews for teenagers, and police protection attitudes toward certain municipal areas.

3. Delineate three values esteemed by contemporary U.S. culture as evidenced in recent media infomercials, commercials, and music videos. Explain how each of the values may be ethically but not morally acceptable in United States today. For example, the advertisement for condoms may be considered ethically acceptable by United States culture but has been soundly denounced as morally unacceptable by certain religious traditions.

4. Agree or disagree: Islam and Christianity depict more of a moral system whereas Buddhism is more concerned with an ethical way of life. Explain.

IV. Case Study

"A Universal Religion's Hope in America"

Head bowed, posture stiff, and attitude defensive, Sayidda came hesitantly to the front of the lecture hall. She faced a variety of expressions on the faces of her peers: fear, hostility, boredom, and wary curiosity—but no friendliness. It had been this way for six months. Nothing negative had been done overtly to her, but that was the problem. They just avoided her and treated her with a stony silence that made her feel invisible. There was a long moment of silence, and then Sayidda defiantly raised her head and began her report to the class.

"You do not like me. I do not know if it is because I am black or because I am Muslim or if it is both. There are other blacks in this school, so I know my color doesn't make me that different. So, it must be my dress, which says I am Muslim. I have not figured out why you don't like Muslims."

A derisive voice from the back of the hall shouted, "According to what I've read, you're nothing but terrorists who like to kill Christians and Jews!"

"And there are no white, black, or Asian Christian or Jewish terrorists?" retorted Sayidda. "Yes, some Muslims and some blacks do things to hurt others. But you are lumping us all together as a stereotype. We are *not* here to change or take over America. Islam is more than a religion; it is a way of life. We are here to contribute. A majority of us value what you value. Family is very important to us. Helping our neighbors is very important. That is why my father, Shaheed, agreed to come here to practice medicine in the poorer neighborhoods. He could have earned more money at the big medical center. But my father says we live according to the Qur'an, which is like your Bible, so he chose to come here when he heard there was no doctor for the poor and uninsured of this area.

"People laugh at my head scarf and long dresses and make rude remarks because I do not go dancing or drink alcohol. Our people come from many nations and cultures, from the Middle East, Southeast Asia, and Africa. We speak different languages, and yet we are against abortion, divorce, homosexuality, and premarital sex. I notice that your shops put up bulletproof barriers on the doors and windows at night.

Yet, where my uncle lives in New York City, Muslim stores don't have to hide behind bulletproof barriers. My people work with their neighbors to bring life and hope by helping to keep gangs and drugs out of the neighborhoods. Perhaps you fear because you do not understand. So, I have decided to call my report 'A Universal Religion's Hope in America.'"

Sayidda's case focuses on a growing issue in the United States—the rise of Islam and the United States' cultural response to that rise. Increasingly, people in the United States are becoming aware of what *USA Today* reporter Andrea Stone notes in one feature article: "A new sound is being heard in the USA, a land where church bells have always pealed the loudest. It is the cry of the muezzin, the Muslim call to prayer, beckoning members of what experts say is the nation's fastest-growing religion."[18]

Andrea Stone indicates that as the number of Muslims grows through birth, conversion, and immigration, so too does the Muslim political and cultural influence. Best estimates place the Muslim population in the United States at five million members in 1100 mosques throughout the country. The largely conservative and American value-oriented Muslim majority feel slandered by the media's tendency to sensationalize the more militant and radical Muslim groups. As Sulayman Nyang, a Howard University African Studies professor says, "Most Americans don't have a positive attitude towards Muslims...Most see Muslims through Middle East issues, as fundamentalists, terrorists, anti-Westerners...It is guilt by association" (2A). As a result, the positive and significant influences and contributions that Muslims are making in communities across the country are not known by a majority of Americans.

And so, like two sides of the same coin, the United States is being forced to come to grips with the two faces of Islam: that of the warrior/terrorists who bombed the New York World Trade Center and a busload of Jewish school children in Israel, and that of the persecuted Muslim peacemakers of Bosnia and urban areas of the United States who seek to instill the hope that life and peace know no religious barriers—only those erected by ignorance and intolerance.

Case Study Discussion Questions

1. Given the chapter's discussion of personality development, how would you characterize Sayidda's personality? What have been the most influential factors on her personality development?

2. Agree or disagree: The problem Sayidda is experiencing with her peers is based more on a lack of understanding of the moral and religious tenets of Islam than on a cultural bias against a particular race and religion that is different.

3. Compare and contrast the values with which Sayidda has been socialized with those she claims Islam has in common with United States culture. Are there values esteemed by the United States that Sayidda has missed and that are not shared with Islam? Are there other reasons that may be more to the root of the problem that Sayidda is experiencing?

CHAPTER II

THE EMERGING SOCIAL SELF

Overview
The Tale of the Unfinished Tapestry

I. The Relational Model of Covenant
  A. Covenantal Models
    1. Jewish Biblical Vision of Covenant
    2. The New Testament Vision of Covenantal Love
    3. Covenant Vision of the Indigenous Peoples
    4. Contemporary Perspectives on Covenant:
      — An Ecological Perspective
      — A Feminist Perspective
  B. Establishment of Moral Codes
    1. Jewish Moral Code
    2. New Testament Moral Code

II. Civil and Moral Law:
    Different Views of Responsibility
  A. Differences in Civil and Moral Responsibility
  B. Law versus Morality

III. Forces That Erode Covenant:
    Personal and Social Sin
  A. The Reality of Sin
  B. Injustice: Contemporary Face of Sin

IV. Case Study: Social Ethics and the Many Faces of
    Violence: The Child of the Twilight

Questions for Research, Reflection, and Discussion

Overview

As a person develops, the family, community, and society inculcate in him or her a sense of right and wrong. This socialization process blends with the person's own experiences, and gradually develops into the person's moral code. Chapter I considered those factors that contribute to the development of an individual moral or ethical code.

However, a person is more than an individual. Concomitant with the developing physical, psychological, and moral dimensions of the individual is an emerging awareness that to be human is to be social, in relationship with others. The implications of what it means to be a social being are contained in society's broader ethical vision. Based on what particular civil and religious communities esteem as valuable moral attitudes and behaviors, the broader ethical vision motivates and guides the person to a consideration of the well-being of others.

The larger ethical vision contains four enduring components: a covenant vision of relationality, a quest for meaning, an esteem for enduring values, and guiding principles. A covenant vision of the world implies a sacred bond or relationship between creation and a greater power. A quest for meaning refers to the human search for that power or value greater than the self. Enduring values are the overarching ideas, motives, and virtues that a society considers as good and essential for the support of covenantal and ethical living. Principles or norms are guidelines that indicate more specifically how a value is to be realized in concrete actions and behaviors.

This chapter will explore a covenant vision of the world, and its implication for a variety of ancient and contemporary ethical visions. The second part of the chapter will consider the impact that the covenant model has had on the development of a sense of responsible morality as articulated in specific moral codes. The remaining three components of a broad ethical vision will be discussed in Chapter III.

The Tale of the Unfinished Tapestry

Absorbed in her own thoughts, the old Native American woman did not hear the giggles of the children behind her. The old woman and her unfinished rug were the subject of derisive jokes within the tribe. For many years, the old woman had worked on the rug, weaving threads and patterns for days; then, suddenly it would seem as if she had lost interest in the rug or simply forgotten how to continue. She might stop weaving for days or months, and simply sit and stare at her handiwork, her head cocked to one side, her fingers and eyes moving silently over every inch of the unfinished tapestry.

And now, as she sat, the old woman's granddaughter approached and placed a hand on her shoulder. The little girl watched as the woman's gnarled fingers reverently picked up some colored threads and began the slow, laborious task of interweaving new threads with the old ones. The stillness was suddenly broken by the old woman's raspy voice.

"They see only an old rug, unfinished and useless. I see the fabric of our lives as a tribe. They see only threads, but I see the lines and patterns that mark the larger story of the joys, struggles, failures, and victories of our people. The different patterns represent the many people and events that have shaped and been shaped by the fabric of our tribal life. Each thread of the pattern represents the unique gifts that each person has been to us.

"Today, I must weave again. Another friend who has been an important part of our lives has died. How shall she be remembered? Which threads shall I choose for the pattern that will tell the story of her gift to us? I choose the threads of wisdom, inner strength, understanding, and fairness. Together they shall create the pattern of a nurturer. Like all women born of the Mother Spirit, she has given life by her very presence. She had the courage to nurture and support life while still encouraging each person to grow and face the winds and storms of the plains rather than cower in uncertainty and darkness. Yet, like the willow tree, the nurturer stands in firm and loving support of all who stand beneath her branches, whispering gentle words of faith and trust, or steely words of love in anger when the promise of one person is in danger of being lost. Yes, the pattern that I shall weave is that of the nurturer, my friend who has and always will be part of the fabric of our lives."

And so, the gnarled fingers reverently picked up the threads and began the laborious task of interweaving new threads with old ones. As she worked, the woman went on to explain to her granddaughter the story of their tribe as woven into the decades-old, unfinished tapestry.

The little girl slowly saw how the individual stories of valiant warriors and women whose personalities and gifts subtly or not so subtly affected the relations and destiny of the tribe were immortalized in the multi-colored patterns.

Many years later, when the little girl was a mother, she brought her own little girl to stand before the unfinished rug. Although the old woman was no longer with them, her legacy to the tribe hung on the old loom, a reminder to who all who came that each thread and pattern, indeed the very tapestry itself, represented the gift of the persons and events that had shaped the total fabric of tribal life.

I. The Relational Model of Covenant

The Tale of the Unfinished Tapestry highlights one of the enduring themes of life—that human beings are both individual and communal beings. Interwoven throughout the tapestry of history are the threads of individual exploits that have shaped human destiny. Threaded around these individual stories, however, are the social and cultural sagas that have not only produced but also supported these individuals, stamping them as moral giants immortalized for their feats of daring and courageous commitment to something greater than self—a tribe, clan, community, or country—despite danger and cost to themselves.

History reveals that each enduring culture or civilization has been motivated by some larger world vision, a vision that has also been guided by a particular definition of the good and the ways to attain it. One such vision has been that of the Jewish and New Testament concepts of covenant, that sacred bond or relationship between the divine and human beings. Although not the main focus of this text, it is important to consider briefly the Jewish and New Testament covenantal visions. An ethical perspective of the world has developed from this covenant concept, and it has spawned a series of evolving relational models that are integral to the enduring pattern in Western thought.

A. Covenantal Models:
1. Jewish Biblical Visions of Covenant
Rooted in the very beginnings of the ancient Judeo-Christian Bible is

Genesis 2, a second creation story, which describes the essence of what it means to be human: <u>We are social or relational beings</u>. In Genesis 2, Yahweh, the Hebrew God, lovingly creates a man and places him in a specially designed garden called Eden. Then God discovers that this seemingly perfect haven is missing something; the man is lonely. Deeply concerned, Yahweh creates the animals and gives them to the man to name, hoping that the man will find a helper as his partner. The animals, however, fail to provide the companionship that the man needs to feel happy. A loving and concerned Yahweh puts the man into a deep sleep, takes a rib from his side, and fashions from it woman, someone intended to be more than a mere helper. She is to be a partner who shares with the man in an intimate way that the animals cannot, in a deep relational bond that makes them seemingly as one.

A closer reading of Genesis 2 gives a hint that the man-woman relationship is modeled on the relationship Yahweh had already established with man at the time of his creation. The man knew Yahweh well enough to be comfortable in Yahweh's presence; in addition, the relationship must have been close enough that Yahweh knew that the man needed more. One can only assume that the creation of the woman only enhanced the sacred relationship, that fundamental bond of personal intimacy established between God and human persons that was supposed to unfold and take shape in the perfect environment of Eden.

In Genesis 3, however, the script is shattered by the first sin. The intimate love relationship between Yahweh and the couple is radically changed, and they know it. The free and easy relationship with Yahweh disappears. Ashamed and fearful, the couple "heard the sound of the Lord God walking in the garden at the time of the evening breeze, and the man and his wife hid themselves from the presence of the Lord God" (Genesis 3:8). Forced to confess their misdeed, the man and woman are ejected from the perfection of Eden. And, as a sign that their lives and their relationship with Yahweh are irreparably damaged, Yahweh places "the cherubim, and a sword flaming and turning" (Genesis 3:24) to guard the garden. Genesis 3–6 records the story of how the ensuing generations display the depths to which human relationships can degenerate. The sacred relationship that linked Yahweh to humankind and humankind to one another became one of continued sacrilege and alienation from self, God, and others.

Separated from though not forsaken by Yahweh, humankind eventually learned newer ways to reestablish relational bonds and roles. Genesis 6 and the rest of the Jewish Scriptures recount how Yahweh took the initiative to reestablish that primordial sacred bond of relationship in a new concept called covenant[1] and how God repeatedly reestablished covenants with humankind despite their constant breaking of the terms of the relationship. Through such persons as Adam, Noah, Abraham, and Moses, the judges, and the prophets, including Isaiah, Ezekiel, Jeremiah, Micah, and many others, Yahweh remained committed to humanity and to creation with the often-repeated vow that "I will maintain my covenant with you and your descendants after you throughout the ages as an everlasting pact, to be your God and the God of your descendants after you" (Genesis 17:7).

For the ancient Hebrews, ancestors to the present-day Jews, covenants were the basic way of understanding the special bond between their God, Yahweh, and Yahweh's chosen people. As Lawrence Boadt explains (174-175), the Hebrew term *berit* is most often used to convey the idea of a binding agreement that can take one of many forms: a solemn contract (Genesis 3:1–44), an alliance of friendship (1 Samuel 18:3), a peace pact (Genesis 14:13), or a marriage bond (Proverbs 2:17). Most often, however, it is used to express the special relational alliance between Yahweh and the Israelite people. Even before their guiding moral vision was codified in the Ten Commandments, Israel had come to know that their national survival and unity depended upon their unswerving obedience, worship, and fidelity to a personal God. In return for their commitment to this relational bond, God pledged to this specially chosen people God's continued love, mercy, and protection.

An essential message about covenant images emerges from the Jewish Scriptures' account of the origins and development of the covenant relationship: Despite humankind's failure to remain faithful to the covenantal bond, God continues to be loyal throughout the centuries. Once the Jewish nation realized and accepted this message, loyalty to the covenant formed an integral part of their evolving morality, which established the norm for human relational bonds that link humans with God, each other, and all of creation. Fidelity to covenant bespeaks a fundamental personal and social commitment to relationship that defines what it means to be human in the world. From the Jewish perspective, covenant relations are maintained by acting right toward *N|D* God, self, others, and all creation.

2. The New Testament Vision of Covenantal Love

As the Jewish Scriptures reveal, covenant is not only a personal relationship toward God; it is also the basis for the sense of human and ecological solidarity initially and irrevocably established by that first covenant. Incorporating the essential elements of the Jewish vision, the New Testament vision of covenant enlarges the concept of covenant to include such ideas as incarnate love, reciprocity, and solidarity.

Christians see the fulfillment of this ongoing covenant, or love relationship, in the life, ministry, saving death, and resurrection of Jesus the Christ—a relationship Christians are called to reenact daily in their personal and social relations. Jesus took the ancient, covenantal, relational bond between God and individuals and broadened it to wider dimensions. He emphasized the immanent nature of God, who was not only a mysterious, transcendent power, but also a personal, incarnate God who lived and loved within everything created.

Jesus also insisted that the sacred love and relational dimensions of covenant were a radical and new calling to solidarity and reciprocity— to a covenant extending beyond one tribe or people and including all human beings and all of creation. As Jesus envisioned it, to be related to God was not just an alternative way of being religious or spiritual; it was a personal, social, and political call to change lifestyles, which in turn would cause changes in social relationships and eventually in the very fabric of contemporary culture. Initially known as people of "The Way," the early Christians were challenged to be just that—a way of being in the world that called them to ever new forms of relational loving and caring.

Whether it be peers, friendship, family, neighborhood, work, or church-based relationships, human beings find themselves involved in multiple relationships throughout their lifetime. Jesus' life, ministry, and death became for humanity a model of how to handle the responsibilities, sacrifices, and obligations demanded by covenantal love and relationships. For those relationships imbued with mutual love, caring, and respect, the extension of covenantal love in the spirit of Jesus' example is not usually difficult. However, Jesus' message about the depth and extent of covenantal love relationships is more challenging when the relationships are not of our choosing, involve people and situations where love and relating are very difficult, and include all of humanity and creation. Jesus' vision of covenantal love can best be understood through one of his parables or teaching stories.

The Parable of the Good Samaritan

"...He said to Jesus, 'And who is my neighbor?' Jesus replied, 'A man fell victim to robbers as he went down from Jericho to Jerusalem to Jericho. They stripped and beat him and went off leaving him half dead..." (Luke 10:29–37).

So begins the famous story of the good Samaritan, the third stranger to happen upon a luckless victim of assault and robbery. The first two strangers were religious representatives of Judaism who would be expected to have been models of what a "neighbor" was all about. Yet, they hurriedly passed by the victim. It took the third stranger, a Samaritan, the traditional enemy of the Jews,[2] to demonstrate the true meaning of neighbor. The Samaritan stops, tends to the wounds of the stranger—who, it is implied, is Jewish and therefore supposedly an enemy to the Samaritan—and then takes the wounded man to an inn. After caring for him, the Samaritan leaves money with the innkeeper, who is commanded to continue to care for the stranger.

Was it something more than human compassion and mercy that caused the biblical good Samaritan to stop and aid a stranger who was an ancient enemy? History informs us that the people of Samaria were descendants of what used to be the ten Northern Israelite tribes. Until the aftermath of the Assyrian captivity in 722 B.C.E.,[3] these Northern Israelite tribes were well versed in, and steadfast practitioners of, the Israelite religion. At the core of the Israelite religion was the ancient and enduring concept of *covenant*,[4] that eternal, enduring bond of relationship that bound the Israelite to Yahweh and to others. Future generations of Jews believed that the Northern tribes had defiled the covenant by their subsequent intermarriage with the pagan Assyrians. In the eyes of the Jews of the South, therefore, the Northern tribes of Samaria had diluted the purity of the Israelite covenant with "pagan" beliefs and practices. By the time of Jesus, this had all become part of the generations-old, fierce contempt that the Jews of the South had for the Samaritans. However, that the Samaritan stopped to care for a member of a group that held him in contempt indicates that the ancient concept of covenant had endured within the Samaritan people in spite of their ostracism.

3. Covenant Vision of the Indigenous Peoples

The covenant vision of the indigenous peoples is both similar to and different from more well-known Western and Eastern traditions. Like other spiritual and moral systems, indigenous peoples affirm the need for community, love, and service. Unlike their counterparts in other traditions, these people are more attuned to the rhythmic patterns of the land and nature; consequently, they see the road to healing and health not through technological advancement but through a personal and social quest to live in harmony and balance with their own inner nature and with the environment.

Often oppressed by their stronger and more technologically advanced conquerors, deprived of their lands and natural resources, and lacking in sociopolitical and economic influence, the native or indigenous peoples of the world are nevertheless the possessors of an important wisdom, mythology, and spirituality that are just being rediscovered by the West.

Tapping into the mythological and spiritual traditions of indigenous tribes, anthropologist Angeles Arrien's *The Four-Fold Way*[5] presents an ethical vision, a way of achieving the good and of living healthfully in the world. After years of extensive study of the world's agrarian and indigenous peoples, Arrien discerned three important universal threads for moral living: a deep, abiding respect for change, environmental reverence and management, and a recognition of the interdependence between the human and the non-human (4-5). Arrien asserts that when we listen to these people,

we are listening to our oldest selves. Indigenous cultures support change and healing, transition and rites of passage through mythic structures and through the incorporation into daily life of art, science, music, ritual, and drama (6).

Arrien says that to achieve inner harmony as well as environmental balance, the shamanic traditions draw upon the power of four arche-types: the Warrior, the Healer, the Visionary, and the Teacher. Although expressed differently from their Western and Eastern counterparts, these archetypes do draw upon universal human themes available "to all humankind, regardless of context, culture, structure, and practice" (8). These themes also reflect the ethical and moral attitudes and behaviors that the indigenous peoples believe are necessary for promoting personal and social good.

Integrating the attitudes and behaviors of each archetype into one's lifestyle is both a lifelong process and the end goal. For example, the way of the Warrior is characterized by an attention to each situation that enables the person to access the human resources of power, presence, and communication. Always attentive, the Healer is able to access the powers of love, gratitude, acknowledgment, and validation. The Visionary lives by non-judgmental truthfulness, which radiates an authenticity based on inner gifts of vision and intuition. The Teacher uses the gifts of wisdom and objectivity, which lead to non-attachment and a flexibility to choose among any number of alternatives instead of maintaining a rigid adherence to one method or direction.

Combining theory and practical tools for implementation and empowerment, *The Four-Fold Way* explores the four principles, each based on an archetype, that Arrien contends are the heart and soul of the shamanic moral vision (7-8). Drawing upon many cultural perspectives, Arrien blends many mythic and ritualistic threads, such as direction, season, instrument, creature, right ways of living, and human resources, into diverse patterns. Arrien weaves the patterns together and presents a tapestry that richly captures an ethical vision encompassing many indigenous and agrarian cultures. In fashioning a broad ethical vision for the late twentieth century, Arrien reminds humanity that

> spiritualism is the highest form of political consciousness. The native peoples of the West are among the world's surviving proprietors of that kind of consciousness. They are here to impart that message. It is important to use it wisely and well as we go into the twenty-first century—a time of bridging ancient wisdoms into the creative tapestry of contemporary times (11).

Self in the
Morally developed Self

God
Self
others

N/B

Although developed by different cultures in different times and
places, the covenant visions of the Jewish, New Testament, and indigenous communities share many common themes: 1) a belief that
strong covenant or communal relationships, which are founded on and
promote mutual love and service to a supreme being, to others, and to
all creation, are essential for the well-being of all; 2) a belief that morality, more than right behaviors, is the possession of right personal and
social attitudes; 3) and an understanding that inner harmony and environmental balance are the best ways to achieve personal and social
health. Taken together, these threads form an important part of the relational pattern in the broader ethical tapestry.

4. Contemporary Perspectives on Covenant

The beauty of the covenant model lies in its ability both to evolve
and to reflect the changes in communities and their relationships over
time and in varied cultures. In modern times, the covenant model continues, but it is changed and transformed by the contributions of diverse insights from the ecological, feminist, and liberation perspectives.
The ecological and feminist perspectives are explored below, and the
liberation perspective will be discussed in Chapter IV. The ecological
and feminist perspectives are presented in an attempt to show how
these two views have broadened the covenantal relationship model to
include the diverse ways that men and women are challenged to fashion covenantal relationships, not only between themselves, but also between human beings and all of creation.

An Ecological Perspective

Relationships among humans and humanity's relationship with God
have received a great deal of emphasis in religious writings throughout
history. Much less emphasis has been given to humanity's relationship
with the rest of creation, especially the non-human parts. Recent writings in the field of ecological theology and environmental ethics have
attempted to awaken humanity's consciousness to the broader dimensions of the covenantal bond.

For centuries humanity has pointed to and celebrated the biblical ex-
hortation to "be fertile and multiply; fill the earth and subdue it. Have
dominion over all...the living things that move on the earth" (Genesis

1:28–29). As the ecological perspective points out, human technological advances celebrate the short-term success in mastering ourselves and creation. Humanity, however, has forgotten that while it is master over creation, it too is part of the multi-billion year, long-term process of growth and development of the planet. This long-term goal has not been as seriously pursued as have the short-term technological advances, and the ecological and environmental problems plaguing the world have been increasing as a result.

In June 1992, the world received an important wake-up call. The "Earth Summit," the U.N. Conference on Environment and Development, held in Rio De Janeiro and attended by over 130,000 people, dramatically underscored the vital message reiterated in the works of environmentalists: An ecological revolution must occur that challenges all nations to make global policies that deliberately acknowledge the interdependence among ecology, human production, and non-human reproduction.

The nature and function of this global ecological revolution is the subject of Carolyn Merchant's *Radical Ecology*.[6] Echoing the rediscovered contributions of the indigenous peoples, the covenant perspective of Merchant and others represents a growing movement by environmentalists to combat the increasing "contradictions (tendencies to be contrary to each other's continuance)" (9). She sees these contradictions as a reason for the global ecological crisis of the late-twentieth century. Merchant cites two examples of these globe-threatening contradictions: the tensions between economic forces of production and local ecological conditions, and the tensions between processes of human production and non-human reproduction. She notes that the ecological revolution needs to do more than address these contradictions in practical ways; the revolution must transform human consciousness so that humanity's ways of representing nature through myth, cosmology, religion, philosophy, and art—as well its ethics, morals, taboos, and rituals—are all "translated into actions and behaviors that both affect and are affected by environment, production and reproduction" (13).

Merchant is convinced that radical ecology is the method by which this ecological revolution can occur. Radical ecology is a comprehensive approach not only because it offers theories and practical options toward solving current environmental problems, but also because it challenges those aspects of political and economic order that prevent the fulfillment of basic human needs...pushes social and ecological systems toward new patterns of production...and supports social movements for removing the causes of environmental deterioration and raising the quality of life for people of every race, class and sex (9).

In her recent book, *The Body of God: An Ecological Theology*,[7] Sallie McFague echoes the calls of Merchant and the Earth Summit. Framed within a theological and ecological metaphor of the planet as the "body of God," McFague links another biblical theme, that of vocation or a sacred calling, to covenant in order to remind all of humanity that it is called to use its energy and talents to further a covenantal interrelatedness and interdependence that encompass all beings and processes on the planet. McFague sees humanity's primary vocation and moral issue as the short- and long-term decisions concerning

whether we and other species will live and how well we will live...The planetary agenda takes the wide and long view: it is concerned with the well-being of the diverse, rich plenitude of beings, human and nonhuman, that inhabit the planet, not just for the present and the near future, but...for as long as we can imagine...Increasingly we are recognizing the world as a tribal village, at least as it refers to all human inhabitants of the earth. But that recognition needs to be extended to all other living creatures and to the ecosystems that support us all (8-9).

Merchant, McFague, and others who espouse an ecological view of covenant represent another important strand in the larger relational pattern of the ethical tapestry. Just as an ethical act flows from broader ethical vision and values, so too, daily actions of planetary conservation must flow from a long-term vision that includes attitudes and behaviors imbued with a sense of sacred calling that makes covenantal interrelatedness the core of planetary life and survival.

A Feminist Perspective
From feminist and psychosocial circles comes another thread of the tapestry: the feminist perspective. This perspective emphasizes that al-

though men and women are united in a vocation or calling to covenant, their response is at heart diverse. Feminists attribute this diversity to the complexity of gender-based influences. As previously discussed in Chapter One, there are many factors that combine to produce differences in the personal and ethical perspectives of men and women. Using these differences as a starting point, feminists contend that men and women by nature have different values for their ethical vision of the world and use different methods to bring this vision or agenda into being. Feminist studies by Beverly Harrison and Rosemarie Tong[8] illustrate the gender distinctions in the ways that males and females approach such things as relationships and ethical/moral language.

For centuries, the cultural, social, and ethical methods of society have tended to favor a male-dominated imagery, which often emphasizes the mechanical, logical, and manipulative perspectives and methods of dealing with life and relationships. In her essay on "The Power of Anger in the Work of Love," Beverly Harrison[9] underscores one strain of feminist thinking that seeks to affirm a different but complementary perspective: the intimate, nurturing, organic, active, and relational contributions of women (9-12). Harrison believes that women are ideally suited to the most basic and human of the works of love— "the work of human communication, of caring and nurturance, of tending the personal bonds of community" (12). Unlike what has often been seen as the male human need to rule and master, women's vocation and contribution to an understanding of covenantal ethics may very well be the deepening and extension of human relations. Beginning first with the individual, Harrison contends that the grounding of relational building and maintenance in personal self-respect and dignity results in an ever-widening extension of respect and dignity to other humans, to communities, to nations, and to non-human creation.

In summary, the covenant model is basic to a variety of ancient and contemporary models of relationality. From this model have evolved a variety of moral codes that highlight the attitudes and behaviors necessary to promote a covenantal ethical vision.

B. Establishment of Moral Codes

Covenantal systems of morality presume a sense of responsibility. A responsible moral attitude involves a consideration of a human action

and whether it sustains or disrupts human good, welfare, and relationships. Usually, individual and communal behaviors are measured
against a set of moral norms based on a variety of values, principles,
and rules that flow from the overall moral vision adopted in any given
historical time. For example, the moral visions of the Jewish people and
of the Roman Catholic community illustrate how covenantal moral
codes are based upon a particular people's ethical vision and moral tradition of a covenant model of relationality.

Jewish Moral Code

Amid their growing awareness of the covenant bond, the Israelites,
ancestors to the Jewish people, experienced the Exodus, one of the most
profoundly influential events in ancient Israelite history. Enslaved under the Egyptians, the Israelites prayed for centuries for deliverance.
Their prayer was answered in the person of Moses, a charismatic leader
who, according to the book of Exodus, was born Israelite, raised as an
Egyptian noble, and was later accepted by his native people after a
desert conversion experience with the Israelite God, Yahweh. Finally
convinced by Yahweh that he, Moses, was the answer to the Israelite
pleas for deliverance, Moses eventually persuaded the ruling pharaoh
to let the Israelites leave Egypt for a land promised to them by Yahweh
(Exodus 1—11).

On their last night of slavery, the Israelites renewed their covenant
relationship with Yahweh and commemorated their "passing-over"
from slavery to freedom by celebrating the meal known today as the
Passover Meal (Exodus 12). The memorial Passover Meal, and the subsequent experiences of the Exodus and the conquering of the Promised
Land mark

> ...the real beginning of the history of Israel as a people...a nation
> unified by faithfulness to a God who chooses them for a special
> role. There now become two clear focal points: a single God and a
> single people bound together for better or for worse...This divine
> act of liberation (the Exodus) was motive enough for a group to
> pledge itself to this God in a binding covenant. The exodus mir-
> acle had proven the love and power of Yahweh and shown that
> he was worth trusting...Thus the tradition is threefold: 1) de-

liverance, 2) binding covenant, 3) conquest of a promised land...
(Boadt 155-56).

Freed from slavery, Moses and the Israelites spent many years in the
desert while moving toward their promised land. It was that desert experience that transformed them into a unified people whose bonds were
eloquently expressed in the Sinai Covenant, or the Ten Commandments.
This famous code of ten action guidelines state the covenantal attitudes
and behaviors expected from Israel (Exodus 20:1–17).

The first three commandments deal with divine and human relations, recognizing Yahweh as Israel's only God to be worshiped in fidelity and love:

> I am the Lord, your God, who brought you out of the land of
> Egypt, out of the house of slavery...you shall have no other gods
> before me. You shall not make for yourself an idol...You shall not
> bow down to them or worship them;
>   You shall not make wrongful use of the name of the Lord your
> God...
>   Remember the sabbath day, and keep it holy...But the seventh
> day is a sabbath to the Lord your God; you shall not do any work
> (Exodus 20:2–8).

Yahweh is a personal God whose willingness to be bound in this
personal relationship is both a free gift to Israel and also a demand for
single-minded loyalty and trust. In return, Yahweh promises a pro-
tective love that brings not necessarily material property, wealth, and
renown, but "freedom from fear in the promised land, the fruitfulness
of children and crops, permanent peace and the joy of knowing God is
near" (Boadt 175).

As the last seven commandments indicate, the covenant between
Yahweh and the individual also affects the relationships between individuals.

> Honor your father and your mother...
> You shall not murder.
> You shall not commit adultery.

You shall not steal.

You shall not bear false witness against your neighbor.

Your shall not covet your neighbor's house; you shall not covet your neighbor's wife...or anything that belongs to your neighbor (Exodus 20:12–17).

In specifying that underlying attitudes and behaviors like murder, lying, stealing, and coveting persons and the possessions of another are detrimental to the covenantal bond, the Ten Commandments also forge the bonds of solidarity and justice so crucial to the understanding of covenant. Because the religious and civil aspects of life were one in Israel, the Ten Commandments became the foundation for future moral and civil norms that act as guidelines for the personal and communal covenant relations of Israel.

New Testament Moral Code

Not only did Jesus affirm the Ten Commandments, but in Luke 10:25–28 he summarizes these traditional norms into what he called the two greatest commandments: love of God and love of neighbor. A study of his life and teachings also reveals that Jesus established love as the first essential covenantal attitude and responsibility. In Matthew 5, the Sermon on the Mount defines this love not as emotional affection for another, but rather as an active and abiding respect that considers all of humankind as worthwhile and valuable.

Blessed are the poor in spirit, for theirs is the kingdom of heaven...

Blessed are those who hunger and thirst for righteousness, for they will be filled.

Blessed are the merciful, for they will receive mercy...

Blessed are the peacemakers, for they will be called children of God.

Blessed are those who are persecuted for righteousness' sake, for theirs is the kingdom of heaven.

...You are the light of the world...Let your light shine before others...

...But I say to you, love your enemies and pray for those who persecute you... (Matthew 5:3–14).

Therefore, a true follower of Jesus is one who is able to model for others a love that embraces and forgives even an enemy, and who is committed to working for peace, mercy, and justice even in the face of persecution.

Service, the second essential attitude of Jesus' covenantal ethics, can be found in one of his early preachings in the Nazareth synagogue:

> The Spirit of the Lord is upon me, because he has anointed me to bring good news to the poor. He has sent me to proclaim release to the captives and recovery of sight to the blind, to let the oppressed go free, to proclaim the year of the Lord's favor (Luke 4:18–19).

Love and service, therefore, are the two essential elements of Jesus' New Testament covenantal ethics. Through love and service, Christians are called to liberate themselves and others from situations of injustice and oppression. That this is true can be seen in Jesus' linking of the two great commandments to his parable of the good Samaritan (Luke 10:25–37).

Finding answers to the questions "How do I love and serve God and neighbor?" and "Who is my neighbor who is blind, poor, captive, and oppressed?" are the challenges that face each generation of Christians. One response is suggested by David Hollenbach, S.J., in *Claims in Conflict: Claiming and Renewing the Catholic Human Rights Tradition*.[10] Hollenbach provides a historical view of the Roman Catholic Church's rich history of social teachings, especially since the last century, concerning such issues as human rights, social and political justice, and poverty. A second response is articulated by Karen Lebacqz's *Six Theories of Justice: Perspectives from Philosophical and Theological Ethics*,[11] which presents both a variety of religious and non-religious perspectives on the particular issue of justice and its implications for the world. Another contemporary application of Jesus' covenantal ethics was given by the Second Vatican Council, a gathering of Roman Catholic Church leaders from 1962-65. Guided, the church believes, by the Spirit of God, the Council was to update the church by defining its nature and mission for this century and beyond.

One of the major documents of Vatican Council II is *Gaudium et Spes*, also known as *The Pastoral Constitution on the Church in the Modern World*.[12] In that document, the dual covenantal norms of love and service are reiterated as absolutely essential for contemporary covenantal ethics:

...this Council lays stress on reverence for man; everyone must consider his every neighbor without exception as another self...In our times a special obligation binds us to make ourselves the neighbor of absolutely every person, and of actively helping him when he comes across our path, whether he be an old person abandoned by all, a foreign laborer unjustly looked down upon, a refugee, a child born of an unlawful union...or a hungry person who disturbs our conscience... (# 27).

...It grows increasingly true that the obligations of justice and love are fulfilled only if each person, contributing to the common good, according to his own abilities and needs of others, also promotes and assists the public and private institutions dedicated to bettering the conditions of human life (# 30).

A specific application of the guiding ideas of *Gaudium et Spes* and the other Vatican Council II documents regarding social justice, poverty, and loving service is offered by a publication of the United States Catholic Church's Campaign for Human Development, *Sourcebook on Poverty, Development and Justice*.[13] Intended to be an educational tool for consciousness raising among U.S. Catholics, the *Sourcebook* reminds Catholic Christians that even though conditions, economies, and immediate causes of events change over time and place, the Christian is faced with the continued need to "recall the basic reality of the Church, the teachings of the Lord Jesus, the vocation of discipleship—and by applying these to current times and lifestyles...to choose forms of action which manifest...basic transcendent themes of Christianity" (5). The first two of these transcendent themes are the calls to love all people and to give life to the world primarily through works of love and service (5-8).

Summary
The Jewish covenant vision has affected the establishment of moral

codes by its contribution of the idea of covenant relationships that is proscribed by external specific action-guides. The New Testament covenant vision and the documents of Vatican Council II challenge Jesus' followers to move beyond a fixed, literal adherence to time-bound rules and toward a more internally motivated spiritual response whereby the love that undergirds the covenant relationship is continually seeking expression in actions that bespeak service, forgiveness, mercy, solidarity, and justice. A third perspective, the covenant vision of the indigenous peoples, seeks to blend internal and external dimensions into a personal and social quest that equates ethical and moral health and goodness with harmony and balance among all of creation.

A covenant vision of relationality and the moral codes based upon covenant have in turn affected the development of civil law. Ideally, a society's legal code is informed by its ethical and moral codes. The particular expressions of how covenant love and service are to be enacted are culturally and historically influenced; so too are the complementary but different legal expressions of what is right and wrong for individuals and communities. In any given situation not only may the civil and moral law differ, but there may also be a difference in the extent of the individual's moral and legal responsibility.

II. Civil and Moral Law:
Different Views of Responsibility

A. Differences in Civil and Moral Responsibility

As a community or society develops, the twin forces of law and ethics work to fashion a system for the orderly maintenance of the group. Ethics should provide a consistent standard by which laws are made for the good of the people. Ethics should also provide the basis upon which the rightness or wrongness of a law is judged by the individual and the society. In his contemporary exploration of the Vatican Council II documents and teachings, Dennis Doyle[14] notes that

social institutions and human cultures have sets of meanings at their very core. These meanings can be detected as presuppositions and formulated as beliefs. For example, the judicial system of the United States rests upon a set of beliefs about the meaning and importance of justice...Religious beliefs shape one's understandings of the meaning and purpose of life (102).

Despite their common goal of community law and order, differences exist between a society's or community's civil and moral codes. There are many reasons for these differences. The first is that human views of right and wrong relational behaviors have been developing over thousands of years. As a civilization moves at uneven rates—from primitive concerns over basic survival needs to a more sophisticated awareness of and sensitivity to what positively and negatively affects relationships—what that civilization considers as legally and morally right and wrong also changes. These changes are reflected not only in the diverse moral codes and the social norms and mores of each society but also in the basic human "rights" or needs that a particular society considers essential for healthy individual and social living.

In some societies, cultural customs and traditions, as well as socioeconomic and educational development, provide a different legal and moral context for behaviors than would be acceptable in other societies. For example, in certain countries in Africa, bigamy and sexual mutilation are morally and legally acceptable; in the United States both these acts are legally and ethically unacceptable. In the West the usual penalty for despoiling of property is either a fine, jail time, a form of restitution, or all three; for the same crime in some Asian countries the penalty is more severe and entails either whipping the person or cutting off a finger or a hand.

A second reason for the potential difference between moral and legal norms is the separation of church and state in some societies. In the case of the earlier societies, like that of the Hebrews or Israelites, or the Puritans of colonial New England, religious and civil bodies were intertwined; what was legal and what was moral were one and the same. However, once a separation of church and state is established, differences begin to occur between civil and moral laws. In general, good civil law, like moral law, attempts to foster the good and the welfare of society. On some issues, societies may even share a universal legal and moral norm, such as the prohibition against the killing of another human being without just cause. In the United States, however, capital punishment is legal, even though many members of certain religious traditions (Islam and Christianity, for example), view capital punishment as immoral.

A third reason for differences between a society's moral and legal codes is that laws are culturally and historically bound; they reflect the legislators' perceptions and interpretations of right and wrong at a given time. However, their perceptions of what is legally right or wrong may not coincide with what is morally the best or worst way to express covenantal ethics. Slavery is a good example. In the ancient civilizations of Greece, Rome, Egypt, and India, slavery was a legally and morally accepted custom. Similarly, in parts of the United States before 1860, slavery was considered legal as well as moral. However, since the end of the Civil War in 1865, slavery is no longer legally and morally permissible in the United States. What had been a two-century-old legally and culturally accepted practice was changed as the country and its legislators came to see the inherent evil of slavery.

B. Law versus Morality

What happens when law and ethics conflict? What are the individual's and the collective group's responsibilities when faced with a law that they consider unjust or immoral? These are the precise questions of the famous MyLai trial. In March 1968, during the course of the United States involvement in Vietnam, a United States Army platoon was ordered by their platoon officer, Army First Lieutenant William Calley, to attack the Vietnam village of MyLai and to kill all the inhabitants. The platoon proceeded to do this, although the men realized that the inhabitants were mostly children and old men and women. When details of this execution-style killing reached public notice, Lt. Calley was court-martialed. His defense was partially based on the idea that his military superiors had given the orders that he was to destroy the village, and that he was only following their orders. The basic moral, legal, and ethical principle of this defense is that the blind obedience demanded by authority somehow excuses the individual from the dictates of morality. As the subsequent conviction of Lt. Calley to life at hard labor attests, blind obedience to authority in no way replaces the individual person's responsibilities to weigh all actions against basic ethical codes of right action.

This belief is also repeated in a variety of religious traditions, especially the Roman Catholic tradition, which is very clear that a Christian is not morally bound to obey an unjust and immoral law; in its *Declaration on Religious Freedom*,[15] Vatican Council II reminds all individuals that

> in all his activity, a man is bound to follow his conscience faithfully in order that he may come to God, for whom he was created. It follows that he is not to be forced to act in a manner contrary to his conscience. Nor, on the other hand, is he to be restrained from acting in accordance with his conscience, especially in matters religious (#3).

In conclusion, a covenant vision of relationality entails a responsibility to support the civil and moral law codes that have developed to sustain and nurture communal relationships. At times, civil and moral law codes conflict as to the extent of the duties and responsibilities incumbent upon the members of the community. When such a conflict arises, some moral traditions dictate that the individual and society as a whole are bound to consider more than external rules; each person is also bound to follow an inner code for ethical living, called conscience. The nature, development, and function of conscience will be discussed in Chapter IV.

III. Forces That Erode Covenant: Personal and Social Sin

A. The Reality of Sin

In "The Power of Anger in the Work of Love" Beverly Harrison remarks that

> like Jesus, we are called to a radical activity of love, to a way of being in the world that deepens relations, embodies and extends community, passes on the gift of life...We are called to confront, as Jesus did, that which thwarts the power of human personal and communal becoming, that which twists relationship, which

denies human well-being, community, and solidarity to so many in our world. To confront these things, and to stay on the path of confrontation, to break through...the prevailing distortions and manipulations in relationships and the power of relationships is the vocation of those who are Jesus' followers (18-19).

Within the Christian tradition, that which Harrison describes as the thwarting and twisting of relationships and the severance of covenantal relations with God, self, others, and the rest of creation is called sin. The biblical concept of sin can be expressed by two Hebrew words: *hatta't*, which means a missing of the mark, a failing in what is expected in relations with another, and *ma'al*, which means infidelity or a breach of a freely undertaken obligation to another.[16] Thus, sin is defined as any individual or social act or failure to act, any thought or intent, that is deliberately intended to harm one's covenantal relationship with God, self, others, or creation.

Judeo-Christian history is replete not only with examples of human infidelity and missing the mark in personal and social relationships, but also with diverse myths about the initial manner and causes for the divine-human alienation. Despite the diversity of these myths, the story line seems to be the same. Begun by what the Judeo-Christian Scriptures describe in Genesis 3 as the temptation of Eve and the first sin, that initial, personal rupture of the divine-human covenantal bond is quickly followed by an ever-widening breach in human relations, so that by Genesis 8 all of creation is so corrupted and alienated by the effects of sin that Yahweh destroys much of what was created in Genesis 1–2. When eventually choosing to reestablish relationships with creation, Yahweh begins with the faithful family of Noah. The Judeo-Christian Scriptures are full of these new beginnings, quickly followed by a repetitive cycle of human sin, human repentance, and divine liberation. With mercy and forgiveness Yahweh always moves to liberate human beings from bondage to sin while challenging them to use their liberation to create a more just world through love, service, repentance, renunciation, conversion, and reparation.

B. Injustice: Contemporary Face of Sin

I have long been convinced that injustice is our lived reality, and that it is therefore the primary category. Justice emerges as the cry of revolt against injustice. Justice must begin with injustice (10).

So begins Karen Lebacqz in *Justice in an Unjust World,*[17] which explores the many forms of injustice, the contemporary human sin. Lebacqz draws upon a rich biblical tradition to help define the current forms of injustice and the strategies involved in a covenantal ethics. She unmasks the current faces of sin: racism (ethnic injustice), rape (sexual injustice), repression (political injustice), robbery (economic injustice), territorial removal (cultural injustice), and rhetoric (verbal injustice) rampant in individual and social lives. The results of this sin are the dehumanization of persons and the ruination of the world through a web of injustices that, Lebacqz contends, feed one another:

> Political injustice reinforces economic injustice. Verbal injustice supports ethnic and sexual injustice. Ethnic injustice is used to undergird political injustice. The result is a web of injustice that ensnares and destroys those within it. The result is the ruination of a people: locked in a pen, with chains around their necks, they can be likened to goats (35).

Lebacqz notes that when Yahweh reestablished the covenant with Noah, Yahweh also established a new sign for the covenant: the rainbow (Genesis 9:13). As Lebacqz interprets it, the rainbow

> signifies the re-establishment of right relationship between God and human beings...between God and all living creatures. It is a joint covenant of life with life...Above all, the rainbow is God's commitment to the struggle against human injustice, and God's call to humans to join that struggle and to reestablish right relationship or righteousness (85).

Righteousness, the central concept upon which justice is based, involves the fulfillment of mutual obligations. Therefore, injustice implies *hatta't,* a failing in what is expected in relations with another, and *ma'al,* a breach of a freely undertaken obligation to another. In other words, injustice in all its forms is another way of characterizing the ancient moral concept of sin. As characterized by Lebacqz, Yahweh's response to instances of human injustice can be described as reticence, rebuke, requisition, and the covenant call to mutual responsibility (70-85). Lebacqz envisions the expected human response to injustice to be formulated in terms of rage (the justice of anger), repudiation (the justice of rejection), resolve (the justice of determination), rebellion (the justice of revolt), and remembering (the justice of solidarity) (86-102).

Lebacqz's treatment of biblical and contemporary forms of justice and injustice reveals that the lines often blur between personal and social sin; one eventually affects the other. What began in primitive cultures as personal and social interconnectedness has, in our contemporary world, advanced to encompass an ever increasingly complex web of political, economical, and environmental interdependence. To speak of sin and injustice is to look beyond the personal acts of the individual human heart to the very social and political structures created by humans themselves. As Dennis Doyle notes,[18] Catholic social teaching and such Vatican Council II documents as *Gaudium et Spes* refer to the sin of social structures:

> Catholic teaching also recognizes that the results of individual sins pervade our institutions in such a way that the institutions themselves are in an analogous sense "sinful" and help to lead individuals to sin (282).

That the pain and hurt of sinfulness are still being felt is evidenced in the daily media onslaught of experiences of hatred and indifference; educational, economic, and political injustices; personal hatreds and greed; and multinational wars. There is cause for hope, however. Jesus concluded his call for the liberation of the "poor, imprisoned, blind, and oppressed" by announcing that "the year of the Lord's favor" (Luke 4:18–19) had arrived. Using the lens of liberation theology, Lebacqz's contemporary interpretation of this phrase is portrayed through the image of "reclamation,"[19] which implies "a conviction that the present injustices do not have to reign...It is possible to be brought back from wrongdoing. Justice can be done in the midst of injustice" (127). Reclamation will take concrete form in the two still unfinished yet enduring responses—justice responding to injustice, and love and service responding to sin—that mark the threads of an ethical vision of covenant.

In summary, the concept of the good Samaritan reminds humanity ~~summary~~ that covenant is crucial to an understanding of a broader personal and social ethical vision. At the level of this larger, broader moral vision, covenant is one of the major traditional patterns in the ethical tapestry. As people called to a covenantal ethical vision, we are also challenged today to step back and evaluate, individually and socially, how individual threads like love and service, sin and evil, justice and injustice are coloring the contemporary broader ethical vision of life as well as particular moral actions. In articulating new visions of what is good and what is possible for people as a nation and as a world, Paul Ramsey exhorts humankind in his preface to *The Patient as Person*:[20]

> Man is a sacredness in the social and political order. Justice, fairness, righteousness, faithfulness, canons of loyalty, the sanctity of life...are some of the names given to the moral quality of attitude and of action owed to all men by any man who steps into a covenant with another man—by any man who, so far as he is a religious man, explicitly acknowledges that we are a covenant people on a common pilgrimage (xii-xiii).

IV. Case Study:
Social Ethics and the Many Faces of Violence

The Child of the Twilight

Ms. Darren, the court-appointed counsel, stood and watched as her newest client, Raul, a young boy of 16, was being escorted across the courtroom. What struck her was not the poor quality of the faded clothing, not the multiple scars on the boy's arms and neck, but the blinking eyes in a face that struggled to adjust to the sunlight and varied sounds echoing about the large courtroom. As Raul caught sight of the sea of strange faces surrounding him, a look of awe and then intense fear crossed his face. It was as if he were not used to being in the presence of bright light, let alone other people. As the boy sat, a young woman came and sat beside him; Ms. Darren recognized Lisa, the Court's Spanish translator.

As Ms. Darren began her opening remarks, the story she told soon shocked the judge and spectators out of their complacency and into the realization that this was about more than the usual adolescent crime. Raul, who did not know English, was an orphan abandoned ten years ago by Juanita, a Nicaraguan mother who had died of drugs in the city's back alleys. Initially brought to U.S. to work as an undocumented nanny for a wealthy couple, Juanita was quickly terminated when she became pregnant. Abandoned by Raul's father, Juanita spent six years trying to find work in the city's sweatshops, whose employers, by physical and mental abuse as well as sexual harassment, took advantage of the workers, many of whom were undocumented aliens. Juanita's lack of legal and socioeconomic status, poor wages, and lack of education locked her into an unending cycle of poverty, malnutrition, and, finally, drug dealing. Little Raul helplessly watched as his mother fell into the cracks of the city's life of drugs and crime.

By the time Juanita died of a drug overdose, Raul was already familiar with prowling the city streets for survival. By the age of nine he was streetwise beyond his years, having learned to scavenge and con for food in increasingly ingenious ways. His home was nowhere and everywhere; in summer he favored the large drainage pipes near the docks—until the bites of river rats when he slept forced him to find lodgings in various ghetto areas. As he grew older, his lack of language, manners, education, and decent clothes brought ridicule from the well-dressed adults and rejection from any legitimate work places. He soon took to hiding during the day, coming out at twilight to forage for odd bits of rubbish and cans that he could recycle for food money.

The night was also forbidden to him, as Ms. Darren pointed out, for it belonged to the organized street gangs who had marked Raul as "bait"—those unlucky victims who were open season for fledgling gang members who needed to prove themselves. Their goal was not to kill the "bait" but to beat him and leave a signature mark upon the victim's body. Raul had had two such experiences before the age of ten; he had learned the lesson of never lingering on the streets at night.

On the night of Sept. 6, however, Raul lingered beyond sunset because Mrs. Kim, the 68-year-old owner of a small convenience store, who had befriended him some months before, had asked him to escort her home. In return for doing odd jobs and protecting her while she walked to and from the store, Raul got the leftover sandwiches and empty cans to recycle. When she had not come out of the store at the usual time, Raul entered it quietly from the back alley. He found Mrs. Kim surrounded by Marcus and his gang.

Noting only that Mrs. Kim was doubled over, Raul unthinkingly charged Marcus, knocking him and Mrs. Kim against the canned goods display. Before anyone could resist or retaliate, shouts from the front of the store alerted the boys that they were no longer alone. Two off-duty policemen had stumbled upon the scene. Marcus and his friends rushed out the back door, but one of the policemen recognized Marcus, gave chase, and eventually captured him. The other policeman found Raul bending over the dead body of Mrs. Kim. Assuming him to be one of Marcus' gang, the officer arrested Raul.

Both Marcus and Raul were charged with murder. Marcus, however, already had two felony convictions. If convicted this time, he faced life imprisonment under the state's "Three Strikes" crime legislation. Therefore, Marcus' attorney would contend that it was Raul who had murdered Mrs. Kim before Marcus and his friends, who had come in to buy soda, could stop him.

"And so, Your Honor," Ms. Darren concluded, "I move for dismissal of the charges against my client for two reasons. First, the coroner's report is inconclusive as to whether Mrs. Kim's death by cardiac arrest resulted from the shock of Marcus' intimidation or from my client's attempt to protect her, which led to her being accidentally pushed into the canned goods display. Second, the death of Mrs. Kim involves more than Marcus and Raul. Mrs. Kim's murder involves the wealthy white couple that lured Juanita here with promises of a new life and then abandoned her, alone and pregnant. Our social and political institutions, the welfare and social services programs are as guilty as those employers who exploited Juanita's vulnerability and made it impossible for her to survive through legitimate means. Our inability to control this city's crime and gang life enabled the drug dealers and Marcus and others like him to prey upon and violate the unprotected Rauls of this city. I contend that it was not Raul who killed Mrs. Kim, but the many faces of violence that pervade this city."

Questions for Research, Reflection, and Discussion

1. Research current legislative efforts, such as "The Three Strikes and You Are Out" laws, to combat crime in the United States. Explain:

a. which crime-combatting efforts are favored by what sociopolitical groups.

b. how these efforts to combat crime may or may not be too narrowly focused on just the wrong actions of criminals and perhaps fail to address other important factors discussed in this chapter: the influence of individual and social sin upon the environment; the interdependence of differing concepts of relationality upon the establishment of moral codes, and the interrelationship between civil and moral law codes in a society.

2. Research the creative efforts with which a particular community has experimented in its efforts to combat crime in a socially, morally, as well as legally responsible way.

3. List the many types of violence that mark the personal and social sins described in the case study. Select one and research how a social, political, or economic system may contribute to the continuance of violence in the United States.

✳4. If you were the judge and you strongly believed that the law should be tempered by a covenantal ethic as described in this chapter, would you dismiss the case against Raul? Explain your answer.

5. Agree or Disagree: Ms. Darren was correct in stating that, although not legally responsible, their city had failed its moral responsibility to Juanita and Raul and is guilty of the social sin of injustice. Explain your answer in light of the chapter's contents.

6. If the coroner's report had ruled conclusively that Mrs. Kim's death was caused by either Marcus' assault or Raul's attack on Marcus that accidentally pushed Mrs. Kim into the display, explain, in light of this chapter, how Raul and Marcus may have varied degrees of moral, if not legal, responsibility for Mrs. Kim's death.

7. Research the Vatican II documents to compare and contrast *Gaudium et Spes* with *Lumen Gentium* ("Light of Nations," also known as *The Dogmatic Constitution on the Church*) concerning the documents' vision of how Jesus' covenantal ethics of loving service can be witnessed to in the contemporary world.

8. Research a possible connection between loving service and the

theme of social and political justice as captured in the contemporary writings of Reinhold Niebuhr, José P. Miranda, John Rawls, or Robert Nozick.

9. Who would you identify in the United States today as "the poor, the blind, the captive, and the oppressed"? Research the history and treatment of one such group within the United States and whether or not there is or should be legislation to help that group. What concrete social and ethical steps should be taken by individuals and by society that would express the Christian vision of covenantal ethics to that group? For example, contemporary examples of "the oppressed" are the many millions who lack health insurance or the millions of un-documented aliens who lack the basics for survival.

Chapter III

A Quest for Meaning and the Development of Values and Principles

Overview

I. Quest for Meaning:
   The Second Pattern in the Ethical Tapestry
   A. Meaning Defined
   B. Ethics, Faith, and Morality
   C. The Role of Reason
   D. Stages of Faith Development

II. Values: The Third Pattern in the Ethical Tapestry
   A. Values Defined
   B. Basic Human Values
      1. The Dignity of the Human Person
      2. Stewardship
      3. The Common Good

III. Principles:
   The Fourth Pattern in the Ethical Tapestry

IV. Feature: Business Ethics and Academia

Questions for Research, Reflection, and Discussion

Overview

The development of a person's individual and broader social sense of ethical living and decision making involves the nurturance of attitudes and actions that are characterized by four interrelated threads: a covenant vision, a quest for meaning, esteemed values, and guiding principles. Chapter II considered the nature and role of the first of these threads—a covenant vision of relationality. Chapter III will consider the nature and role of humankind's quest for meaning. For some, that ultimate search for meaning is encapsulated in a relational image with a transcendent power known as God; for others, ultimate human meaning and fulfillment are found in the pursuit of virtues or goods that move the individual to transcend self. This chapter will also consider the third and fourth threads of the ethical tapestry—esteemed ethical values and action-guiding principles. These threads flow from and are influenced by one's vision of relationality and quest for meaning.

Culturally and historically colored, all four threads form an ethical tapestry that influences an individual's and a society's vision for ethical living and decision making. Ethical maturity requires an awareness and understanding of not only the evolving multidimensional nature of a person's growth but also the interrelated development of an ethical sense that is influenced by each of the four threads.

I. Quest for Meaning:
The Second Pattern in the Ethical Tapestry

"Good morning," said Professor Grant. "Today's lecture will explore the theological and psychosocial relationships among one's image of self, one's image of authority, and one's image of God. Recent research indicates that the development of an individual's self-image and the faith response within a particular religious tradition are both significantly influenced by the effects important authority figures have had on the individual. For example, I would like you to think back to your earliest recollection of receiving help from a significant person in your life..."

As Professor Grant continued, Taylor's mind flew back to long-forgotten memories of a time when, in Taylor's mind, her mother

Carolyn had been the center of her world. As a single mother, Carolyn had been faced with raising a daughter and trying to earn enough money as an entry-level bank teller to support them both. Taylor's earliest memory of Carolyn was centered around Taylor's fourth birthday when Taylor had blithely demanded that her whole day care class be invited to her party because that was the size party that Susan, her best friend and daughter of the mayor, had received. At that early age Taylor had no idea of the enormous cost such a party would entail; in her mind, Carolyn would provide as she had always done. And Carolyn *had* provided a party, though not as lavish as Susan's.

The next images, of Carolyn struggling to fix Taylor's broken bicycle or train set, reminded Taylor that she used to think of her mother as a wonder-worker; Taylor smiled over the memory of boasting to her boy friends that her mother could do anything that their fathers could do.

As the years passed, it seemed that what had been infrequent but firm disciplinary sessions became more routine, and Carolyn became in Taylor's eyes "the boss" whose rules and "dos and don'ts" seemed to multiply with the years. Always independent and stubborn, Taylor's entry into adolescence seemed to intensify these traits. Taylor's image of Carolyn at this time reflected the typical adolescent view of parents: Carolyn knew nothing, her ideas and standards were outdated, and she failed to appreciate her child's opinions and need to be treated as a full-grown adult. Continual battles with Carolyn over drinking, dating, curfew, and educational goals often found Taylor storming from the house to retreat to her best friend Marilyn's house until the storm had passed. It had been mostly through the efforts of Marilyn's mom that Carolyn and Taylor had entered therapy together. Now, five years later, as Taylor entered her sophomore year at the university, her relationship with Carolyn had begun to change for the better. No longer the little girl, Taylor had become in her mother's eyes an adult, a unique individual with needs, feelings, and gifts to contribute. For Taylor, Carolyn had become someone whom Taylor could trust, and a friend with whom she could talk on a somewhat equal footing...

"Similarly," continued Professor Grant, "consider the first time you were presented with the idea of a supreme being, of God. Usually, this concept is presented as a mysterious figure in symbolic, mythical language. Studies show that because of the developmental stage at which children are usually first introduced to the idea of God or a supreme being, they tend to make an automatic identification of God with significant figures in their lives..."

Head nodding in agreement, Taylor's mind again flew back to her first morning at Sunday school, where Mr. Christopher had talked about God, this unseen, mysterious person who was all loving, knowing, and powerful. Taylor remembered thinking at first that he must have been describing her mother, for her mother certainly had loved her, had provided everything for her, and had seemed to be able to do anything and everything. Then, unbidden, came the later memory of junior high years and learning about obedience and responsibility to God; Taylor had thought that Carolyn and God must often confer about making her life miserable by concocting as many rules as possible. And just as Carolyn used to list Taylor's failings whenever there was a confrontation, so too Taylor thought this unseen God must sit in his black robes like the famous television judge, listing in his master book Taylor's sins and failings. So, it was no surprise that, in high school, as Taylor came to view her mother as an enemy, God, too, became an enemy to be ignored...

"Therefore," continued Professor Grant, "by the time individuals have reached adolescence, they have formed both conscious and unconscious "images" of who God or a supreme being is or is not for them. And this image seems to parallel closely the conscious and unconscious images that individuals have formed about significant adults in their lives. And just as life experiences continually cause us to accept, modify, question, doubt, reconsider, and accept or reject the images we have of these significant adults, the same thing should (though it often does not) happen with this image of God. Because we are talking about covenantal relationships where one of the partners in the relationship is the mysterious or transcendental figure known as God, these images of God are always incomplete, always in process and in need of altering as the person grows and develops throughout life.

"Your assignment for the next class," continued Professor Grant, "is to explore as we have done in class the parallel development of your self-image and your image of God. You are also to discuss how your lifestyle, values, goals, and future expectations may or may not be influenced by your image of God and covenant relationship."

As Taylor left the lecture hall, she was struck by how little thought she had given to her relationship with God. Unlike the positive and growing relationship with her mother, Taylor's relationship with God had remained fixed back at the angry, negative, enemy stage of adolescence. Although life experiences had enabled her to reconsider her relationship with her mother, she had taken little time to explore and reevaluate what those same life experiences may have been teaching her about God and the mutual relationship that bound them together. What were her beliefs about God, about faith, and about a commitment to living out those beliefs in an ethical lifestyle?

The preceding vignette highlights the second major thread in the tapestry of an overarching ethical vision: a quest for individual meaning. If a broad ethical vision is grounded in covenantal relationships, then a primary relationship to be considered is the relationship between God, as the ultimate source of meaning, and the individual, and between communities and God. The very term "God," however, carries a diversity of meanings and implications. For Islam or Judaism, God signifies a transcendent single being; for Christianity, the word connotes a transcendent and incarnational being; for Hinduism, there are many transcendent beings or gods. For Buddhism, there is no god as known in Western terms; like the ancient Greeks, the Buddhists seek a highest good, which is described as a super-consciousness, a spirit of wisdom and compassion that enables the individual to live in the world as a better person while simultaneously achieving a higher level of spiritual development.

Besides the traditional and constantly changing notions of "God," our contemporary age of pluralism supports the views of atheists and agnostics who envision the realization of humankind's quest for meaning as lying in the search for an ultimate good or virtue. For these people and others, the Judeo-Christian traditional concept of a covenantal relationship that includes a bond between the individual and a higher power or deity may not exist. Still, because we are human beings, each individual and community as a whole must consider and decide what ultimate meaning or purpose undergirds the relationships, human values, and principles that should be chosen and integrated into individual and collective lives in order to achieve the best possible growth and development.

A. Meaning Defined

There is something within the human person that compels us to search for a power or value greater than the self. In the process of that search, the person creates a conscious and unconscious image of this power or force that gives meaning to life. Victor Frankl declares in *Man's Search for Meaning*[1] that this meaningful image of a greater power or good is the primary force in human life, the force for which human beings live and die (154). As Frankl defines it, meaning is found in limitless potentialities or "in something confronting existence…values that pull man" (157), whether these values be "a cause to which he commits himself, or for a person whom he loves or for the sake of his God" (158). Arguing that a person is always free to accept or reject the challenge to search for and integrate those values by which individuals and communities find their ultimate meaning, Frankl states that meaning is essentially and continually found in each individual's ability to respond, that is, to explore the potentialities for those values, powers, or beings such as God that move the individual to transcend self. For Frankl, meaning in life can be discovered in three self-transcendent ways: through accomplishments, through experiencing something such as a work of nature, and by experiencing someone through love and suffering (176). Ultimately, each individual and community must make a choice "…for better or worse, what will be the monument of his [and their] existence" (191).

While humankind is called to find and live by a life-meaning that draws individuals and communities outside of themselves, Frankl argues that there is also the need to make a commitment to this life-meaning. Faith is this commitment to that which gives ultimate meaning.

The nature of faith has also been considered by many other writers, including James Fowler, a pioneer in religious education. According to Fowler, faith is founded in trust and mutual dependence; it is an attachment, commitment, and loyalty to the complex levels of relationships and values that bind individuals to each other and to the wider community. As Fowler explains in "Faith and the Structuring of Meaning,"[2] viable and lasting communities have a triadic faith structure—involving shared loyalties and trusts among the individual, the community, and "centers of supraordinate value" (17). As Fowler envisions it, creation is moving toward a total transformation or "ultimate environment," much like the Christian and Jewish concept of the "kingdom of God" (18). For Fowler, God is the "center of power and value which unifies and gives character to the ultimate environment" (18). Just as the individual is able to affirm or reject experiences of trust and commitment to ordinary relationships, so too will these same experiences affect the individual's ability to establish and maintain commitments (faith) with larger and more comprehensive relationships (like those with family, neighborhood, country, world) and with supraordinate values (such as justice and God). Ultimately, faith is, in Fowler's words,

> an irreducibly relational phenomenon. It is the active mode of knowing and being in which we relate to others and form communities with those whom we share common loyalties to supraordinate centers of value and power...which unify and give character to an ultimate environment (19).

Whether it be a "highest good," "supraordinate centers of value and power," or supreme being(s), the term "God" will be used in this text to refer generally to a being, power, ultimate good, or value outside the individual or community. Faith is both an internal assent to the presence of this center of meaning in one's life and an external, active commitment and loyalty to the supraordinate centers of power and value in an ethical life centered in covenant relationships.

B. Ethics, Faith, and Morality

Ethics—defined as the way individuals and societies should best order their lives in order to attain maximum growth and development—is shaped and informed by the conscious and unconscious images of this being, power, or ultimate value that influences individual and communal relationships. Faith in and loyalty to this image moves the individual and community to self-transcendence through commitment to an overarching ethical vision. Thus, one does not have to be "religious" or committed to a belief in a traditional concept of God in order to fulfill the human mandate to be ethical.

For many, however, ethics and faith also involve being religious and moral. As defined in Chapter I, "religion" refers to the moral and spiritual tradition to which an individual and community adhere; this tradition provides the best answers to life's ultimate questions for the individual and community. Today in the West, because of the influence of Islam, Judaism, and Christianity, religion involves faith practices, worship, rituals, and devotion focused on a central being—God—who is seen as absolutely good and loving. Faith in, beliefs about, and worship of this God are expressed in religious writings and stories, such as those found in the Bible and Qur'an, and have been further expounded throughout the centuries by theological traditions and teachings of the mosque, synagogue, and church.

Richard M. Gula,[3] a Roman Catholic moral theologian, argues that what God enables and requires of human beings becomes the basis of morality. According to Gula, a moral life informed by faith is human moral striving which

> ...ought to be responsive to God and to be governed by what we can know of the goodness of God and of God's own good activity...Morality itself (from "mores" or "customs") means to make "customary"...in the actions of our lives the experiences which we have of knowing and being loved by God...[Believers] cannot do justice to moral experience and moral world view without seeing all things as being dependent on God...God is the horizon within which the believer sees and values all things. As a result, the morality of those whose imagination is influenced by the religious beliefs of the Judaeo-Christian (and Islamic) traditions has a distinctly theological element to it (44-45).

Religion grounds an individual in a system of beliefs and morality that entails faith in and an ethical commitment to a particular set of experiences of God and a specific image of God. Faith provides a distinctive context, a religious motivation, and a self-understanding that form the basis of a relationship among God and the individual and a community of like-minded people. The mosque, synagogue, or church community concretely expresses its religion and morality in symbols and rituals. Like all relationships, however, the relationships among God and the individual and the community must remain open to change. Time, different experiences, and increased understandings between God and the individual not only affect the relationship but also alter the symbolic and ritualistic expressions. Thus, the community becomes a people of both belief and action; it dynamically witnesses to the faith relationship and moral enactment of the believers' experiences of a good and loving God.

C. The Role of Reason

A faith commitment to one's source of ultimate meaning is not the only basis for ethical living and decision making. Sound ethical decisions are also achieved through the use of the distinctly human faculty of reason.

As noted in Chapter I, Erikson and Kohlberg view life as a process of moving through sequential stages of psychosocial and moral development. The development of reason is one of the faculties that an individual must acquire in order to make intelligent and informed decisions. Sidney Callahan's *In Good Conscience*[4] contends that the mental operations so essential to the working of conscience—memory, focused attention, information processing, and abstract thinking—also develop gradually and build upon the mastery of previous capacities (184). Callahan states that, in terms of a cognitive approach to moral development, moral reasoning involves more than a passive memorization of rules and norms. Moral reasoning involves, first of all, being able

> ...to initiate, use, and appropriately apply mental strategies or operations. It is necessary to focus attention for extended periods of time and yet also to be mentally flexible enough to go backward and forward in time and imagine the problem from different perspectives...One has to be able to take the elements of puzzles apart and put them back together in meaningful, new wholes. If one cannot think flexibly then one cannot meet new contingencies in the environment with new solutions (184).

A certain level of intelligence and rational competence is also necessary if the individual is to master the beliefs, morals, and ethical rules of a faith community. Callahan contends that moral development is enhanced through new social experiences, especially where the individual experiences conflict and discrepancies between his or her own development and that of others. Conflicts and differing views seem to stimulate the individual to search for "a better, higher, more adequate and inclusive level of reasoning" that seems to be distinctly human (185). The result is that, as the individual matures and successfully develops reasoning capacities, there is an increasing movement to higher and higher levels of cognitive and moral reasoning that are characterized by a heightened ability to imagine the perspectives of others, to retain more information, to compare the information for logical inconsistencies, and to evaluate the application of values, rules, and principles to specifics. As Callahan views it, moral maturity is signified by not only the successful achievement of higher cognitive capacities, but also

> a moral sensitivity and quality of the individual's interpretation of what is at stake in an observed situation. Not seeing a dilemma, or not noticing anything morally relevant in a morally problematic situation, is as indicative as other outward signs of moral immaturity or moral tone deafness (185).

Faith requires an ability to commit to a power, value, or reality greater than oneself. Reasoning is the ability to discern and connect with realities outside oneself. Callahan defines moral reasoning as "successfully discerning, resonating to, and approximating …something as rationally true and real." She defines reality as "something that is not the product of one's own cognitive functioning—something that exists beyond one's ken or say-so" (28). Through reasoning, the individual can reach an impartial, universal moral truth, can experience a desire for goodness and an attraction for values, and can experience a compulsion to seek that which enables human beings to appreciate such virtues as love, goodness, beauty, and truth.

In summary, reason informed by faith, but not necessarily the faith commitment to an organized religion, enables individuals and communities to search for and commit to a reality or value greater than the self. Faith, like reason, is not an inherited ability; both capacities require communal guidance, education, and training of human capacities that seem to develop and progress sequentially through the human life span. Unlike reason, however, faith is the ability to risk belief in and commitment to a reality or value that is greater than self and that defies human reasoning capacities.

D. Stages of Faith Development

James Fowler's six-stage theory of faith development is an example of those constructs positing that faith development occurs in sequential stages and is also mutually affected by many of the same factors that positively and negatively affect the moral and psychosocial developmental stages. In *Stages of Faith*[5] Fowler identifies six stages in the development of faith throughout a person's life span. Fowler's study also explores the lifelong development of a person's images of God.

Cognizant of the works of Kohlberg and Erikson, Fowler notes that the degree of trust and autonomy a person experiences as he or she moves through the sequential stages of moral and psychosocial development also influences the person's religious development. For example, in Fowler's Stage One, or the Intuitive Projective Stage, faith for the child of two to seven years of age is at the "fantasy-filled, imitative phase in which the child can be powerfully and permanently influenced by examples, moods, actions and stories of the visible faith of primally related adults" (133). If the child's early experiences have engendered love, trust, and autonomy, then the child becomes more able to intuit a God who loves, trusts, and respects his or her personal autonomy. If the experiences have been the exact opposite, then the God that will be imagined may be a more intimidating and punishing figure who, like parents, must be rejected in order to achieve personal autonomy and freedom. At this stage, the child's imagination enables the child to intuit through stories the feelings and meanings of ultimate realities like God, death, life, and love.

Many budding relationships with God have been permanently scarred or destroyed by negative images or parallels that the child has consciously or unconsciously made with the help of experiences with significant others in the child's life. Brennan Hill, Paul Knitter, and William Madges have noted in *Faith, Religion & Theology*[6] that in the Intuitive-Projective Faith Stage, faith is

as we experience it from others. Since children tend to mirror the actions of those around them, they reflect the faith life that they experience in the significant people in their lives, especially parents. The faith of children is not so much their own personal faith as it is the faith that is modeled for them by others. If a child sees a parent devoted to God, that faith deeply affects the piety of the child. On the other hand, if a parent is filled with fear of God and divine punishment, this attitude can move the child to become very intimidated by God (38-39).

In addition to these negative experiences that affect the child's image of God at this first stage, there is another danger to the development of a moral imagination. As they attempt to reinforce doctrinal expectations or social taboos, adults can exploit the young child's imagination with images that evoke terror and anxiety. Because a child at this stage lacks the ability to use logic and analysis to sort out the truth, the emerging imagination "is extremely productive of long lasting images and feelings (positive and negative) that later, more stable and self-reflective valuing and thinking will have to order and sort out"(133).

As the child of eight to twelve years moves into the second stage, that of Mythic-Literal Faith, he or she leaves behind intuitions and fantasy and employs narratives, symbols, and concepts to devise a concrete and literal interpretation of faith commitments and loyalties. God is envisioned in anthropomorphic terms, which again reflect past and present experiences of significant adults (141). External structures of fairness, for example, are constructed in terms of the loving, caring, fair, or just ruler/parent. As in Kohlberg's Stage Four, rewards and punishments are reciprocal: Goodness is rewarded and badness is punished (142-45).

Arrival at adolescence corresponds with Fowler's Stage Three, or Synthetic-Conventional Stage. At this stage the adolescent is becoming increasingly more critical of personal and social relationships. The emerging ability for reflection and myth making about self, God, values, commitments, and relationships is tied to the individual's struggle to achieve a sense of identity and worth, which is strongly influenced by the affirmation and approval of significant others (154). From a psychosocial perspective, the adolescent is caught in the double bind of achieving an identity and independence apart from significant others while also needing the approval and support of these same people..

Just as views of and relationships with significant others undergo diverse changes during adolescence, so too must the relationship with God be reevaluated. Fowler contends that "the adolescent's religious hunger is for a God who knows, accepts, and confirms the self deeply, and who serves as an infinite guarantor of the self with its forming myth of personal identity and faith" (153). The adolescent tends to view the ultimate in terms of a personal, all-knowing God who is also accepted or rejected depending upon the parallel experiences with significant others. The individual adheres to or rejects the beliefs and convictions of significant adults and his or her religious tradition as a means of asserting or rejecting a sense of commonality and solidarity with others (167).

The Individuative-Reflective Faith, or Stage Four, ideally occurs in early adulthood, in a person's twenties. For some, however, this stage may not occur until a person has reached the thirties or forties. For a few, this stage is never reached. The stage of Individuative-Reflective Faith is a time of critical examination of the very values and beliefs tacitly accepted but unexplored in the previous stages. The sense of self and relationship to others is regrouped in terms of choices and exclusions and "in a qualitatively new authority and responsibility for oneself. External authority and systems of values must now be chosen and internalized as one's own. Roles and relations once constitutive of identity, now being chosen, become expressions of identity" (181). There is a genuine awareness of social systems and institutions; the individual no longer sees social relations as merely the extensions of interpersonal relations but can now see them as influenced by impersonal laws, rules, and social standards. Control is important and, in terms of faith, is expressed in the tendency to demythologize symbols and myths into conceptual meanings that the individual deliberately accepts or rejects. Beliefs and values are no longer tacitly accepted as a means of solidarity; explicit acceptance or rejection becomes part of a larger need to reconcile other developmental tensions: personal identity versus the larger group membership, self-fulfillment versus the call to serve others, and a sense of personal commitment to what is immediate and present versus a commitment to a possible greater force or power.

Fowler's Stages Five and Six transcend age and are not automatically achieved. They have more to do with a way of being in the world than with a chronological age progression. As the individual develops within Conjunctive Faith, or Stage Five, there comes a gradual realization that truth has opposites and paradoxes, that relationships are a balance of initiative and control, and that a part of life is seeking to be part of a larger movement of spirit or being that moves a person toward a solidarity and selflessness heretofore unthought of. Reminiscent of the shamen and medicine men of the indigenous peoples researched by Angeles Arrien in *The Four-Fold Way*,[7] this stage becomes a time of reconciling the conscious and unconscious, a "seeking of an intimacy and knowing that celebrates, reverences, and attends to the 'wisdom' evolved in things as they are, before seeking to modify, control, or order them to fit prior categories" (185). Individuals who have caught the meaning of this stage have an ability to encounter people, relationships, and beliefs that are different and to see in them truth and values that transcend tribe, class, religious tradition, and nation. The ultimate goal of this stage is the capacity to see and to live in one's own community and belief system while recognizing that they are "relative, partial and inevitably distorting apprehensions of transcendent reality" (Fowler 198). Conjunctive Faith enables the individual to see and accept truth as more multidimensional and interdependent than previously considered.

Similar to Kohlberg's Stage Six, Fowler's last stage, Universalizing Faith, is rarely attained. It calls for an individual's ability and willingness to move from self as central to a faith identification with, or participation in, the Ultimate:

> They have become incarnators and actualizers of the spirit of an inclusive and fulfilled human community. They are "contagious" in the sense that they create zones of liberation from the social, political, economic and ideological shackles we place and endure on human futurity. Living with felt participation in a power that unifies and transforms the world, Universalizers are often experienced as subversive of the structures...Many persons in this stage die at the hands of those they hope to change...Their community is universal in extent. Particularities are cherished because they are vessels of the universal...Life is both loved and held to loosely. Such persons are ready for fellowship with persons at any of the other stages and from any other faith tradition (201).

Epitomized in the past by Muhammad, Jesus Christ, and the Buddha, and in contemporary times by Mohandas K. Gandhi, Martin Luther King, Jr., and Mother Teresa of Calcutta, the universalizers of Stage Six have achieved a commitment and loyalty to relationships and values that transcend a particular value system, community, or religious tradition. They have consciously chosen values and beliefs about self, God, and others that are based on universally agreed upon ethical values and principles. Universalizers are role models and leaders of contemporary religious and ethical lives, moving this world slowly toward an ultimate goal: a total spiritual transformation. According to Fowler, their lives reflect H. Richard Niebuhr's "radical monotheism," which Niebuhr defines as a form of faith in the transcendent reality of God who is exerting a transforming influence upon the world (204). Fowler identifies this description of Niebuhr's radical monotheism with the Judeo-Christian concept of "the Kingdom of God," a hope founded in the Jewish covenant relationships and transformed by Jesus who was

> steeped in the Jewish vision of a covenant relationship with God...that will redeem, restore, and fulfill God's creation in a kingdom of right-relatedness between God and humanity, between peoples and between people and nature. Niebuhr saw Jesus as the "pioneer and perfecter" of the faith to which we are called (Fowler 206).

James Fowler, like Victor Frankl, H. Richard Niebuhr, and many others, envisions human beings as involved in a dual challenge. The first challenge calls individuals to progress through a variety of moral, psychosocial, and faith levels of development while pursuing personal life meanings or goals. These levels of development eventually lead the individual to the realization that the self is bound by many types of relationships, all of which are essential for individual and communal growth and well-being.

Simultaneously, the second challenge is for human beings to transcend particular quests for ultimate meaning so as to participate in an overarching ethical vision and ultimate goal that have the ability to move people to transform the world. These people envision a common

Summary Chart of Fowler's Stages of Faith Development

Stage Value Shapers	Faith System	Method of Decision Making
I. Intuitive-Project Faith		
Imaginative, fantasy-filled view of a supreme being that mirrors eclectic qualities of culture & significant others	Internalization of images, symbols and values from Bible, fairy tales and religious stories	Fluid and magical; lacks deductive and inductive logic.
II. Mythic-Literal Faith		
Transcendent being who is anthropomorphic representation of qualities of significant adults; – reflects cultural and religious influences	Beliefs, morals, rules and attitudes are appropriated literally from religious narratives and significant others	Intuitive sense of natural system of right and wrong; – justice based on cause and effect
III. Synthetic-Covenantal Faith		
Interpersonal relationship with transcendent being who is mysterious and omniscient; knows human beings intimately	Images and values are shaped by expectations of outside authority figures; beliefs and values are tacitly held	Unexamined reliance on and obedience to existing outside system of values and rules
IV. Individuative-Reflective Faith		
Critical questioning and reflection on once tacitly held image of transcendent being, religious symbols, and ritual; – deliberate choosing of ideology and affiliations	Relocation of authority within oneself; – awareness of impersonal set of law, rules and standards	Reflective adherence to impersonal set of law, rules, and standards

Summary Chart of Fowler's Stages of Faith Development

Stage Value Shapers	Faith System	Method of Decision Making
V. Conjunctive Faith		
Transcendent reality only partially known through one's chosen beliefs, values and image of this transcendent reality	Values one's own experience of truth; – values order and institutions; – seeks a justice that transcends tribe, class, and country	Self becomes a valued authority; –decisions based on conscience and compromise
IV. Universalizing Faith		
Belief in and need to incarnate in self and world a transcendent reality. – deliberate choosing of ideology and affiliations	Spending of self and energies in actualizing values, justice, and unconditional love standards	Conscience; – Universally agreed upon ethical values and principles.

goal to which all of creation is gradually but inexorably moving, "a universal, shared future of all being...grounded in a divine-human partnership that bears the weight of ultimate truth" (Fowler 210).

How persons and societies respond to the dual challenges will be mirrored in the images of God, or power greater than self, that they project. Together, this image of God and the vision of relationality held by a person or society become important indicators of the values or goods that a person and society hold as necessary for continued growth and survival.

"Image of God" has been discussed as a person's internal vision of and faith in a power or value greater than the self. "Faith" is defined as relational trust in and commitment to this "image of God." According to Fowler, each person's acquisition of the interrelated realities of an image of God and faith in this image depend upon a concomitant sequential process of psychosocial and moral development. The chart, pages 82-83, summarizes the discussion of the salient points of Fowler's stages of faith development.

II. Values: The Third Pattern in the Ethical Tapestry

I say to you today, my friends, so even though we face difficulties of today and tomorrow, I still have a dream. It is a dream deeply rooted in the American dream.

With these impassioned words ringing over the massive 1963 rally at the Lincoln Memorial in Washington, D.C., Martin Luther King, Jr., poured out his vision to the rapt audience of over 200,000 people and millions of others watching on television the world over. This dream or "vision" captured the essence of an eight-year struggle for civil rights and bespoke a deeper understanding of the civil rights struggle that went far beyond the initial 1956 bus boycott by blacks in segregated Montgomery, Alabama. King's immortal "I Have a Dream" speech continues today to provide the underlying meaning to both the civil rights movement, in particular, and to the world's quest for greater equality and dignity for all peoples and nations.

Similarly, a year prior to the delivery of King's historic speech, and many thousands of miles away, another man saw his "dream" come to life; in 1962 Pope John XXIII opened the first session of the Second Vatican Council. Elected in 1958, Pope John was expected by many to be a "caretaker" pontiff, one who would maintain the status quo during a brief reign. However, guided by many years of pastoral experience, this 77-year-old man brought to his papacy a joy for life and a passionate vision of God's love for and involvement with humankind. Molded by the needs of the times and his own inner understanding of God's call for the church, John XXIII's vision for Vatican II went beyond rule and practice changes; the vision of Vatican II involved a deeper realization of what and who the modern Roman Catholic Church should be for its members and for the world.

The dreams of Martin Luther King, Jr., and Pope John XXIII have outlived these men who provided the initial impetus to movements that changed their worlds. There are at least two possible reasons for their enduring power. First, these visions and dreams reflect an overarching ethical vision that these men believed would transform the world, if taken seriously. Second, their ethical vision captures the four enduring threads that are interwoven into the ethical tapestry that we have been examining: covenant relationships, a quest for meaning, esteemed values, and principles. The first two threads have already been discussed.

The third and fourth enduring ethical threads are the values and principles that human beings establish as a result of the influences of a vision of covenant and and search for meaning. Values are esteemed ideas or motives, and principles are particular norms or action guides that express how covenant relationships are to develop and be maintained, as well as how ultimate meanings and ethical goals are to be achieved. Human values and principles do more than transcend the boundaries of time, race, and creed; they also reflect the overarching ethical vision, the sense of the moral good that is larger than individual actions.

A. Values Defined

As defined in Chapter I, values are the broader or overarching ideas, motives, and virtues that a society considers as good and essential for the support of life. Values affirm not only a particular individual or society's vision of the good but also a way of being that actively moves individuals and societies toward developing an internal and external awareness of the larger world ethical vision of life. Donald Walhout points out in *The Good and the Realm of Values*[8] that each society within its own historical time period articulates a system of values based on individual and communal biological, psychological, ethical, spiritual, and social needs, and on senses of variety, imagination, curiosity, and aesthetic appreciation (41). Learned and cultivated within the individual, values, says Walhout, are "biological and spiritual, individual and social, private and communal, persistent and temporary" (44). Life, bodily and psychic health, and freedom are examples of basic values. Similarly, there are negative realities that are not esteemed as values that support human well-being: Pain, suffering, hunger, thirst, illness, ignorance, prejudice, and segregation are a few examples.

Rooted in common experiences that society considers independently good, supportive of life, and necessary for continued growth and survival, values are, as William Frankena[9] explains, "traits of 'character,' rather than traits of 'personality' like charm or shyness. They are all dispositions to do certain kinds of action in certain kinds of situations, not just to think in certain ways" (49). They guide human beings toward the ideal of becoming the best possible human beings that they can become. Ethical values challenge individuals and communities to be responsible and accountable for the achievement of certain attitudes and behaviors that will achieve the ideal. For example, the value of respect for life leads to the cultivation of traits within the individual and society that affirm life in all its stages. Filled with this attitude of respect for life, the individual makes choices and decisions that underscore that value. Therefore, an attitude that respects life is not disposed toward, nor does it behave in a manner that promotes, murder—the unjustified taking of the life of another human being.

In *Principles for a Catholic Morality*, Timothy E. O'Connell[10] notes that although important in and of themselves, values also possess four other essential qualities. First, they are real and part of the objective world; as such they keep human beings in contact with and accountable to objective reality (162-64). Ethical living based on values seeks to do that which is generally considered as supportive of human growth and welfare; values prevent legalism and the whims of the individual from becoming the bases of ethics.

Second, values involve choosing certain goods that result in the rejection of other goods. Constricted by a natural limitedness of insight and opportunities, individuals and societies know that selecting certain values means rejecting other possible values. This results, according to O'Connell, in a tension and awareness that ethical judgments are evaluations "of and choices among, relative (not absolute) goods" (167). As circumstances change, insights grow, and other opportunities emerge, present values may be discarded in favor of new ones, some of which may have been among the values previously rejected.

O'Connell notes a third quality: Values are susceptible to change because they are historically bound evaluations of right action rather than absolute dictums carved in immutable stone. As situations change, as awareness and experiences increase, and as other values affect the situation, values change in relative importance (170). For example, many persons tend to place more value on work than on time spent with significant others. These relative values often change, however, when a person is faced with a life-threatening experience such as a plane or automobile crash. Suddenly priorities shift, and work recedes behind the need to maintain important relationships. Thus, not only is the priority of values subject to change, but the final evaluation of which values are chosen in a particular situation is also subject to change.

A fourth quality of values is that they are grounded in the essence of ethical living (174). In Chapter II of this text, the essence of ethical living is presented as a personal and communal commitment to covenant relationships. Values point to both internal attitudes (character or disposition) and external behaviors (action) that are expressed in and by covenant relationships. Values also reflect the ultimate meanings as well as the broad ethical vision that inspires the commitment to covenantal living.

B. Basic Human Values

Embedded in the history of humankind are examples of individuals and communities who seek to establish basic human values that reflect their overarching ethical vision. Sometimes known as "metavalues" (Walhout, 90) or cardinal virtues (Frankena, 50), these basic values are goods considered essential for human flourishing; from them all other values flow.

In *Spheres of Justice: A Defense of Pluralism & Equality,* Michael Walzer,[11] a distinguished Jewish political philosopher, notes that a study of history, philosophy, and theology reveals that there seems to be no consensus throughout history as to what constitutes a universal set of basic values or goods esteemed by every culture during every age.

> There is no single set of primary or basic goods conceivable across all moral and material worlds...A single necessary good, and one that is always necessary—food—for example—carries different meanings in different places (8).

As times and societies change, the basic values that they have esteemed may be added or dropped. For example, in his *Short History of Ethics,*[12] Alasdair MacIntyre notes that for the Greeks of Aristotle's time, the concept of happiness was the primary goal of life. A life exemplified by virtues such as wisdom, intelligence, prudence, and temperance enabled certain individuals to achieve this ultimate goal (62-63). The medieval world of Christianity extolled the values of the moral equality of all members of the Christian community, obedience to the religious laws and teachings of the church, and adherence to the virtues of faith, hope, and charity. If rightly lived, these values would enable the individual to achieve the true goal of life: the eternal reward of heaven (115-118). Influenced by the scientific and philosophical revolutions of the seventeenth and eighteenth centuries, communities like the Puritans came to esteem such economic values as property, financial thrift and planning, and material prosperity (150-51). In the nineteenth century the German philosopher Hegel extolled personal freedom and spiritual development as central values (203), while Marx advocated personal and social freedom from oppressive economic structures (211-213).

Another important development occurred in the mid-twentieth century when, for the first time, nations joined to declare a united political and moral stand for basic human values. In 1948 the United Nations issued its "Universal Declaration of Human Rights,"[13] which proclaimed in the contemporary language of "rights," those basic human values necessary for the flourishing of peoples of all nations. Among the rights recognized in the thirty articles of the Universal Declaration are life; liberty; security of person; freedom of thought, conscience, religion, work, and leisure; and enjoyment of the arts. The late-twentieth century considers these rights not only fundamental for personal, social, and economic welfare of all peoples, but also essential for the political stability of the world. Like all political systems, however, this declaration of rights can change as united nations progress to a deeper understanding of those values necessary to human life and development.

However, among the values supported by the United Nation's Universal Declaration are three enduring values that, as Albert C. Outler and James M. Gustafson[14] contend, echo the writings and teaching of Judeo-Christian tradition: 1) the dignity of the human person, 2) stewardship, 3) the common good. These three values may not provide an exhaustive listing of the values that are significant for all times and cultures; they do, however, provide some firm examples of what can be considered as basic human values integral to the visions of ethical life throughout much of human history.

1. The Dignity of the Human Person

From a non-religious perspective, the 1948 Universal Declaration represents what countries like the United States and France have long affirmed in their sociopolitical struggles for democracy: the essential and basic human value of life, especially self-conscious life.

> The peoples of the United Nations have in the Charter reaffirmed their faith in the fundamental rights, in the dignity and worth of the human person and in the equal rights of men and women and have determined to promote social progress and better standards of life in larger freedom (Preamble, Universal Declaration of Human Rights).[15]

From a religious perspective, the valuing of the human person is rooted in the scriptural vision of each person being created in the "image and likeness of God" (Genesis 2). For the followers of Islam, Judaism, and Christianity, this means that, above all, human life is a gift that, according to James Gustafson, has an

> author and a source beyond itself, and we and all other forms of

life are dependent on that source. Life is given to us...Since the *sine qua non* of other relative values and of valuing is the existence of human physical life, it is valued and is to be valued with a high priority (123).

According to this value, then, human life possesses a dignity and sacredness that each human being must always uphold. Human beings share in the creative power of what H.R. Niebuhr calls "the One beyond the Many" (Gustafson 123) and are challenged to fashion a world in which life flourishes.

For example, founded in 1976, Habitat For Humanity, an ecumenical Christian housing project, seeks to support human dignity and a basic human need for shelter by providing no-interest homes that are sold to those who can not otherwise afford one. Funds, building materials, and labor for the homes are donated by volunteer organizations, churches, and individuals who work along with the designated family to produce what is often the first real non-substandard home that family has known.

The religious perspective recognizes that the gifts of reason and creativity are two ways in which human beings express the dignity and sacredness of the human person. Reason gives one the ability to imagine, think, and plan. Donald Walhout defines creativity as the quality of "being alive, being aware of constructive possibilities, being imaginatively and resiliently productive" (93). In the cultivation of reason and creativity, and in the pursuit of science and new developments to transform the world, human beings reflect an innate sacredness and dignity that mirror the image of the God who initially authored life.

In the late-twentieth century, however, human beings are now beginning to become sensitized to the idea that if "life" is a precondition of value, then "life" must always be viewed in terms of the unified or organic nature of the universe; the multi-leveled nature of the universe demands that human beings never forget that they are radically interrelated and interdependent with all other forms of life. Life in general and human life in particular are to be considered a primary basic value, and other values, such as belonging, worth, and appreciation are cultivated so as to support this respect for the dignity of life in all its forms.

Founded in 1971 by a group of Canadian environmentalists, Greenpeace International exemplifies a nonviolent and direct effort by over 40 national groups to preserve life by working to change governmental and industrial policies and practices that threaten the world's non-human resources. Prevention of air, land, and water pollution; arms control; the protection of animal habitats; and support of alternative sources of energy are some of the areas of interest supported by Greenpeace International.

2. Stewardship

Viewed from a non-religious or an ecological perspective, human beings are to be the responsible managers, not the masters, of personal and planetary resources. As prudent managers, human beings are held accountable for a wealth of resources that include the physical and material goods around us, the gift of mind and body, the gift of life, and the gift of the power of bringing new life into the world. Prudent management means that human beings must ultimately see that the human powers and created resources are not endless, and that the true valuing of these resources is to be found in respecting the dignity of everyone and everything. Abandoning the traditional notion of humankind's vocation to master the earth, this perspective reinterprets human management as a basic way of life that is oriented toward a responsible respect for, and development of, life in all its forms. For example, over the past twenty years, international congresses have convened to explore prudent management of the earth's resources. As discussed in Chapter II, the 1992 United Nations Conference on Environment and Development represents efforts to confront a variety of threats to the environment. The 1994 Cairo Congress on Population and Development is illustrative of nations attempting to combat one part of the human threat to planetary well-being: the debilitating effects of overpopulation on current and future planetary needs and resources. Experts at the congress warned that, if left unchecked, increased overpopulation could lead to endemic poverty and mass starvation in less than a century.

Flowing from a religious perspective of the value of human life is the value of human accountability or stewardship. Gustafson explains that, like a good household steward or manager, each person is held ac-

countable to God for the stewardship of his or her own life and the
lives of others for whom the person is responsible. Each person is
called to preserve the dignity and sacredness of life and to make it
fruitful. As humanity uses its gifts, especially the gift of reason, to meet
the challenge of fashioning a world in which life flourishes, it cannot
assume unwarranted sovereignty over life, itself a gift. As Gustafson
notes,

> Man is accountable to the author and source of life for his use and
> cultivation of life, including human physical life. He is re-
> sponsible (in terms of accountable) to God for the ways in which
> he cares for, preserves, sustains, cultivates, and, in his limited ca-
> pacity, creates life around him. His disposition is that of the free
> servant; not servile but acknowledging that his human vocation is
> under God (123).

3. The Common Good

From prehistoric times, humankind has recognized the need to band
together and work cooperatively in order to ensure survival, growth,
and development. The evolution of the state, of social, political, economic, and religious structures, and of codes of law all point to the
goal of affirming the value of the common good for the welfare of the
planet. Although there is a strong espousal of individualism in the
United Nations Declaration, it also reflects the common human experience that human growth and welfare depend upon a continued recognition that individual rights and freedoms, although good in and of
themselves, must be continually balanced with the rights and freedoms
of all peoples.

Article Twenty-nine of the Universal Declaration captures the concept of solidarity or concern for the common good:

> Everyone has duties to the community in which alone the free
> and full development of [individual] personality is possible. In
> the exercise of [individual] rights and freedoms, everyone shall be
> subject only to such limitations as are determined solely for the
> purpose of securing due recognition and respect for the rights
> and freedoms of others and of meeting the just requirements of

morality, public order and the general welfare in a democratic society (164).

Religious tradition also esteems the value of the common good. The basic tenets of Islam, Judaism, and Christianity all remind their followers that if believers are to be good stewards, then they must look beyond the immediate implications of what they do as individuals and ask how their actions affect others. The good of society as a whole must always be taken into account. If the good of the whole is lessened, the good of its parts—that is to say, its members—is lessened. The dignity of the individual cannot be upheld unless the dignity of society is served.

And who shall teach thee what the steep is? It is to ransom the captive, or to feed in the day of famine, The orphan who is near of kin, or the poor that lieth in the dust;
    Beside this, to be of those who believe, and enjoin steadfastness on each other, and enjoin compassion on each other.
    These shall be the people of the right hand... (*The Koran* 90:12-19).[16]

In summary, the notion of the common good is concerned with the integral ordering of all goods so that they contribute to the harmonious flourishing of the entire planet. The resources and gifts given to individuals must be seen as gifts meant for all. When evaluating technical abilities, for example, individuals and communities must look at more than just what these aptitudes will accomplish for certain individuals; they must also consider what effect these skills have on society as a whole—on the customs, values, and institutions, such as family, schools, corporations, and religions. The critical question to ask is whether the development and use of any gifts is for "the benefit of all."

III. Principles: The Fourth Pattern in the Ethical Tapestry

The basic human values that flow from a broad ethical vision and covenant relationships are further delineated in guidelines. Known as norms or principles, these guidelines indicate more specifically how a value is to be realized in concrete terms. For example, the value of the "dignity of human life" is reframed in a specific norm or principle that outlaws slavery because it reduces human beings to the inferior status of property.

In *Reason Informed by Faith,* Richard M. Gula discusses three other qualities of principles or norms. First, principles or norms are reflections of various aspects of covenantal living. As the "moral memory of the community, they are the repository of its collective, experiential wisdom" (284). Through time and a variety of situations, humanity has experienced certain actions and judged their consequences as having humanizing or dehumanizing effects that cannot be ignored. Therefore, out of experiences of social relations, humanity has learned that the telling of untruths leads to the undermining of trust and solidarity, both of which are crucial to social cohesion.

Second, norms or principles provide consistent guidelines of what are right and wrong behaviors. Because they are based on shared human experience and wisdom, norms provide a "reliable point of reference and direction" (284) for ethical living. These reliable points of reference allow for ready and consistent decision making; they save one from having to figure out what is the right or wrong direction to take in every new situation.

Third, norms challenge ethical living by "giving expression to the good toward which we ought to strive" (285) as individuals and as a collective whole. From an individual perspective, norms enable each individual to evaluate and to correct his or her actions when they fall short of enabling the person to develop as fully and healthfully as possible. From the communal perspective, norms represent "a broader vision...challenging us to take into account the accumulated experience of the community and to consider the collective consequences of our behavior as well" (285).

Traditionally, principles or norms have been categorized into two types: formal or general norms, and material or behavioral norms. The first type, formal or general norms, relates to one's inner character or attitude as an ethical person: what one ought to be or become. Formal or general norms are, as Louis Janssens,[17] a Roman Catholic moral theologian, has noted, the "animating element of our conduct" (207).

Formal norms challenge, motivate, and guide one to become the best that he or she ought to be as a human being. For Janssens, the fundamental attitude that should affect human relationships and activities is an ethics based on the principle of love (agape) of God and others. Love is not the emotional attachment or affection usually equated with the word. Rather, because every human being is created in the image of God, love is the equal and impartial regard for every person as having value, dignity, and worth (220). However, this basic attitude of love also needs the support of other moral virtues or formal norms, such as justice, sincerity, honesty, prudence, compassion, and gratitude, to name a few, and the avoidance of vices or the attitudes opposite to virtues. As Gula notes, formal norms

> ...do not give us specific information to answer the practical moral question, "What ought I to do?" But they encourage us to be a certain sort of person...They remind us of what we already know and encourage us to do what is right and to avoid what is wrong (289).

Material or behavioral norms—the second type of norms or principles—relate to the sorts of actions one ought to perform as an ethical person. These norms challenge a person to apply formal norms to specific instances of behavior. They ask that one bring a certain valued disposition to a concrete situation. However, because material norms relate to actions that human beings should do or should avoid, they have limitations. They must, as Gula cautions, always be evaluated in light of three interrelated factors: the historical times, the concrete circumstances surrounding the action, and the intentions of the actors (290-91). Just as values are susceptible to change because they are historically bound evaluations of what is good or right action rather than absolute dictums carved in immutable stone, so too people and the behavioral norms they choose to follow are affected by historicity and a particular context. As situations change, as awareness and experiences increase, and as other values affect the situation, the behavioral norms change in relative importance.

Summary

The general ethical tapestry has been traced in Chapters I through III. We have laid out the four threads: covenant relationships, quest for meaning, esteemed values, and guiding principles that shape and are shaped by individuals and communities. Now that each of the basic threads has been discussed, we can shift our focus from the large tapestry design to the old Native American woman as the particular weaver of the tapestry. In other words we will concentrate less on the broad, the external, and the communal, and more on the specific, the internal, and particular dynamics of the individual as an ethical and moral agent. Just as the old woman's communal experiences brought a unique dimension to her weaving, her individual character also had a definite impact on every phase of the tapestry making. Chapter IV will focus on the unique dimensions that each individual brings to each particular act of ethical decision making. The discussion will focus on issues such as freedom, responsibility, conscience and authority, conflict and doubt, and ethical theories, and how these influence each person as a moral agent attempting to live and choose ethically within a communal context.

IV. Feature: Business Ethics and Academia

When the phrase "business ethics" is used, the implied reference is usually to the world of corporate America. Closer to home for most readers of this book, however, is the business world of higher educational institutions. Universities and colleges have stated educational goals as their primary objectives. Like their corporate counterparts, however, these institutions of higher learning face strong national and international competition for clients, in this case students. Therefore, in order to survive and be successful in a competitive business and academic milieu, academic institutions must be run according to sound legal and ethical business practices. They must devise persuasive public relations and advertising programs to draw customers (students) and use big budgets to attract well-trained staffs to deliver the primary product (educated persons). And because financial resources are always limited, educational institutions must go beyond student tuition and fees and cultivate a variety of funding sources: the federal government, state and county agencies, private donors, private businesses and corporations, alumni, and community groups.

Each of the following vignettes features a conflict among the educational, ethical, and business values and principles of a university and its students.

Questions

Consider the following questions for each vignette.

1. What are the values/norms in conflict?

2. What values and norms are potentially being violated?

3. What moral virtues and behavioral norms should be considered as the basis for resolving the ethical conflict?

4. How might the other two broad ethical concepts—covenant relationships and image of God—influence a resolution?

Vignette 1

Darius is the senior editor of the university's student newspaper. Now a graduate student, he has worked on the paper since his freshman year. His goal is to pursue a career in national or cable television. His work as a feature reporter and editor has already come to the attention of two television networks who have made job offers following graduation.

However, Darius and his editorial staff have become embroiled in an escalating conflict over a plan to run a series of feature articles on serious animal rights violations by the university's large medical research department. The topic is a hotly debated one on campus and the focus of protest by a variety of community animal rights groups. Darius and a majority of his staff favor running the articles as planned. Darius believes the paper has an ethical and humanitarian duty to expose the results of its investigation. Because local news agencies have expressed some interest in carrying the features locally and nationally, Darius also sees publication as a way possibly to solidify his promising career in television.

The university administration is opposed and has already applied some pressure on Darius and the editorial staff. The administration does not want the feature articles run, as they could prove damaging to

upcoming government research grant awards that the university needs
to remain competitive.

Vignette 2

Although admission quotas are illegal at the university, Tom, a student member of the Admissions Board, learned of an unwritten rule
whereby the Admissions Board favors the children of alumni and certain ethnic and socioeconomically advantaged groups over others. As a
scholarship student, Tom knows that if he reveals these policies and an
investigation ensues, he may well lose his scholarship and his chance at
a degree from this big name institution. Yet Tom knows at least four
other students who will not have any chance of an education because
of the Board's unwritten and discriminatory policies.

Vignette 3

As a business major, Sherry, a senior at the local university, is the
first ever chosen from this university to work as a summer intern at a
nearby printing company. While entering some data in the company's
accounting files, Sherry accidentally uncovers some accounting discrepancies that imply that in exchange for business, the company is
making unreported donations to the university to support its nationally
competitive sports program. When Sherry reports the discrepancies to
two of her supervisors, she is told to "forget it." The next day, after receiving a phone call from the printing company, the dean of her business college meets with Sherry. He tells her of the favorable impression
she has made at the company, and implies that, should she agree with
her supervisors at the company, she will be sure to receive a job offer
from one of the Big Eight international accounting firms.

Vignette 4

In an attempt to raise consciousness concerning ethnic and gender
discrimination, the university's Dance, Art, and Drama Department decides to sponsor a series of combined productions featuring controversial pieces on issues of racism, homosexuality, and gender bias.
After a protest by a few community and student groups, Sabrina Ferris,
the department's faculty advisor, is warned by the administration that
unless the production is altered or canceled, the department will lose

future university funding. The president also implies that Dr. Ferris will be removed as advisor and her own career placed in jeopardy, as there could be a reduction in her department's size and funding for the next academic year.

Questions for Research, Reflection, and Discussion

1. Research, compare, and contrast how the concept of God or the good had a profound affect on the ethical vision of two societies or nations in the course of history.

2. Research the basic values of an unfamiliar religious tradition or philosophy and the effects those values have or do not have on the tradition or philosophy's ethical system.

3. A variety of health care reform plans have been proposed to address the need for better health care coverage. One health care reform plan was based on six values and principles: security, simplicity, savings, choice, quality, and responsibility. Research another major piece of legislation to discover the values and principles upon which the legislation is based.

4. How would socioeconomic and financial status, gender, age, and ethnicity affect the formation of an individual's character and disposition in terms of ethical decision making?

5. What position would you take regarding Kohlberg's and Fowler's contention that their highest stages of moral and faith development are rarely attained?

CHAPTER IV

THE ROLE OF CONSCIENCE AND ETHICAL DECISION MAKING

Overview

Influenced by a sense of personal and social awareness, each individual seeks to do that which ideally brings ultimate meaning, happiness, or fulfillment to self and others. People need to be trained to follow ethical or moral standards designed to promote individual and social good and to avoid evil. This training entails, among many things, the development of conscience, which is that unique capacity within each person in which the broader ethical vision is uniquely woven together with the particular character of the person as a moral agent and the individual's unique analysis of the particular situation.

Chapter II began with The Tale of the Unfinished Tapestry. In this imagery, conscience is like the old Native American weaver who both shapes and is shaped by her culture, historical times, life experiences, covenant relationships, quest for meaning, values, and principles. Like the old weaver who, when faced with making a particular addition to the unfinished tapestry, must make particular choices that affect the overall pattern, conscience, too, molds and brings the components of self, covenant, quest for meaning, values, and principles to bear upon particular ethical or moral decisions.

Chapter IV will explore the nature and function of a sound conscience. Conscience is viewed as a three-dimensional entity within each person that enables the person to learn right from wrong, to use the reasoning process correctly, to evaluate each particular situation in light of the person's own unique individual and social experiences and ethical training, and to commit finally to a particular course of action. Also considered in this chapter are such issues as the role of conscience, the nature of freedom as involving choice, determination, and responsibility, the right use of freedom, the function of one's personal obedience to and dissent from civil and moral authorities, and the influence of evil on conscience.

Responding to Conscience

The heat was oppressive. The multitude of sounds—raucous vendors, snarling dogs, the incessant babble of human voices—could not be blocked. The sights were even worse. From her bedroom window she looked upon streets filled with squalor, poverty, and disease. She saw abandoned babies, the elderly, lepers, and destitute people dying. What even seemed worse was their seeming invisibility to the passers-by who callously stepped over the prone bodies. Distressed by these experiences, she took her concerns to prayer.

In September 1946 her prayer was answered by a new call from God. She was to leave her work of teaching in a cloistered convent and become actively involved in relieving the plight of these nameless, destitute human beings in the slums of India's cities. By 1948 her white sari with a blue border and a cross on the shoulder had become a familiar sight as this diminutive woman trudged the slum streets, caring for the dying and destitute. Limited in medical experience and lacking financial and medical resources to make a seemingly impossible task possible, this woman was seen by most observers as insane and doomed to ultimate failure.

The world knows her as Mother Teresa of Calcutta. A native of Yugoslavia, educated in Ireland, and trained as a Roman Catholic sister, Mother Teresa spent 17 years as a member of the Loreto Sisters, a cloistered religious order in Darjeeling, India. However, in 1946 her world changed drastically as she received permission from her religious superiors to leave a world of isolation to become an advocate for India's poor. In 1950 she founded a new religious order, the Missionary Sisters of Charity, whose work is devoted to care of the poor of the world. Desmond Doig's *Mother Teresa: Her People and Her Work*[1] testifies to the successful record of this faith-filled woman and her religious community, which by 1978 had grown to over nine hundred members working in sixty-one foundations in India and twenty-eight abroad. At that time they staffed eighty-one schools, sixty-seven leprosy clinics, twenty-eight homes for abandoned children, and thirty-two homes for dying destitutes (100).

Mother Teresa's life and work illustrate the concepts of ethical vision and living that have been explored in the first three chapters in this text. In answering the dual ethical questions of what to become and how to act, Mother Teresa's individual actions and life are guided by a conscience and vision of life formed and shaped by her spiritual call as a Roman Catholic woman religious. The nature and function of this call are in turn continually informed by Mother Teresa's search for meaning, which is grounded in an image of God incarnated in Jesus Christ, a faith commitment, and a life of prayer and meditation that have provided compelling images of love and service that impel her to make choices and commitments to the poor and the destitute. She is a woman whose covenant relationships encompass the world. In Frankl's terms, Mother Teresa has found meaning or faith in a power and in values outside of herself and to which she has tirelessly devoted herself. Through committed service to others, her life reflects the values and principles of love, service, esteem for the worth and dignity of all human beings, and compassionate commitment that in turn are models and inspiration for others.

Besides revealing Mother's Teresa's larger ethical vision, Doig's biography also illustrates how this vision has been shaped within the context of her overall psychosocial, moral, and religious development. As developed in Chapters I through III of this text, the development of each person involves a complex interweaving of many individual and social processes, which, if effective, enable the person to come to a special self-awareness comprising two parts: 1) an understanding of his or her human nature as historical, relational, embodied, unique, rational, and creative and 2) a view of self as to broad ethical and social demands embodied in the concepts of covenant, search for meaning, and values and principles. Empowered with this special self-awareness, the individual now realizes that to be an ethical person involves more than right choices and actions; it also involves a "being in the world" that is continually informed by this self-awareness.

I. The Nature of a Sound Conscience

- "Your conscience tells you what is right and wrong."
- "You must judge according to your conscience."
- "Look at her behavior. It is obvious she has a guilty conscience."

We have all heard statements like these. They reveal that conscience, like love, is a widely used term, but its definition is ambiguous, and its role and function are difficult for individuals to grasp precisely. Traditionally, conscience was defined more as a mechanical function of the individual's will or intellect that enables a person to know right and wrong or to exhibit certain skills in good decision making.

In accordance with contemporary ethicists Richard Gula and Timothy O'Connell,[2] conscience is defined here as a single entity with three dimensions: a capacity, a process, and a judgment. This definition differs from the traditional one in that conscience is now seen as more than an intellectual, skilled exercise in right decision making. Rather, a more contemporary understanding of a sound conscience considers it as comprising both a fundamental attitude or way of living that adheres to the good or the right, plus a fundamental way of acting that results from the correct use of reason and sound decision-making skills.

Gula notes that, as a capacity, conscience enables a person to learn and to do what is good and to avoid what is evil. This fundamentally human orientation to the good also gives a person a sense of moral value and responsibility toward life. As a process, conscience involves accurate perception and moral reason so as to be able to search out accurately the "objective moral values in each specific situation in order to discover the right thing to do" (131). Informed by its sense of the good (capacity) and its ability to perceive and select relevant moral values and principles (process), conscience uses its judgment dimension to evaluate and to decide what each unique person must do in a particular situation; the judgment dimension of conscience also enables the person to commit to that decision. Because each person is unique, the judgments of conscience are ones that can be made only by that person. Conscience, defined as a combined capacity, process, and judgment, expresses the whole person, or as Gula describes it,

> "...me coming to a decision." It includes not only cognitive and volitional aspects, but also affective, intuitive, attitudinal, and somatic aspects as well. Ultimately, conscience is the whole person's commitment to values and the judgment one must make in light of that commitment to apply those values (131).

II. The Development of Conscience

Just as human growth and development is a process needing formation, so too, conscience needs to be educated, formed, and examined so as to achieve right thinking and to avoid error, narrowness, and ignorance. Similarly, just as the individual is formed through a complex community process of socialization, so too conscience is molded by many of the same factors that affect the other developmental dimensions of the person: one's culture, race, ethnicity, family, peers, socioeconomic environment, and educational, psychological, and spiritual resources. In addition to these are the various sources of moral wisdom that a person's conscience experiences as it learns what it means to perceive and act in an ethical way.

There are many sources of moral wisdom. These include the culture and social life of a community, the sacred writings and teachings of past and present world moral giants, and the rituals, stories, visions, authoritative teachings, and rulings of leaders and experts in the world's religious traditions. Other rich sources of moral wisdom, whereby the conscience of individuals and communities are constantly being enriched and enlarged, are the ethical, philosophical, theological, anthropological, spiritual, and psychological contributions of thinkers of all cultures and ages.

The narrative is another rich source of moral wisdom. Theologians, ethicists, and religious thinkers are reexamining these personal and community biographies for their importance and influence upon the ethical life. The writings of Stanley Hauerwas, Michael Goldberg, James W. McClendon, and Sidney Callahan[3] re-emphasize something seemingly forgotten by traditional ethics: Ethical choices are not made in a vacuum; they are made by people whose lives are continually being shaped and motivated by choices that are based on changing perceptions, experiences, and interpretations. Viewed from the perspective of each life story or narrative, these choices are a reflection of the underlying character of the person, and as such, provide insights into the status of ethical living in the contemporary world. For example, in *Naming the Silences,* Stanley Hauerwas examines the lives of terminally ill individuals who he believes contain sources of moral and ethical wisdom for individuals and communities faced with life and death questions.

Not only do individual biographies reflect moral or ethical character, but each life or narrative is also an embodiment of the images, visions, values, beliefs, and habits of the character of the community that nurtured the individual. As Michael Goldberg explains in *Theology & Narrative,*

The character of the community in which an individual is fostered and nurtured is part of the heritage—for better or worse—of his own character. Obviously, for his part, the individual may develop a character which may affect—for better or worse—the character of the community in which he lives (67).

In summary, conscience development, like personality development, is a lifelong process that shapes, and is shaped by, many influential factors. And just as the right environment is needed to nurture the sound growth of the person, so too must the right environment exist if a sound conscience is to emerge. Freedom and knowledge are two important environmental conditions that must be present if a sound conscience is to be nurtured and maintained.

A. Freedom

A person's conscience must operate in an environment of freedom in order for the conscience to develop and to act ethically or morally. Freedom involves two human capacities: freedom of choice and the power for self-determination. Although related, these two capacities involve different requirements and both are necessary components for responsible ethical decision making. In *Love & Conflict: A Covenantal Model of Christian Ethics*,[4] Joseph L. Allen, using Reinhold Niebuhr's philosophy regarding human nature, defines the two-pronged nature of freedom:

> ...God has created us with two fundamental characteristics. One is freedom, in the sense not only of the ability to decide between alternatives, but also and especially of having the capacity for self-transcendence—standing "outside ourselves," so to speak, of needing to interpret our existence, and of having to decide upon the total direction of our lives...(92).

1. Freedom of Choice

Freedom of choice, or the ability to make responsible choices, involves a number of complex internal and external realities. One internal reality is the mental capacity for competency. This involves independence of judgment, an ability to make voluntary choices among different alternatives. Independence of judgment, however, can be limited or obstructed by real or imagined pressures from other persons, groups, or agencies, which in turn leave the person with the awareness that the decision-making alternatives are limited.

For example, in *Black Womanist Ethics*,[5] Katie G. Cannon explores the nature and role of the freedom, faith, and ethics of the black woman. Using a mixture of black historical and literary traditions, Cannon concludes at the end of her study that the need to survive forms the basis of black women's ethics. Such an ethic was born out of the black woman's moral situation, which Cannon characterizes as one of non-freedom, as a "struggle to survive in two contradictory worlds simultaneously, one white, privileged, and oppressive, the other black, exploited, and oppressed" (8). In other words, given the context of a long history of oppression, exploitation, sexism, and racism, the black woman has been deprived of her independence to evaluate and choose freely the ways by which she can realize the three things that Cannon argues are necessary for a black woman's sound moral growth: dignity, community, and interrelatedness with the entire human community (168-174). In the case of the black woman, historical and social factors have shaped an ethical context that has severely limited her independence of judgment and her liberty to make choices about her life.

Freedom as competency also involves the possession of cognitive skills enabling one to make an informed and intelligent choice in any given circumstance. As Sidney Callahan notes,[6] these cognitive skills, which are keys to conscience and decision making, involve

> ...self awareness, a sense of identity, an ability for self-regulation (control) and self-direction, a capacity for self-evaluation, and an affective desire, or caring commitment, to measure up and act according to some perceived standards of moral worth. Such qualities require highly complicated mental, emotional, and social abilities...(38-39).

The impairment or lack of these complex cognitive skills reduces a person's competency to make free, realistic, and informed decisions; such is the case for mentally ill, mentally retarded, or brain diseased persons. For example, Greg, age 24, has been diagnosed as schizophrenic for two years. As long as he adheres to his medication and therapy protocol, Greg is competent to hold down a minimum wage, part-time job and to function independently while living at home. However, when stress levels become too high or he fails to remain on his medication, Greg experiences the delusions, illusions, and social and emotional withdrawal characteristic of schizophrenia. At these times, Greg is not capable of competent decision making.

Competency has layers of meaning and degrees of abilities within philosophical, medical, legal, and psychiatric circles. Despite a lack of consensus in these professions, James F. Childress and Tom L. Beauchamp offer, in *Principles of Biomedical Ethics*,[7] a standard for defining competency: "A person is competent if and only if that person can make reasonable decisions based on rational reasons" (83). Childress and Beauchamp note contemporary efforts to establish standards for judging competence based on situation-specific criteria (80-81). For example, the criteria for a person to stand trial for murder are different from the criteria for a person to go grocery shopping or to choose a meal. Similarly, because competency exists along a continuum from full competence through various levels of incompetence to total incompetence, the criteria for judging competence must also take into account the particular circumstance, the type of decision required, and the emotional and chronological age and condition of the person. A frightened, slightly emotionally retarded adult, for instance, cannot be expected to make an emergency room decision about amputating a limb; the same individual, however, can, under normal circumstances, make simple dietary and monetary decisions while shopping (84-85).

The external realities to freedom of choice involve the social, political, economic, and cultural environment within which the person faces the possibility or lack of possibility of freedom of choice. For example, the amendments to the United States Constitution guarantee freedom of speech, religion, and press. These freedoms and the rights to life, liberty, and the pursuit of happiness cannot be taken away from United States citizens except through legal means. Within this constitutional context, United States citizens are free to make personal choices so long as they do not impinge upon the rights and freedoms guaranteed by the Constitution and laws as belonging to other individuals, the states, or federal government.

In contrast, other countries and cultures limit or prohibit to varied degrees the political, religious, social, and economical freedoms and choices of their citizens. Bender and Leone's *The Third World: Opposing Viewpoints*[8] presents a variety of compelling and opposing viewpoints that explore whether modernization in parts of South America, Africa, and Asia has resulted in real freedom or in further limits of freedom that had already been restricted by the countries' ideologies, governmental structures, and economic policies. If modernization has resulted in a further limit of political, socioeconomic, or physical freedoms, then freedom of choice is an illusion for millions of people in these countries.

In summary, freedom as a freedom of choice involves both the sound mental faculties that enable one to make a competent choice and the supportive environment that permits one the independence to make decisions after consideration of a variety of possible alternatives.

2. Freedom of Determination

He is an eleven-year-old boy who had the misfortune to sneak a cigarette in the wrong place at the wrong time. His experience brings him face-to-face with a suicidal lawyer who reveals confidential, incriminating information about a Mafia client. For Mark Sway, the eleven-year-old in John Grisham's novel *The Client*,[9] the results are life changing: His younger brother becomes psychologically traumatized, his mother loses her job, their home is blown apart by a bomb, and Mark is the object of a simultaneous hunt by the media, the FBI, and the Mafia. Suddenly his juvenile world of fishing, television, movies, and petty pranks evolves into a deadly game for survival. Everyone has ideas about what Mark should do: His lawyer advises him and his family to disappear by entering the FBI protection program; a supportive judge wants to incarcerate him for his own protection; the Mafia in New Orleans wants to kill him; the politically aspiring D.A. wants him to appear before the New Orleans Grand Jury.

Mark is only eleven years old, and with so many experienced legal and illegal groups forcing him to act as an adult in a violent world, his expected choice might be to follow the adults' easiest and safest road for survival. Instead, this young hero provides an interesting study in self-determination. From the beginning of the novel, Grisham portrays

Mark as street-smart and world-wise beyond his years. His addiction to television crime stories and police movies and his strong independent streak enable him to visualize choices and to determine a course of action for his life and those of his family.

Mark's choices and actions highlight the human capacity to view self, events, people, and circumstances within a certain context and to choose a certain path. This capacity is what Richard Gula defines as self-determination or

> ...the freedom to decide about oneself and to make someone of oneself...The more we are able to become aware of ourselves and possess ourselves, including all the determining influences, the more we will experience ourselves as responsible for what we do and who we become (77).

The Client is the story of freedom and the ways that each person must learn to handle it. As Mark's life becomes more complicated, he decides that he needs advice that he can trust; so he sets out alone to retain a lawyer. His life soon becomes intertwined with that of his lawyer, Reggie Love, who wisely gains Mark's trust by allowing him to make his own choices and to determine his destiny as much as possible. To do so, Reggie must also model the very virtues that she is trying to help Mark espouse: honesty, integrity, responsibility, and courage in the face of overwhelming odds. This is illustrated when Mark asks Reggie's advice as to whether he should lie about what he learned from the suicidal lawyer. Mark's very question pinpoints Reggie's own ethical dilemma: to advise him to remain honest could result in psychological traumatization by the D.A. or death by the Mafia. To advise him to lie, however, would violate Mark's trust as well as her own professional standards of protecting the best interests of her client.

> She'd thought about this for hours, and still had no answer...As much as she wanted to, she could not advise him to lie. A lie would work just fine. One simple lie, and Mark Sway could live the rest of his life without regard to what happened in New Orleans. And why should he worry...? He was just a kid, guilty of neither crime nor major sin (190).

Reggie's subsequent advice and actions on Mark's behalf illustrate that there are limits to self-determination. Historicity, genetics, culture, economic and sociopolitical structures, institutions, and other factors limit each person's range of choices and ability to determine the course of life. Despite the limitations of present circumstance, as personified in Mark, all human beings face the challenge to choose responsibly and ethically. In Mark's case, he is able to look at those limits and then navigate himself creatively through an adult world full of pitfalls. Mark's strong sense of freedom, as evidenced by his stubborn self-determination and continued evaluation of available choices, also reflects his developing moral character and conscience.

In summary, implying freedom of choice and cognitive abilities to make decisions, the freedom of self-determination goes the next step by enabling one to decide about oneself and one's future. The more a person is free to make choices and to determine one's own destiny, the greater is this person's ability to make responsible decisions.

3. Freedom and Responsibility

Freedom also entails a correct understanding of two of its correlates: license and responsibility. One of the marks of maturity is the ability to see that freedom is not license—the unrestrained ability to act regardless of social rules and laws. Rather, freedom always involves responsibility. In *The Nature of Moral Responsibility*,[10] Stephen Ross characterizes responsibility as a pervasive, fundamental, human, moral attitude of each person whereby one

> ...has accepted the commitment embodied in the moral life, a commitment with no beginning and no end, no boundaries and no restrictions. We are obligated by the demands of moral commitment to certain actions, and when we fail we are responsible for our failures...The moral life [is] a perpetual questioning and responding, testing and retesting, evaluation upon evaluation, in which nothing is finished or irrelevant (230-31).

So, for example, even at age eleven, Mark Sway, the hero of *The Client*, provides evidence of his willingness to accept the responsibility for his choices; after receiving advice to the contrary from Reggie, Mark voluntarily draws a court citation for contempt when he refuses to reveal information that he believes will only further hurt himself and his family.

Throughout the history of the Western world, philosophers have examined this idea of freedom as responsibility versus freedom as license. In his historico-critical survey of Western thought on the human will, Vernon Bourke[11] notes that the concept of freedom as responsibility emerged in the works of such Greek philosophers as Plato and Aristotle, who always viewed human freedom from a political and social context. As Plato remarks in *The Republic,*[12] the decisions of human beings are directed toward true happiness, which can only come from the right development of the human personality as a rational and moral being who esteems the virtues of justice, temperance, courage, and wisdom:

> ...the simple and moderate desires which follow reason, and are under the guidance of mind and true opinion are to be found in...the best born and educated...this (justice) is the only virtue which remains in the State when the other virtues of temperance and courage and wisdom are abstracted;...this is the ultimate cause and condition of the existence of all of them (Book IV, 121, 123).

Freedom of choice and freedom of determination play a part in human development; however, as Plato warns in Book IV, freedom is not license to do as one likes (109). Rather, the Platonic sense of freedom always entails the ability to act not only in accord with justice and reason but also for the common good (Book IX, 276); human beings are, foremost, social beings whose use of freedom and ultimate happiness and development occur only within responsible social living (Book IX, 269, 286).

This latter thought is echoed by Aristotle in *Nicomachean Ethics.*[13] In this work he reminds his listeners that life's ultimate goal of happiness can only be achieved through the development of reason and of one's individual potential, which are then harnessed into responsible service for the further nurture and maintenance of society:

The good of the state is manifestly a greater and more perfect good, both to attain and to preserve. To secure the good of one person only is better than nothing; but to secure the good of a nation or a state is a nobler and more divine achievement (Book I, Chapter 1, 1094 B, 385).

Centuries later, the philosopher John Locke reiterated this same train of thought: Human beings are by nature equal and free. They have certain freedoms or liberties that are characterized by moral responsibilities and not license. In his second *Treatise of Government*,[14] Locke contends,

But though this be a state of liberty, yet it is not a state of license, though man in that state have an uncontrollable liberty, to dispose of his person or possessions. Yet he has not the liberty to destroy himself, or so much as any creature in his possession...The state of nature has a law of nature to govern it which obliges everyone; and reason, which is that law, teaches all mankind...that being all equal and independent, no one ought to harm another in his life, health, liberty, or possessions (Chapter II, 6, 270-71).

Similarly, from a Judeo-Christian theological perspective, responsibility and freedom are linked to the biblical notions of a creation made in the image of God and related through covenant. Roger Burggraeve[15] contends that because human beings are created as responsible, it is their "creaturely responsibility" (120) and their God-given mandate to channel their gifts of reason and freedom so as to fashion loving relationships and creative situations that will transform the world:

This does not mean that we can do as we please with the world, catering to our individual existence, aiming solely at our own self-development...We must take care of the world in the way that God wishes it to be guarded (Burggraeve 120).

In *Responsibility in Modern Religious Ethics*,[16] Albert Jonsen, S.J., concludes that freedom as responsibility was an essential theme in the writings of the philosopher Robert Johann. According to Jonsen, Johann characterized the responsible, moral, human life as one that shapes and is shaped by a world that is essentially interrelational:

> ...The responsible man is not the one who is merely concerned with the personal character of his action, but much more importantly with its adequacy to the demands and exigencies of the occasion...We must seek the demands and exigencies of our moral life in this world of interpersonal relations (156).

Human beings are challenged continually to be open to a reality that is ongoing, engaging, and rejecting. Summoned to act responsibly in the concrete situations in which individuals find themselves, persons are called to "dialogue," that is, to use their experiences of self, others, and all creation (160), to act freely and responsibly in making evaluations about the world's needs and conditions, and finally to make decisions that will increasingly bring about a universal community (161). According to Johann, this community

> ...grows out of the continuing free response to the presence of the other, who continually presents himself in new revelations, making new demands, in the light of new conditions. The promotion of being is precisely the effort to work toward the wholeness and coherence of experience, in which self is known as self, other as other, self and other in intersubjectivity which transcends itself (165).

Johann then defines the basis of morality as the freedom to love, which always seeks to promote the uniqueness of self and others, to intervene in those concrete situations that deprive others of beingness and hinder the advance of genuine community (167).

To summarize, freedom of conscience is an essential ingredient for ethical decision making and living. Freedom is not license. Because human beings are social beings, freedom of conscience entails the ability to respond maturely, to experience alternatives, and to decide independently about oneself and one's destiny within socially agreed upon limitations. Freedom promotes the well-being of others; to the degree that freedom and conscience are impaired, lacking, or prohibited, then the real ability to develop as an ethical person in community is curtailed.

B. Knowledge

1. Types of Ethical Knowledge

✗   Integral to the psychosocial and moral development of each person is the attainment of a knowledge of self, others, and the world. Erik Erikson[17] argues that the search for self-knowledge, or a sense of identity, is the central task of adolescence. From a theological and ethical perspective, Paul Schotsmans[18] notes,

> ...the individual can only become a self by searching for his or her own identity...The individual constructs the self with a view toward meaningful existence. With the knowledge of what one is and what one can become, one puts everything into the service of one's own life project (170).

The acquisition of knowledge that contributes to identity development also involves the ability to master and integrate two different types of knowledge that are sometimes called knowledge of the "head" and knowledge of the "heart." Knowledge of the "head" pertains to the observable and known facts and data about self, others, and the world. It also involves acquiring the skills to understand and master social, ethical, and moral rules, values, and principles. The development and use of cognitive skills and reasoned reflection characterize the traditional use of "knowledge of the head," or reason, to acquire knowledge in general and to make ethical decisions in particular.

Knowledge of the "heart" goes beyond the facts and observable data. This type of knowledge is gained through personal life experiences and reflection. Because it is a "felt" knowledge, it cannot be taught through rules or formulas. Rather, knowledge of the heart is born of one's experience and intuition; it has to do with apprehending the essence of a person, object, or event without the use of logic or reason. It has more to do with an inner sense or ideas that are best explained by tactile images. Callahan describes intuition as a moral signal that is

...more like a faint odor; we might say, "I sniffed a bad odor about the whole thing." We might refer to the sense of touch— "My skin crawled at the suggestion"—or in a positive vein—"I tingled with the sense that this was what I have been longing for" (87-88).

Knowledge of the heart eventually moves the person to choose his or her own important facts, relationships, emotions, and values rather than to depend upon compulsion or outside authority.

As explained in Chapter I, there are differences in the way males and females approach life. One of these differences surfaces in the ways that men and women acquire, interpret, and implement knowledge of the head and knowledge of the heart. Studies of children's differing styles of play may account for these differences. Little boys engage in active, competitive, structured games whose rules are clear and concise and whose goals can be concretely measured by the successful advance of, for example, the football into the end zone. Little girls form small groups whose games tend to involve a great deal of talking, like playing house or dressing dolls, which causes them to become more attentive to one another's feelings. The result is that males will tend to lead with knowledge of the head and attend more to changes in action, ideas, or the rules. Women will be more attuned to and comfortable with employing knowledge of the heart, which acquires its information less factually through changes in feelings conveyed through verbalization or more subtly through body language and gesture.

There is no doubt that men and women use both knowledge of the head and knowledge of the heart. History is replete with examples of how knowledge of the heart or intuition, sometimes called "inspiration," enabled men like Edison, Einstein, and Oppenheimer to create scientific and industrial inventions that have changed the world. However, because of women's relational base, which emphasizes mutuality, empathy, flexibility, and receptivity, they, more than men, may be open to using and trusting knowledge of the heart in any type of decision making.

Taken together, however, knowledge of the head and knowledge of the heart comprise a blend of rational, intuitive, and emotional knowledge of self, others, and world that is integral to the development of a sound conscience and ethical decision making. Informed decision making consists in an awareness of and a willingness to be flexible enough to apply both types of knowledge in a particular context.

2. Acquiring Ethical Knowledge

The following question has been raised throughout the history of morality and ethics: How does one gain the best or correct knowledge by which to shape one's identity, moral character, and life direction in an ethically or morally sound way? One answer is found within the Christian tradition, which delineates three methods: reasoned reflection and dialogue, the natural law theory, and fundamental stance. All three methods are informed to some degree by both knowledge of the head and knowledge of the heart.

a. Reasoned Reflection and Dialogue

Dialogue or communication requires constant interaction with others. It is a means by which information about self, others, and the world is exchanged for a variety of purposes. Reflection is that capacity of the person to use one's faculty of reason to ponder, review, and evaluate personal and social communications in order to make better and more informed choices. In *The Human Center*[19] Howard Harrod describes human beings as moral agents possessing the powers of interpretation and projection, that is, as beings who possess an awareness of identity and integrity that enables them to perform the distinctly human capacities of thinking, choosing, and acting freely. Harrod contends that it is through the use of interpretation and projection that human beings are able to employ their complex reasoning processes to declare personal and social needs and wants, and to make deliberate choices between right and wrong (96-113). We arrive at ethical decisions by employing a complex cognitive process known as reasoned reflection. In this process each person's conscience combines the integral skills of self-consciousness, self-direction, control, self-evaluation, affective desire, and the ability to make a caring commitment, with a process of dialogue and reflection.

If correctly formed and informed, conscience, with its ability to use reasoned reflection, enables the person to shape identity, moral character, and basic life direction. According to Sidney Callahan,

...reason and rationality are a real way to truth, and we participate in something real beyond ourselves...Through reasoning,
a rational mind can reach an impartial, universal moral truth,
which logically must be the same for anyone in the same situation. We see it and cannot deny it, and this rational necessity provides the force of the moral imperative (28).

As one way of acquiring ethical knowledge, reasoned reflection
tends to focus upon the inner cognitive abilities of a person to reason,
dialogue, and reflect about external experiences. In this way, moral
knowledge is gained through sound interpretation and use of one's interactions with self and others.

b. The Natural Law Theory

A second way of gaining and using moral or ethical knowledge in
the Christian tradition is offered by the theory of natural law, which is
a name for a long, complex philosophical and theological tradition.[20]
For example, the Roman Catholic understanding of the natural law theory draws heavily upon the synthesis of philosophical and theological
themes by the medieval Roman Catholic theologian Thomas Aquinas.
Aquinas's articulation of the natural law theory is a combination of two
threads of thought rooted in various books of the Judeo-Christian bible,
in the Greek philosophy of the Stoics and Aristotle, and in the Roman
law as interpreted by Ulpian (Gula 222-223). Although both threads of
Aquinas's thought are found in contemporary Roman Catholic moral
theology, each thread represents a very different view as to the source
and function of freedom, reason, and ethical decision making.

The first thread posits that there is a generic "order of nature"
whereby both the human and animal worlds are governed by physical
and biological structures, laws, and properties. Sometimes known as
physicalism (Gula 226), the moral system based on this strain sees God
as speaking directly through nature; the structures and functions of
creation are an expression of God's intentions for creation. Therefore,
sound moral living and decision making require an examination of natural biological and physical laws. Once a person grasps the arrange-
ment and purpose of this "order of nature," one is able to acquire
knowledge upon which to evaluate one's physical actions. Ethical liv-

ing becomes automatic acquiescence to, and following of, these biological and physical laws regardless of the input from the human capacities for freedom and reason.

For example, one of the natural inclinations of creation is procreation. Adherence to the "order of nature" thread of natural law theory demands that created beings, especially humans, promote good by
doing nothing to frustrate this reproductive capacity. Moral evil is anything that frustrates the inclinations of this natural capacity. Therefore,
according to natural law theory, contraception and sterilization are considered morally evil because their intent is to prevent the natural inclination toward reproduction.

It is in his comprehensive manual of moral theology, the *Summa
Theologiae*[21] that Aquinas diverges from this first strain of natural law
thought and its originators, the Stoics, the Roman jurist Ulpian, and
Aristotle. Aquinas asserts:

> The injunctions of the law in us by nature are to reason planning
> action...The first premise in reason's planning of action is that
> good is to be done and pursued and evil avoided. And on this are
> based all the other injunctions of the law in us by nature, which
> command us to do whatever reason, when planning action, nat-
> urally grasps to be good for man (*Summa*, IaIIae, Question 94, p.
> 286-87).

According to Aquinas, the good that befits human nature, and toward which human beings are inclined, is characterized by the tendencies to preserve life, to procreate, and to use reason to seek truth
and to live a sound social life (*Summa*, IaIIae, Question 94, p. 287).
Anything that prevents the realization of these natural inclinations is
evil. Therefore, suicide is condemned by Aquinas as frustrating the natural inclination to love and cherish life (*Summa*, IIaIIae, Question 64, p.
389), and speaking falsehoods is wrong because it violates the natural
human inclination toward truth (*Summa*, IIaIIae, Questions 109-111, p.
418-419). Furthermore, because nature is the result of and ultimately
subject to God, the laws of nature are unchangeable. The implication is
that human beings are expected to conform to physical and biological
laws and structures as a matter of fate or God's will; morality becomes

a blind following of what nature requires in order to fulfill some inherent design of God or destiny.

Simultaneously, there exists within Aquinas's natural law theory a ✗ ②
second strain or "order of reason," which originates from such ancient
thinkers as Aristotle, Cicero, and Gaius (Gula 223). Aquinas synthesizes
the works of these ancients into a fundamental teleological standpoint:
God is the ultimate end or goal of human existence,

> ...for God is the ultimate goal of all...Men attain their goal by
> coming to know God and love him; other creatures are incapable
> of this, but attain their goal by existing and being alive and
> aware...We call man's way of attaining his goal being happy
> (*Summa*, IaIIae, Question 1, p. 174).

As creator and ultimate end, God is also the ultimate and eternal
source of moral value, law, and decision making. Just as the human
will is naturally inclined toward the good, so the human intellect is naturally made for knowledge and truth acquired through reason and ultimately satisfied by the experience of God as the source of all truth:

> Man's intelligence is his highest power, and its highest object the
> good that is God, an object of contemplative not practical intelligence. So happiness is above all the activity of contemplating
> the things of God...The proper object of mind is truth, and God
> alone is essentially true; so it is contemplation of God (the source
> of all being and light), that makes us completely happy (*Summa*,
> IaIIae, Question 3, p. 178).

According to Aquinas, if the ultimate goal for human beings is the
development of their fullest potential, then it is God's intent that hu- ✗
man beings use their God-given gift of reason to attain such a goal.

Sometimes known as personalism, this second strain of natural law
thinking implies, according to Gula's contemporary interpretation of
Aquinas, the "totality of the human tendency to want to know the
whole of reality and come to truth" (224). Truth becomes the continual
human search for, and use of, those resources that human beings need
in order to develop to their fullest potential as individuals and as social

beings. The way to gain truth is through all the dimensions of reason that Sidney Callahan underscores in her work *In Good Conscience*: research, intuition, affection, and common and aesthetic senses (126).

A moral system based on this perspective challenges the person to use the physical, spiritual, emotional, intellectual, and psychological dimensions and faculties of life so as to grasp at any historical time what it means to be fully human and to live a moral life. This entails a morality that is sensitive to the changing aspects of human experiences, to an evolving personal and communal sense of the good, and to the responsibilities and consequences incumbent upon a covenant community that is called to a life based on ethical values and principles. According to Gula, a modern worldview of contemporary morality favors a personalist view of natural law in which nature is not fixed but evolving, and in which human beings creatively and reflectively seek

> to discover moral value in the experience of the reality of being human...The human person does not have to conform to natural patterns as a matter of fate. Rather, nature provides the possibilities and potentialities which the human person can use to make human life truly human. The given physical and biological orders do not dictate moral obligations; rather, they provide the data and the possibilities for the human person to use in order to achieve human goals...The "nature" which reason explores is no longer separated from the complexity of personal, human life in all its relationships (235).

In conclusion, moral values, obligations, and decisions will vary, depending upon which perspective a person adopts. This choice will also have decidedly different implications for individual and covenant life. An understanding of natural law as seen through the Roman Catholic tradition provides insights into two different perspectives for gaining and using moral or ethical knowledge. Adoption of the first perspective, the "order of nature" strain of natural law, results in a person's continued struggle to make moral decisions based on the discernment of a fixed physical or biological order. Such a view prohibits the creative use of freedom, reason, and knowledge, for the created order is static and unchanging. In sharp contrast, the second perspective, the "order of reason" strain, continually challenges humankind to discover new possibilities in an ever-evolving world. The need for continual choices amid ever-evolving possibilities and realities is similar to a third way of acquiring ethical knowledge.

c. Fundamental Stance

Ethical knowledge can also be acquired through what Timothy O'Connell terms a "fundamental stance" of life,[22] the idea that an ethical or moral life is reflected in more than a one-time choice for good or for evil. Each person's life is directed by a lifelong choosing and evaluating that reflects a direction that is essentially positive or negative.

For example, Jake, aged 14, looked and fit the stereotypical role of gangster. A native of the ghetto area streets of Brooklyn, N.Y., Jake sought to mold his identity according to the callous and rough-tough image of his Mafia leader uncle. He took great pride in being able to strip cars, rob stores, and coordinate drug deals with a speed and efficiency that earned him tangible material rewards from his uncle. When asked once when and why he chose this lifestyle, Jake responded

> When I was nine, I always wanted to do this stuff. My Uncle Joey and his friends was always coming by to brag to my old man about how he was coming up in "the organization." For me, it started out as a game. Uncle Joey used to teach me things so I could get extra dough on the side. My folks worked hard and honest, but it never got them anywheres. So, when I was nine, I decided to go to the top. I was going to be even better than my uncle. And I ain't never looked back since.

By age 14 not only had Jake identified with the gangster lifestyle, but his whole life had become directed toward achieving this goal. His moral character, his knowledge of head and heart, and his values were all keyed toward one thing: becoming the best Mafia leader that he could become. Committed to this direction, he repeatedly made choices and performed actions that reflected and reinforced his basic trend toward a life of crime. Jake's actions and overall direction freely and consistently demonstrated a stance or direction that defined not only his identity but also his life's goal.

From a faith perspective, the experience or realization of a power, force, or good greater than oneself provides a different source of identity and life direction. In *Conscience and Responsibility*,[23] Eric Mount, Jr., notes that the Judeo-Christian tradition uses the concept of covenant. Because human beings are created out of love and for love by a gracious God, the basic stance or direction of human life is toward covenant. To agree to live according to this covenant is not only an act of faith but also an orientation toward the use of freedom and the acquisition of knowledge supportive of that fundamental stance. However, the choice to live in covenant is not a once-in-a-lifetime decision. It requires constant choices and affirmation amid the positive and negative circumstances of life. Identity and moral character are forged over a lifelong process of experiences and choices; so, too, is the fundamental stance to orient oneself and one's life in the direction of covenantal relationship with a good, power, or force greater than self.

In summary, a mature and sound conscience is one that has developed a reasoned and informed capacity, process, and judgment. Through the development of cognitive skills, reason, and reflection, conscience is able to use a variety of experiences and sources of moral wisdom with which to guide the person in sound, ethical decision making. Diverse types of knowledge, especially knowledge of the head and knowledge of the heart, and an understanding of the natural law tradition, enable conscience to use its gift of freedom wisely to determine a life's course amid a variety of ever-changing alternatives. Through the exercise of conscience, a person's identity, moral character, and fundamental life stance are revealed.

III. Authority and Conscience

Erich Fromm, noted developmental psychologist, remarked in "Human Nature and Character"[24] that the character of the developing child is molded by the character of the parents; the parents and their methods of training are also a reflection of the social structures and historical times within which they live. "...The average family," he says, "is the 'psychic agency' of society, and by adjusting himself to his family, the child acquires the character which later makes him adjusted to the tasks he has to perform in social life "(334).

Fromm's comments highlight a central fact of human development:

Significant adults and society play an essential role in the psychosocial and moral development of the child.[25] It is from these significant people that the child learns the personal and social values and principles that guide his or her future life. The developing child is taught to conform to external authority figures or institutions of social and moral education. By the time the child reaches adolescence, however, the process of questioning what has been the mostly unquestionable dictates of a variety of external authorities becomes more frequent and overt.

Simultaneously, the process of moral development is also affected by authority figures. Lawrence Kohlberg noted in "Moral and Religious Education and the Public Schools: A Developmental View"[26] that the ultimate goals of his proposed stages of a sequential moral development, and of any sound program of moral education, were twofold: the capacity to make genuine moral judgments, and the ability of the child then to apply his or her own moral judgment, rather than that of some other person or agency, to evaluate individual actions (179). Again, the child's ability to achieve these two goals is very much dependent upon past and present experiences with authority figures. Ideally, sound moral education will facilitate the development of a mature conscience that moves from a child's dependence upon external rules and authority figures to the mature adult's ability to make decisions that seek justice and moral value in shared, universally applicable standards, rights, or duties (171). Such a conscience also consults and dialogues with the writings, teachings, traditions, and moral codes of religious authorities so as to make creative and constructive choices that compel the individual to act in an ethical manner.

Part of the successful achievement of psychosocial and moral independence is the ability of the individual to accept responsibility for his or her own judgments and decisions. The phrase "following one's conscience" is but another way of saying that the person's conscience is able to engage in reasoned reflection and dialogue on personal and shared common experiences, to understand the alternatives, to make a binding decision, and to accept the consequences freely. This moral imperative to follow one's conscience is accepted by most civil and religious communities and is insightfully described by Gula:

...If a person truly believes in his or her heart (i.e., with one's whole person) that one line of action rather than another is God's objective call, then that line of action is no longer simply one action among many. It becomes the morally required line of action for that person to take. [This is] what we mean by being bound to follow one's conscience...it cannot be violated (133).

While it is true that, ultimately, the decision of conscience is binding, one must do everything to insure that such a decision is the fruit of a "well-formed" conscience and not the result of blind or purely intuitive or arbitrary assertion of autonomy. With respect to ethical and moral decisions, the free exercise of conscience always entails a process of reasoned understanding and dialogue with various sources of moral wisdom. This includes consultation with knowledgeable people and groups, employment of sound principles of moral guidance, and the guidance of one's religious tradition and its religious writings and moral teachings.

Conflict, Dissent, and Obedience to Authority

Individuals exist within a communal environment that has developed civil and religious codes for human development and welfare. Personal and communal survival depends upon obedience to the reasonable demands of civil and religious authority. Conflict arises when the individual or group questions or refuses to obey established civil and religious codes. Historically and culturally bound and interpreted, these codes, and the designated authorities that make and interpret them, have a varied ability to tolerate conflict and dissent. Meredith McGuire notes in *Religion: The Social Context*[27] that within religious groups, conflict over religious ideas and practices "frequently centers on the issue of authority, which implies control both of the religious organization and over the articulation of central beliefs and practices" (193). McGuire cites examples of internal dissent regarding the role and function of authority that have caused schisms and divisions in Christian, Hindu, Islamic, and Shinto religions. The eleventh-century split between Eastern (Orthodox) and Western (Roman) Catholicism, the split, evolving during the eighth-eleventh centuries, between Sunni (the dominant form of Islam) and Shiism (the most powerful of the challenging sects of Islam), and the modern civil and religious strife in

Northern Ireland are a few of the examples (193-97).

From the religious perspective of the Judeo-Christian tradition, obedience as a moral value is always viewed as colored by the individual's relationship with God and by a belief that this God is potentially knowable in and through every human experience. Through a process known as discernment, the individual seeks continually, but especially in times of ethical decision making, to discover, as Richard Gula states, "what God is requiring and enabling me to be and to do" (263).

The response to this question becomes very important at those times when the free exercise of conscience brings a person into conflict with civil or religious authority. The ability of any civil or religious law to place an ethical claim on an individual conscience is possible only to the extent that the individual discerns that the law is a genuine guide to answering what God requires of the individual at that specific time. As Gula notes

> ...even though we listen to privileged mediators of God's word with special deference, none of us is thereby dispensed from personal discernment about whether and to what extent one is hearing the word of God in this instance. Since obedience is directed only to God, the challenge of living in society is to determine which claims coming from the wide range of legitimate authorities over us can be integrated into our obedience to God. This is the challenge of discernment (263).

Since the end of World War II, the notions of civil and religious dissent have gained prominence throughout the world. In *Civil Disobedience and the Christian*,[28] Daniel Stevick explores the crucial distinction between law breaking and morally responsible civil disobedience. It is Stevick's contention that morally responsible civil disobedience is more than mere law breaking; it is a last resort action with specific aims that are taken to reform a law and promote public welfare. Although Stevick is addressing civil disobedience, his insights can also be applied to religious disobedience. Based on a deep reverence for law, civil or religious, disobedience seeks to make that law more responsive to the changing contemporary needs of the people for whom the laws are designed.

IV. The Question of Evil

With so many inherent capabilities and external supports, ethical decision making and living might seem as if it should be easy to achieve. And yet human beings learn from an early age that this is not the case; there is something within or without that "we experience as regrettable, harmful, or detrimental to the full actualization of the well-being of persons and of their social relations" (Gula, 269). Humankind has labeled this something, "evil."

The nature and source of evil have been subjects of speculation by religious and non-religious disciplines throughout the course of human history. An examination of the literature and elaborate religious codification of evil and sins throughout the centuries leads to three general interrelated notions that seem to summarize the thinking regarding the existence and nature of evil: evil as a reality, as an absence of good, and as a deliberate negative choice.

A contemporary depiction of all three notions is found in *An Interrupted Life: The Diaries of Etty Hillesum*,[29] which chronicles the life of a young Jewish woman living in the Netherlands during the Nazi occupation. Through these diaries the world can observe the gradual transformation of Etty in a spiritual journey that enables her continually to refuse the safety of hiding so as to remain and finally die with the condemned Jews of Westerbork and Auschwitz. Etty wrote,

> I don't want to become a chronicler of horrors. Or of sensations…It all comes down to the same thing: life is beautiful…I have broken my body like bread and shared it out among men. And why not, they were hungry and gone without for so long…We should be willing to act as balm for all wounds (192, 195, 196).

In May 1940, evil emerged in the form of the Nazis, who took over the Netherlands and systematically began to isolate and persecute Dutch Jews. In April 1942, the Nazis started to move Dutch Jews to Westerbork, a transit camp, which, although not an extermination camp, was the last stop before Auschwitz. In July 1942, Etty (Esther) Hillesum voluntarily chose to go to Westerbork to work with the trapped Jews. From August 1942 until September 1943 Etty remained in the camp, working in its hospital and, with special permission, returning to Amsterdam many times to bring messages and to pick up much needed medicines. In her August 1942 entry, Etty describes evil personified in the figure of the Westerbork commandant, who in his stylishly decorated uniform and iron gray smile, walks along the crowded transport trains with an attitude that declares

> ...He is the absolute master over the life and death of Dutch and German Jews here on this remote heath in Drenthe Province...He is inspecting his troops: the sick, infants in arms, young mothers and shaven-headed men...Then he makes a gesture, like royalty in an operetta...The train gives a piercing whistle, and 1,020 Jews leave Holland (217-219).

Etty's diaries also captured the second concept of evil—an absence of good. In her July 1943 entry she comments on the lack of good and the all-prevailing horror of the Westerbork camp:

> ...The misery here is really indescribable. People live in those big huts like so many rats in a sewer. There are so many dying children...One night last week a transport of prisoners passed through here. Thin, waxen faces. I have never seen so much exhaustion and fatigue as I did that night. They were being "processed": registration, more registration, frisking by half-grown NSB men, quarantine, a foretaste of martyrdom lasting hours and hours (197).

Despite the horrors that she sees and the absence of good—as characterized by the deliberate dehumanization of thousands by the Nazis—Etty is able to see beyond this evil to a core of inner truth that enables her to survive in spirit, although her body is slowly deteriorating from poor health and the rigors of hard camp life. In a later part of the July 1943 entry, Etty acknowledges that her ability to withstand evil comes from the realization that

> ...Life here hardly touches my deepest resources—physically,

perhaps,...but fundamentally you keep growing stronger...And so I call upon you: stay at your inner post...(199).

A third concept of evil—a deliberate human choice that intends or wishes to do harm and, in so doing, negatively affects covenant relationships—is depicted by Etty as the loss of meaning amid suffering. She continually exhorts the people of the Westerbork camp not to let the horrors destroy their inner spirit. Their subsequent inability to choose hope over pessimism and meaning over despair caused a death of spirit that Etty attributes to the force of evil that blinded those it corrupted to seeing beyond this life to another time and place.

...People are dying here even now of a broken spirit, because they can no longer find meaning in life, the young people. The old ones are rooted in firmer soil and accept their fate with dignity and calm. You see so many different sorts of people here and so many attitudes to the hardest, ultimate questions (200).

Throughout her diary entries, Etty continually asserts a faith in God, whom she finds in the deeper, inner recesses of her being (205). Eventually, Etty is no longer able to deny that she too is about to be transported. Just before she leaves Westerbork for Auschwitz and her death on November 30, 1943, she writes:

...I often walk with a spring in my step along the barbed wire...I can't help it, that's just the way it is, like some elementary force— the feeling that life is glorious and magnificent, and one day we shall be building a whole new world. Against every new outrage and every fresh horror we shall put up one more piece of love and goodness, drawing strength from within ourselves. We may suffer, but we must not succumb (198).

No matter what its nature may be, there is a mysterious force known as evil that affects all of creation. One of the challenges of ethical decision making is to realize that although evil might never be eradicated, it can be controlled through positive experiences and responsible choices grounded in a broad vision for ethical living.

Social Evil

Disregard and contempt for human rights have resulted in barbarous acts which have outraged the conscience of mankind (Preamble to the United Nation's "Universal Declaration of Human Rights").[30]

The writing of this statement in 1948 foreshadowed the dawning recognition of a type of evil as old as society itself and yet largely left untouched: the evil bred and perpetrated by unjust social structures. For example, for centuries, areas of Central and South America, Africa, and Asia had been colonized first by the more technologically advanced countries of Europe and then later by the United States. By the mid-twentieth century, the age of direct military colonization gave way to a more subtle form of domination known as "development" or "developmentalism." Less technologically and economically advanced countries, like those of South America, began to compete for financial aid in the forms of direct monetary assistance, military assistance, and corporate buy-outs of native lands and businesses. The goal was to "modernize or develop" these less technologically advanced countries so that their cultural, social, and economic standards of living would approximate those of Europe and the United States.

The positive goals sought by developmentalism did not materialize. Instead, as Gustavo Gutiérrez contends in *A Theology of Liberation*,[31] it was not realized until too late that "development" and "modernism" were synonymous with

> ...misery and exploitation...in Latin America, as a situation of injustice that can be called institutionalized violence...which violates fundamental rights...Institutionalized violence results from a situation of dependence, in which the centers of decision are to be found outside the continent...The underdevelopment of Latin America is a byproduct of capitalist development in the West (108-109).

Rather than fostering native independence and development toward higher standards of living for all the people of these countries, the capitalist countries, through their internationally owned corporations, invested billions of dollars that resulted in further economic gains for the corporations and greater oppression of the native peoples through a cycle of domination, dependence, and exploitation. Native businesses were replaced by large international corporations who paid very low prices for large tracts of native land upon which to build their manufacturing and warehouse facilities; they paid the natives sub-standard wages for long hours of work and contributed nothing to the further educational, political, or socioeconomic growth of the country.

This cycle of oppression was then internally supported by military governments and corrupt social institutions established and controlled by the international conglomerates. The result has been an endless, dehumanizing poverty for a majority of the native population, whom Robert McAfee Brown[32] describes as not only economically powerless, but as

...politically powerless as well, victims of rigged elections, military intimidation, and social structures that function as though the poor did not exist except for purposes of exploitation by the rich. Attempts by the poor to organize are routinely destroyed with whatever brutality a given situation demands. Threats, "disappearances," assassinations, massacres, and torture are run-of-the-mill responses (53).

It was not until the 1960s that the knowledge of social evil perpetrated by technological exploitation emerged into social consciousness. Christian churches began to examine seriously the relation of evil to social structures, and the term "social evil" (sometimes called social sin) came to be used to describe those unjust social, political, and economic structures that oppress human dignity and rights and stifle any legitimate personal, psychological, spiritual, and educational development. The 1965 Vatican II document *Gaudium et Spes*[33] proclaims

...the disturbances which so frequently occur in the social order result in part from the natural tensions of economic, political, and social forms. But at a deeper level they flow from man's pride and selfishness, which contaminate even the social sphere. When the structure of affairs is flawed by the consequences of sin, man, already born with a bent toward evil, finds there is new inducement to sin...(#25).

In July 1966 at Geneva the World Council of Churches Conference on Church and Society began grappling with the interrelated issues of violence in the modern world and the Christian's response to this violence. The conference recognized that one source of violence was the socioeconomic and political structure devised by governments whose objectives were power and material wealth at the cost of oppression, poverty, terror, and death for the more powerless native population. The conference concluded that if a social system is oppressing human dignity and repressing basic human rights,

> ...then it is itself doing violence to the oppressed. This violence by political, economic, and social structures—despite its seeming legality, its subtle, non-violent appearance, its projection by the ruling powers as part of the unchangeable status quo—is the situation which provokes a violent defense, the action of revolutionaries who seek to remove the unjust structures.[34]

The Second General Conference of Latin American Bishops met at Medellín, Colombia, in September 1968 and eventually formulated a response to the social violence and evils being perpetrated in Latin America. The underpinnings of this response reflect the work of a number of Latin American theologians who were discussing what was later to be known as "liberation theology." Influenced by the ideas and writings of liberation theologians such as Gustavo Gutiérrez, Juan Luis Segundo, Ignacio Ellacuría, Leonardo Boff, and José Míguez Bonino,[35] the Christian churches in the poorer Latin American countries began increasingly to organize and speak out against institutional poverty and oppression. Since that time liberation theology has become popularized and influential in the crafting of social teachings by the Christian churches.

Liberation theology has come to represent a unique nonviolent way of being and acting in an oppressive world. Inspired by the Judeo-Christian biblical understanding of poverty as an expression of love, as solidarity with the poor, and as protest against oppression, Gustavo

Gutiérrez envisioned liberation to mean a desire for sociopolitical freedom,

> a movement of struggle for justice, not only to obtain a better standard of living, but also to be able to participate in the socio-economic resources and the decision-making process of the country...[It is] the insistence for oppressed peoples...to control their own destiny (Gutiérrez 109-110).

Despite attempts by various groups to equate this liberation movement with communist or socialist political revolutions, Gutiérrez, Segundo, and others influential in the liberation movement realized that real social and political structural change must first come from a grassroots spiritual renewal. Religious and lay volunteers began by organizing thousands of poor, oppressed peoples into *comunidades de base* (base communities)[36] to read the Bible, pray, reflect, and seek ways to change nonviolently their oppressive world. Their concerted efforts to liberate themselves from centuries of social, political, and economic injustices began to bring results.

Today, the writings and works of the liberation theologians are an articulation of the hopes and goals of these base communities who have sought a spiritual renewal and social response to centuries of sociopolitical and economic oppression. Viewed from a wider perspective, liberation theology is a contemporary nonviolent response to the existence of social evil. Similar to the stance of Thomas Aquinas and his natural law view, liberation theology, as articulated by Gutiérrez in *A Theology of Liberation,* seeks to use reason and all human resources to enable humankind to realize its fullest potential and one true goal, which is

> ...an innate desire to see God...Indeed, the orientation towards God is viewed here as a constitutive element of the human spirit: every act of knowing implicitly contains the desire to know God. This desire defines man's intellectual dynamism. The grace of this vision of God thus culminates a profound aspiration of the human spirit. Man fulfills himself completely only in this communion... (Gutiérrez 70).

For Gutiérrez and liberation theology, this response to social evil represents also a challenge to individual and social consciences to use freedom and knowledge to root out the causes of this social evil and to respond with effective methods to eradicate it. Whatever methods are chosen, they must bring about effective changes in the social order that mirror humankind's call to be a covenanted community whose broad ethical vision and esteemed values and principles enable all of creation to fulfill its greatest potential or attain its greatest meaning. As envisioned by Gutiérrez, the achievement of this ultimate goal entails a process whereby the subhuman gives way to more human conditions, and those people oppressed and exploited by unjust social structures gradually give way to

> ...passage from want to the possession of necessities, overcoming social evils, increase of knowledge and the acquisition of culture. Other more human conditions are increased esteem for the dignity of others, a turning toward the spirit of poverty, cooperation for the common good, and the will for peace...This is the fuller idea of what is human...the profound integration and ordering toward the fullness of all that is human in the free gift of the self-communication of God (Gutiérrez 172).

V. Feature: Setting the Oppressed Free: The Spirituality and Politics of Liberation

•In Brazil, the top 2% of the landowners control 60% of the arable land, while 70% of the rural householders are landless or nearly so. In Guatemala the top 1% of the landowners control 34% of the arable land, while 85% of the rural households are landless or nearly so. (One reason for the Guatemala statistic may be that Del Monte owns 57,000 acres but cultivates only 9,000 acres).

•Whenever the interest rate on international loans is raised by 1%, the indebtedness of the Latin American nations rises by 2.5 billion.

•In 1988, the U.S. gives El Salvador over $1 million a day, most of which goes to sustain the army and feed the death squads.

•Workers in Peru who used to be breadwinners for six persons must now provide for eight persons on less than half the income they formerly had.

•In El Salvador a family of six needs $333 per year to survive, but over half the population earns less than that (Brown 52).

These statistics and more were running through the minds of Ken Lawson and Yvonne Peters as they surveyed the ramshackle, rural, Southern community that they now called home. Four years previously, such information would not have had much impact upon them; then, a group of university sororities and fraternities, along with the seven churches and religious groups in their area, decided to "adopt" a refugee family who had escaped to the United States from a ravaged area of South America. Within months of the arrival of the Torres family, the university and parish groups had been profoundly affected by the stories of poverty, deprivation, and dehumanization that the Torreses shared about their native country.

As the Torreses' story unfolded, Ken and Yvonne began to read and study more about the emerging, nonviolent reform movement known as liberation theology. They began increasingly to see the many destructive faces of poverty as it infiltrated socioeconomic and political structures within their own university community. Their ecumenical social action group had discussed in detail the 1986 U.S. Catholic bishops' pastoral letter entitled "Economic Justice for All";[37] the letter declares "a preferential option for the poor" (#52) and challenges readers to

> ...use the resources of faith, the strength of our economy, and the opportunities of our democracy to shape a society that better protects the dignity and basic rights of our brothers and sisters, both in this land and around the world...The life and dignity of millions of men, women and children hang in the balance. Decisions must be judged in light of what they do for the poor, what they do to the poor, and what they enable the poor to do for themselves. The fundamental moral criterion for all economic decisions, policies, and institutions is this: They must be at the service of all people, especially the poor (#2, 24).

Inspired by these words and those of the liberation theologians, Ken and Yvonne now found themselves part of a volunteer group living in a poor, rural parish in the southern United States. Their town of 8,000 was dependent upon farming controlled by large citrus and tobacco consortiums. The volunteer group's introduction of the ideas of liberation theology into their parish bible group had spread to other home religious and civic support groups. Soon, the poor residents of the town banded together and began to seek reform of some the oppressive socioeconomic and political policies of the company-controlled mayor and city council. When "random" acts of violence against the more vocal residents escalated and the compound housing the volunteer group was bombed, questions emerged for their group: Should they return to the university so as to prevent any further violence? Should they discontinue their nonviolent methods?

Reflection
Consider how such concepts as conscience, freedom, and knowledge were influential in Ken and Yvonne's volunteer group's relocation to a poorer parish.

Questions for Research, Reflection, and Discussion
1. Research further one of the liberation theology writers, such as Juan Luis Segundo, José Míguez Bonino, and Leonardo Boff. According to the writer you research, what inspires liberation theology?

2. Read the 1986 U.S. Catholic bishops' pastoral letter, "Economic Justice For All." Consider three political and social injustices in the United States and the world that would be addressed if the pastoral letter were implemented seriously.

3. Liberation theologians José Míguez Bonino and Gustavo Gutiérrez have both concluded that the future of liberation theology is toward a political ethics for change. What would a political ethics influenced by liberation theology entail?

Chapter V

A Practical Method for Ethical Decision Making

Overview
The Graham Case Study

I. Ethical Discernment of Good versus Evil
A. Three Font Principle of Morality
B. Proportionate Reason

II. Roles and Ethical Decision Making

III. *Prima Facie* Duties or Obligations

IV. A Covenantal Ethic of Care

V. A Model for Ethical Decision Making
Step I. The Acquisition of Information
  A. Naming the Primary Ethical Problem
  B. Gathering and Assessing the Facts
  C. Determining Motives, Naming and Prioritizing the Ethical Values and Principles
  D. Considering Alternative Courses of Action
Step II. Dialogue With Others/ Seek Advice
Step III. Reasoned Reflection
Step IV. Decision
Step V. Implementation

VI. Feature: Biomedical Ethical Dilemmas
Case Studies for Research, Reflection, and Discussion
1. Surrogate Decision Making
2. Organ Donation and Transplantation
3. Allocation of Resources

Overview

Chapters I through IV have explored two parallel movements: 1) the development of a person as a psychosocial, moral, and faith-seeking being; and 2) the emergence of a mutually interrelated broad ethical vision within individuals and communities. Both movements affect and are affected by a person's particular decisions. This chapter will explore other important factors that affect ethical decision making: a lack of clarity concerning what constitutes a morally good or evil action, the influence of role expectations and binding moral obligations (often called *prima facie* duties), and an ethic of care. Because biomedical ethical issues are ones that the reader will most likely encounter in life, these issues are used to illustrate both Chapter V's key points and the practical application of the model for ethical decision making. Other ethical issues will be discussed in Chapters VI and VII.

The Graham Case Study

"That is the most absurd thing I have ever heard! You can't seriously judge Lena's actions as morally wrong," declared Carmen as she angrily tossed her notes onto the table.

"Absolutely. It is against the law to murder someone. She murdered her husband. She admits leaving the medications. She may not have put the pills in his mouth, but she is morally if not legally responsible for Doug's death," snapped York as he sat back and glared at Carmen.

"Look," said Greg, "you two have been at it for over an hour. We're no closer to resolving this case study for our presentation in two weeks. It's late and we need to arrive at a final decision. It's taken us three meetings to lay out the information according to the Method for Decision Making that Professor Michaels outlined in her last lecture. We have gone through all the steps and have enough facts. The final decision is staring us right in the face. Besides, it's not like our decision is going to affect the outcome. We're only students."

"That's the point, Greg," said Brittany, the fourth member of the group. "The final answer is NOT staring us right in the face. Why can't you and York see it? The facts say one thing, but I think you have to look at more than the facts. The case tells us that the Grahams had a good, twenty-five year relationship, that Doug had often helped Lena in her medical research on euthanasia, that he was agnostic while she was Protestant Christian, and that they were socially and politically active in a number of community issues. All this tells me that we have to look beneath the facts. It's my hunch that maybe Doug did finally commit suicide after all, and Lena did not help him."

"York," said Greg, "reread the case study again. Let's try a fresh look before we go through the other objective information on legal factors, motives, principles, values, and *prima facie* obligations."

As the others groaned, York reread the Graham case study. Dr. Lena Graham was accused of killing Doug, her husband, whose suicide she had allegedly assisted by providing lethal doses of medication. Lena had watched helplessly as Doug continued to lose his two-year battle with lung cancer. Doug's condition was also worsened by increasing kidney and liver problems, partial blindness, and heart trouble due to diabetes. As Doug became more debilitated and the pain medications failed to control the pain, he began to speak openly about suicide as a solution. He begged Lena to help him. Lena refused.

As Doug's pain continued unabated and his condition steadily deteriorated, Doug made two unsuccessful suicide attempts. Lena sought appropriate psychiatric care as well as round-the-clock home nursing. Lena's friends and colleagues noticed how difficult it was for her to watch her husband's lingering pain and debilitation, especially when he refused the higher doses of pain medication that would relieve much of the pain, while causing his mind to lose awareness for longer periods of time. After three months of increasing pain and pleading by Doug, Lena finally sat with him one long afternoon to discuss his condition and their future.

Three days later, Lena came home to pick up the evening shift nurse and drive her to the bus station. Because the night duty nurse was late and Doug already seemed in a deep sleep, Lena decided it would be okay to leave him alone for a few minutes. Deciding to leave the night duty nurse a note, Lena opened her briefcase to look for pen and paper. Hampered by the multiple pill samples often left by pharmaceutical representatives, she took them from the briefcase and set them on Doug's nightstand as she hurriedly wrote the note and left it on the bedside table.

When the night nurse finally arrived, she found Doug dead. An autopsy revealed large doses of unprescribed substances in Doug's system. The drugs in Doug's system matched those in the sample pill packets. Lena was charged with assisted suicide. It was the D.A.'s contention that Lena had finally succumbed to the pressures of Doug's illnesses and had arranged with Doug to supply the medications with which he could end his own life.

"Carmen," said York, "we know for a fact that Lena is a physician and she knows it is illegal in this state for a physician to assist a patient's death. We also know that Lena did leave the non-prescribed drugs beside Doug's bed and that she dismissed the evening nurse before the night nurse had arrived in relief. She also knew her husband was suicidal. No responsible doctor would do any of those things."

"And I say," responded Carmen, "we don't know why Lena left the medications like she did. Remember, Lena is Doug's wife. The case says that she cared very much for him; theirs had been a close and loving relationship. And as a doctor, Lena felt responsible for his getting the best of care. This must have been hard on her and Doug. I also wonder what they discussed that last time. Maybe Lena finally realized that Doug was ready to die and there was nothing more anyone could do for him. In light of their last conversation, maybe Doug woke up, saw the pills, and figured this was his way out. I don't believe that Lena did anything ethically wrong."

"Well, that stuff is not relevant," snapped Greg. "It doesn't help us justify whether Lena is morally responsible for Doug's death. Besides, if we follow your ideas, then anyone could kill another person just because they felt sorry for them. Then where would the world be?"

The moral dilemma facing this college study group is complex. Although their assignment involves evaluating and deciding whether Lena is morally responsible for her husband's death, their struggles in arriving at the final decision reveal confusion as to what constitutes a morally good or evil action, as well as over whether Lena Graham should be evaluated in her role as a spouse, physician, or both.

One means of arriving at some clarity is a consideration of the ethical discernment of good and evil.

I. Ethical Discernment of Good versus Evil

A. The Three Font Principle of Morality

Traditionally, ethicists, philosophers, theologians, and moralists have asked whether any act is inherently morally evil, that is, one for which "no intention or set of circumstances could ever justify it. In other words, the moral quality of certain acts are already determined before the person does it in whatever circumstances" (Gula 268). What is implied by calling an action inherently morally evil is that the intentions of the actor or the consequences of the action can never make its performance morally justifiable; the action itself is automatically so evil that nothing will warrant it otherwise.

According to prominent Catholic moralists like O'Connell, Gula Janssens, and McCormick, it is not possible to label an action as objectively morally good or evil by simply evaluating the external action alone. For example, the moral evaluation of Lena Graham's action of leaving the pills on Doug's bedside table cannot be decided simply by virtue of the fact that she did leave the pills within easy reach of Doug. Rather, other factors—that is, Lena's intent, the contextual circumstances (such as the distraction of trying to find a pen and paper to leave a note and the pressure of getting the evening nurse to her bus on time), the degree of forethought about negative consequences in leaving Doug alone, Lena's competency in that circumstance to use her medical knowledge, and her spousal freedom to affect Doug's death deliberately or accidently—all combine to influence the final evaluation of whether or not Lena's leaving the medication on the bedside table was morally evil.

Roman Catholic moralists like those mentioned above have tended to use what they describe as a "three font principle"[1] to determine whether an action is morally good or evil. This principle connotes the idea that the sound, moral evaluation of any act is not complete unless a person scrutinizes the three important, interrelated fonts that constitute the totality of any moral action: *the means, the intended end of the action*, and *the circumstances and consequences surrounding the action*. In the case of Lena Graham, the action of taking pills out of her brief case and leaving them on her husband's bedside table is ordinarily not a problem. By using the three font principle, however, the circumstances

of Doug's deteriorating physical, mental, and emotional status, his suicidal tendencies, and the emotional and spiritual anguish that Lena
must have endured, as a spouse and physician, make two different
evaluations possible.

On the one hand, one would have to scrutinize this action by first
asking about Lena's intention. She could have acted out of a moment of
carelessness and thoughtless preoccupation in trying to find paper and
pen for a note. Based on previous experiences with Doug's sleeping
patterns and her experience as a physician, Lena may have judged that
even if he roused, Doug would be safe for the brief amount of time that it
would take to drive the evening nurse to the bus. Given the contextual
circumstances (that Lena was weighed down with fatigue and expected
the night nurse to come soon) a person could evaluate Lena's emptying
of her briefcase as a rushed and careless action through which the medications inadvertently became the means to end Doug's life.

On the other hand, Lena may have decided that she could no longer
stand in Doug's way and that Doug had the right to end his life if he
ever secured the means. The means toward ending Doug's life would
be the medication samples that Lena's medical training would have informed her would have been the least painful way of aiding Doug.
Although not premeditated, the need to drive the evening nurse to the
bus station and the unexpected lateness of the night nurse, could be
construed as providing an opportunity for an impulsive and fortuitous
use of circumstances to provide indirect assistance to end what had become a tortured existence for Doug.

In summary, the three font principle of morality demands that the
moral judgment of an action can only be made after evaluating the actor's means, intention, and circumstances. However, as illustrated
above, there are a variety of possible means, intentions, and circumstances for any given action. Any or all of these factors affect the final
evaluation of the action as morally good or evil. It is at this point, then,
that some Catholic moralists advocate another criterion to evaluate the
good or evil of the means, intentions, and circumstances: proportionate
reason.

B. Proportionate Reason

Proportionate reason, or proportionalism,[2] considers the relationship of the actor's intention to the means chosen to accomplish some end or goal. The morally good intention of any action is the upholding of basic human values. In any given situation, however, proportionate reason acknowledges that in order to achieve a morally good choice, a certain amount of harm and risk may also be involved. Aided by the skill of prudence, proportionate reason enables the individual to make a wise consideration and an astute evaluation of all the benefits and goods, versus the risks and harms, involved in the situation. As Gula summarizes it,

> ...More broadly speaking, "proportionate" refers to the relation between the specific value at stake and the...limitation, the harm, or the inconvenience which will inevitably come about in trying to achieve that value (272).

A classic example in medical circles is the situation in which a doctor judges that the best way to save a patient's life is by amputating a leg. In the early nineteenth century amputation was considered a necessary evil that brought inconvenience and risk, especially if the patient were, for example, a farmer and father of four. At that time, there were no antibiotic protocols, and amputation was often the only possible, positive choice if the desired good and intention—the saving of the patient's life—was to be realized. Although the doctor was aware that amputation would have serious and debilitating effects on the farmer and his family, he believed that the good or benefit of saving the man's life far outweighed the other risks and consequences.

Given this same case but transferred to a state-of-the-art medical facility in the late-twentieth century, the judgment may become very different. Now the doctor's choice of amputation becomes a morally evil choice if other possible medical alternatives, like antibiotic therapy, have not been first exhausted, or if the doctor's intent is a quick resolution of the case because the patient is poor and uninsured.

In Doug Graham's case, if Lena had knowingly left the pill samples, she may have judged that the good as she saw it—the end of needless suffering for Doug—was worth the personal and professional risks and the potential harm of violating her own beliefs. Perhaps, in Lena's mind, leaving the pills on the bedside table may have served the value of beneficence, or the doing of good, more than it served the value of maleficence, or the doing of harm, which she may have eventually judged was being served by thwarting Doug's desire to end his life.

In summary, sound ethical decision making is a fundamental stance or life direction that reflects more than a covenant vision, the search for meaning, values, and principles. It also involves skills that come from a well-developed and informed conscience that is able to use reason, prudence, knowledge, and freedom to consider and evaluate objectively all aspects of the decision making: the intent, means, circumstances, consequences, benefits, and risks.

II. Roles and Ethical Decision Making

Another influential factor in ethical decision making is the individual and social expectations that are attached to the various roles that each person carries at any one period of his or her life.

As one who chooses and makes decisions, a person also acts out of a number of personal and social roles: son, daughter, brother, sister, niece, nephew, and friend. As we grow and develop we assume more roles—neighbor, student, employee, employer, husband, wife, lover, professional person, etc. According to Margaret Hoopes and James Harper,[3] with the assumption of each role comes

> ...perceptual-behavioral patterns learned and manifested by an individual in order to ensure the individual's physical and social survival. They [roles] are external manifestations of internal patterns of perception about the ways in which individuals relate... (25).

Besides these learned perceptual-behavioral patterns, roles also carry with them another component: a set of expectations placed on a person because of his or her membership in a group. Role expectations usually describe the characteristic and expected social behavior of an individual while a member of a particular group. Lawyers, doctors, teachers, nurses, clergy, for example, have professional codes of practice that articulate role expectations for their particular profession.

In terms of roles as perceptual and behavioral patterns, Hoopes and Harper note in *Birth Order Roles & Sibling Patterns in Individual & Family Therapy* that it is initially within the family unit that the developing child assimilates a variety of roles. It is their contention that by virtue of birth order, each sibling is assigned what has emerged as a characteristic set of role expectations and behaviors. As a result, a perceptual-behavioral pattern of responses can be predicted for each sibling position (25-31). Hoopes and Harper present a functional view of how roles within the family cause the first four siblings to have different role understandings of their jobs, interpersonal responsibilities, and social interactions, as well as differing perceptual awareness concerning cognitive and affective patterns, identity, well-being, intimacy, and conflict (Chapters 4-7).

For example, the first-born child tends to feel responsible for supporting family rules, values, and expectations; this child feels impelled to respond to the expectations of others and has a need to be productive and to take on leadership positions. The second-born child tends to be perceptive about the implicit nuances of family rules and relationships, seeks to have a unique relationship with everyone in the family, and feels responsible for the emotional support of each family member at the cost of personal needs and goals. The third-born child focuses more on the quality of the parents' relationship, seeks to identify family issues, and strives to be the negotiator of personal and social conflicts and relationship rules. The fourth-born child feels responsible for family unity and harmony, and tends to accept the responsibility for family problems or to act out the tensions in relationships; this child forms relationships easily, though sometimes superficially, so as to be in relationship with as many people as possible. Hoopes and Harper note that, with some variations, the fifth child tends to repeat the pattern of the first-born child, the sixth child repeats the pattern of the second-born child, etc. (29).

Given these and other perceptual-behavioral characteristics, each sibling functions in different ways within their family and in social roles outside the home. In turn, the correlating cognitive and affective perceptions tied to each role influence the individual's personal, social, and ethical decision making.

Simultaneously, roles also carry expectations that come from different sources. All of these sources—family, friends, ethnic group, society, and culture—have certain ideas about what behaviors are appropriate and inappropriate for each role. Like the perceptual-behavior aspects, role expectations are age-related as well as culturally and historically bound. For example, what is expected of a four-year-old daughter differs as she becomes an adolescent, a young adult, and an older adult. These same age-bound expectations are also colored by whether she is a daughter in the United States, in Saudi Arabia, or in Japan in 1850, 1910, 1940, or today. Similarly, the historical and cultural influences on roles are also evident in professions such as medicine, law, education, and health care. These professions experience the need for continual updating concerning the duties, functions, and codes of behavior for their members.

In the case being considered by the study group at the beginning of this chapter, Lena Graham is a physician. York and Greg emphasize Lena's role as a physician, and their evaluation of her actions seems influenced by the fact that she is a physician who has failed to conform to an expected set of professional standards and conditions. Carmen tends to view Lena first as a wife; she interprets Lena's external actions through a lens of empathy for a woman who is losing a beloved husband. Greg and York's comments indicate that they and society have higher expectations concerning her behavior because of her professional role; for Greg and York, Lena is more than Doug's wife. They know that physicians are governed by federal and state licensing laws and professional ethical codes. These codes and laws are important in that they articulate society's expectations for Dr. Graham and everyone else who holds membership in the medical profession.

Greg and York's views reflect the contemporary perspective of the role of the physician-patient relationship as a contractual one. This view differs from the more familial context that traditionally mirrored the physician-patient relationship. William F. May, in *The Physician's Covenant: Images of the Healer in Medical Ethics*,[4] explores five images of the healer—parent, fighter, technician, teacher, and covenanter—that are embodied within the centuries-old expectations of what a physician should be and do. As May outlines the role expectations that surround each of these images, he notes that, in modern society, there has been a shift in interpreting social arrangements. No longer seen as a parental figure intimately bonded to the patient by tenets of a covenant steeped in moral and religious significance, the modern physician is viewed as a technician whose covenantal bond is a contractual one, the legal and ethical conditions of which are established by "a huge, impersonal, anonymous mass society that delivers health care to strangers and often in the context of total institutions" (45).

Conflicts or problems tend to arise when people fail to meet role expectations because they either are ignorant of the expectations or simply decide not to meet them. The physician's Hippocratic oath and the medical ethical principles of beneficence (always do good) and nonmaleficence (do no harm) imply that society expects that a physician like Dr. Graham will not deliberately use her medical knowledge or skills to cause the death of another. Likewise, the medical ethical principle of justice requires that physicians treat patients fairly and equally; the principle of autonomy demands that the physician respect the freely chosen and informed plans of the patient for his or her medical care and life.

Today, these traditional expectations are under assault as the concepts of euthanasia and physician-assisted death are being questioned by physicians, other providers of health care, patients, and families. As medical knowledge and technology increase, the traditional concepts of what is good and what is harmful, the meaning of life, the quality of living and dying, and the benefits of caring versus curing are all being reevaluated. As medical technology advances, as people live longer, and as health care resources diminish, the more complex biomedical ethical dilemmas are resulting in the emergence of people like Dr. Jack Kevorkian, a former Michigan pathologist who has openly assisted over twenty terminally ill persons to die. Not only do Dr. Kevorkian's actions challenge traditional societal views, but his actions also challenge the traditional role expectations for physicians. Dr. Kevorkian and people like him raise the question of whether, in terminally ill cases where cure is impossible, it is perhaps more harmful to prolong life and suffering than to ease one toward death.

The study group's deliberations again highlight the conflict resulting from differing ways of acquiring and using ethical knowledge and differing role expectations. As already discussed, the women are approaching the case study with more of a use of knowledge of the "heart," or subjective knowledge, whereas the men are using a more cognitive and reasoned approach. Although all four are not consistent, the women tend to evaluate Lena Graham first on the basis of her role as wife, whereas the men lean more toward evaluating her as a physician. In Dr. Graham's case, Brittany and Carmen's comments indicate a possible role conflict. Is Dr. Graham's action of leaving the pills on Doug's bedside constituted harm or something else that might be more positively construed to be within the performance of the physician's role? Or, as Carmen points out, can Lena's actions be divorced from the fact that her relationship to Doug is not that of physician to patient but that of wife to husband? If the latter is true, Brittany and Carmen are challenging the traditional role expectations of a wife who has a terminally ill and pain-filled spouse. The women are also raising the points of the interrelationship of a variety of roles every person brings to a situation and of the way a conflict in role perceptions and expectations affects a decision. Although the study group makes a distinction, the reality may be that Lena's roles as wife and physician cannot be separated as easily in the legal and medical realms as in the personal.

In terms of roles and ethical decision making, the comment made by Greg that their resolution was not important because they are "only students" reflects a narrow view of the influence of role expectations and responsibilities upon ethical living and decision making. It is true that, as students involved in an academic exercise, the study group's resolution of the Graham case has a vastly different impact than the resolution of the real-life case would have for the physician, family, and all those intimately involved. Despite their being strangers to the Graham case, however, the study group's response is important because the group's basic roles as human beings and covenant members demand that they seriously consider the ethical implications of the case. In time, as husband, wife, mother, father, physician, teacher, or any combination of roles (including first, second, third, or fourth born son or daughter), they may be called upon to act in a similar situation. How they respond now as students provides them with opportunities to prepare for real-life situations of ethical decision making.

In summary, the Graham case and its treatment by the study group highlight the influences of the differing perspectives in the determination of good or evil. It also reveals the impact roles have upon ethical decision making.

III. *Prima Facie* Duties or Obligations

There is a traditionally problematic ethical issue: Should a society's binding rules be seen as absolutes never to be broken? Can they be overridden under any circumstances? Greg and York give the impression that rules and principles are absolutes; they see Lena as bound by marital and professional principles that can never be violated. Carmen and Brittany imply that rules and principles are guidelines and that perhaps there are circumstances that allow a person to override these guidelines.

W.D. Ross,[5] an ethicist concerned with the use of rules to determine the rightness or wrongness of an action, tackles this difficult ethical issue in *The Right and The Good*. Ross takes a position that seems to indicate that certain ethical principles are both rules of thumb and absolute standards of conduct. According to Ross, a person is bound by a *prima facie* duty that is both a life-guiding principle and, on all occasions, absolutely binding unless it conflicts with another *prima facie* duty (19-20). In such conflict situations, the ethical dilemma is how to make a choice between two good principles knowing that ultimately one of the *prima facie* duties will be violated in order to solve the ethical dilemma.

Ross suggests six independent principles or *"prima facie* duties": fidelity, gratitude, self-improvement, justice, beneficence, and non-maleficence (20-22). He then explains what he means by each (21-23).

Fidelity implies remaining true to the promises, both explicit and implicit, that are involved in certain relationships; for example, in conversations there is an implicit promise to tell the truth just as there is an implied promise to present what is true in written pieces of non-fiction. Fidelity also involves the duty to repair in any way the damages done to persons or communities because of wrongful actions.

The second duty, gratitude, flows from the services of one person or society to another. The third duty, self-improvement, challenges each person to use intelligence and virtues to improve life as an individual and as a member of society. Ross contends that the fourth duty, justice, implies receiving a certain amount of pleasure or happiness according to what one deserves or merits. Ross explains beneficence as doing good so that another is able to experience more good or happiness.

Nonmaleficence, as understood by Ross, is a refusal to harm others either through intent or actual deed.

A contemporary understanding of the last three of these *prima facie* duties—justice, beneficence, and nonmaleficence—reveals that they are more complex than Ross initially envisioned them. This complexity is due to the social, medical, and moral dilemmas raised by a complex, interrelated, and technologically advanced world society. For example, as explored by Beauchamp and Childress in *Principles of Biomedical Ethics*,[6] the contemporary concept of justice involves more than merit; it also involves distinguishing between concepts of justice as distributive (that is, the just distribution of goods and services in society [258]), and the concept of formal justice, which attempts to establish material principles for defining the dual principles of fairness and equality, which also seem to be implied by the term justice (260-62). Beneficence is expanded and further defined by Beauchamp and Childress. They distinguish

> ...two principles under the general principle of beneficence. The first principle requires the provision of benefits (including the prevention and removal of harm as well as the promotion of welfare), and the second requires a balancing of benefits and harms...that is, the balancing of benefits against alternative benefits, and balancing harms against alternative harms (195).

Although similar to Ross' definition, nonmaleficence is expanded by Beauchamp and Childress (123) to encompass a variety of types of harm that underlie contemporary moral dilemmas. Implied within the duty of nonmaleficence is the prohibition against intending, causing, and permitting harm, as well the actual infliction of harm. As Beauchamp and Childress remark, however, often the rules prohibiting harmful actions are violated justifiably in order to bring about a good. For example, in a hostage situation where two criminals have barricaded themselves with hostages in a store, the local SWAT team sometimes will have to shoot the criminals in order to prevent them from harming hostages. In such a case, the duty of nonmaleficence as a *prima facie* duty to prevent harm can only occur by doing harm to the criminals.

In situations of conflict between two or more *prima facie* duties, the person's overriding ethical obligation is to consider the particular circumstance, to use proportionate reason, and then, in the words of Beauchamp and Childress, "to locate the greatest balance of right over wrong in the circumstance of conflict between the competing *prima facie* duties" (52). If one *prima facie* duty is violated in favor of another, then, according to Beauchamp and Childress, certain requirements must be followed in order for the infringement to be ethically justified: (1) the moral objective justifying infringement must have a realistic prospect of achievement; (2) there must be no other realistic alternative but to infringe upon a *prima facie* duty; (3) the form of infringement chosen must be the least intrusive; (4) the person must do whatever possible to minimize the negative effects of infringing upon a *prima facie* duty or obligation (53).

The dilemma faced by the study group at the beginning of this chapter is actually a good illustration of a conflict arising between two competing *prima facie* duties or obligations: beneficence versus nonmaleficence. York and Greg expect Lena, as a wife and as a physician, to do nothing that is maleficent or harmful to Doug; they judge Lena's action of leaving the medication as showing a deliberate intent to cause harm to Doug or to allow Doug to harm himself by taking the lethal dose of medications. Carmen and Brittany ask whether Lena's actions intend harm or were a result of carelessness; either way, both women's comments indicate a tendency to view suicide as perhaps beneficial to a person with Doug's prognosis and moral views.

If the study group decides to evaluate Lena's actions according to her role of wife who also has knowledge of medicine, then they will see that Lena has a *prima face* duty to uphold nonmaleficence, that is, "to do no harm." She also has a *prima facie* duty to beneficence, that is, "to do good." The Graham case raises the question as to what Lena considers as more harmful for Doug—being terminally alive with increasing physical and mental debilitation and pain, or being released immediately from what Doug has come to view as a meaningless existence. Lena's response (and the study group's) is determined to a large degree by her overall ethical vision of covenant, quest for meaning, values, and principles as well as her understanding of the nature, role, and function of being a wife and also a physician. Although she is not her husband's primary physician, Lena knows that, as a wife who also knows medicine, she cannot directly aid Doug in committing suicide; to do so would also violate her own moral convictions.

Perhaps, after her long conversation with him, she is confused over what would be more harmful or beneficial for Doug. Because of their joint research on euthanasia, Lena and Doug have considered many alternative courses of action open to terminally ill people. Lena's *prima facie* duty to respect her husband's autonomy also conflicts with her knowledge of his lessening capacity for competent decision making.

In summary, given a particular context, each person evaluates, interprets, and makes choices based on a method of acquiring ethical knowledge, an awareness of one's roles, and the *prima facie* duties that are part of those roles. In the face of conflict or dilemma, a person may also have to evaluate and justify the impinging of one binding *prima facie* duty on another. Sound ethical decision making demands that one have an awareness of how these factors influence the particular circumstances surrounding ethical living and decision making.

IV. A Covenantal Ethic of Care

Any one of the six *prima facie* duties provides a basic reason for acting ethically. In and of themselves, however, they are not enough if one's way of being and acting in the world is covenantal. A covenantal ethic demands more of a person than the following of abstract moral rules and ethical duties. It demands the expression of a fundamental abiding perspective or attitude that permeates a covenant community with a broad ethical vision.

Traditionally, this abiding perspective or attitude was based on an ethic of love. As discussed in Chapter II, the New Testament moral vision considers love to be the essential covenantal attitude and responsibility for ethical living and decision making. Love, as Jesus (among others) seemed to live and preach it, is not an emotional affection for another; rather, love is an active and abiding respect that considers all of creation as worthwhile and valuable. In other words, to love is to possess a fundamental attitude that values and extends care to self and others.

As the countless treatises on "love" testify, however, this amorphous and largely misunderstood word has attracted many connotations, some positive and some negative. Most of these connotations are tied to a variety of affective or romantic states. However, solely affective or romantic bases for love become problematic when one tries to use them as the theological or philosophical basis for a moral code. This is true for two reasons. First, love becomes less an attitude and is quantified to specific emotional states or to rules or measurements of action. Second, there are those who do not subscribe to traditional theological or philosophical underpinnings for an ethic of love. Any moral imperative based on such a love ethic becomes meaningless.

Within contemporary thinking, an ethic of love is reconstructed more specifically as an ethic of care. Care is characterized as an attitude that binds the care-giver and care-receiver in a special relationship that promotes, according to Alastair V. Campbell's "Caring and Being Cared For,"[7] a mutual sense of trust, tenderness, gratitude, and intimacy (270). At its core, this ethic of care bespeaks an attitude of mutual value and respect that is not reliant upon affective or emotional bases. True caring is characterized by behaviors that Stanley Hauerwas describes as helping the person involved to maintain or establish an independent existence and to become "responsive to his own need to care and be responsible for his own life" (265).

The contemporary philosophical and developmental effort of Nel Noddings has established an ethic for action that is based on what she sees as an aspect of love: care. In *Caring: A Feminine Approach to Ethics and Moral Education,*[8] Noddings presents an alternative to traditional ethics; she begins with a moral attitude or natural longing for goodness rather than with the traditional male-oriented idea of an ethics based on moral reasoning and principles. Applicable to both males and females (97), the ethic of caring developed by Noddings is rooted in the feminine studies of human development begun by Carol Gilligan and others, and in the feminine qualities of receptivity, relatedness, and responsiveness. This philosophical understanding of care is grounded in an ethical impetus that precedes action and emerges from within the personality of the individual (28-29).

In defining what it means to care, Noddings uses a combination of three traditional meanings of the word:

...To care is to have solicitude about something or someone...One cares for something or someone if one has a regard for or inclination toward that someone or something...And, again, to care may mean to be charged with the protection, welfare or maintenance of something or someone (9).

Noddings, like Campbell, states that ethical caring arises from two sentiments: 1) the early memories and experiences of natural caring, such as the significant parent-child relationship (128) in which the child or the one cared for consciously or unconsciously perceives caring and tender moments as good; and 2) a condition of longing toward caring as a good that the person unconsciously strives to maintain, recapture, or enhance (79-80, 104). Noddings contends that it is this natural longing for caring—"to be in that special relation—that provides the motivation for us to be moral. We want to be moral in order to remain in the caring relationship and to enhance the ideal of ourselves as one caring" (49).

In a caring relationship, the care given to another is received on a variety of relational levels; the care extended by mother to child or brother to sister can be very different from the care extended by employer to employee or by a person to a stranger. In any kind of relationship, however, the extension of care is dependent upon two important underlying notions.

The first of these underlying notions is the striving toward an ideal self that incorporates a basic view of self as one who strives to care for self and the other as well. The realization of oneself as a care-giver is a developmental process whereby the person sees oneself as fundamentally related to others (18), as receptive or engrossed in the other so as to listen and to extend warmth and comfort (32-33), and as reciprocal or mutually committed to the care-receiver (73).

The second underlying notion to any caring relationship is the awareness that mutual experiences of caring and being cared for are integral if the person is to achieve a sense of the ideal self as a care-giver as well as a sense of what Noddings characterizes as an ethical ideal (80-83). That is, every experience becomes an opportunity to care whereby the care-giver experiences an ethical imperative or a "must." This inner imperative informs the person that caring is what "must" be done in order to achieve one's ideal self as well as the ethical ideal of caring so basic to human existence (99-103).

Covenantal ethics demands an attitude that binds the relationships with something more than rules and standards. Campbell, Hauerwas, Noddings, and others acknowledge that an ethic of care arises out of a natural impulse that defines personal identity and social relatedness. As Noddings characterizes it,

> ...moral behavior arises out of our natural impulse to care. At every level, in every situation, there are decisions to be made, and we are free to affirm or reject the impulse to care...We are ir- revocably linked to intimate others. This linkage, this funda- mental relatedness, is at the very heart of our being. Thus I am totally free to reject the impulse to care, but I enslave myself to a particularly unhappy task when I make this choice...I move into a wilderness of strangers and loneliness, leaving behind all who cared for me and even, perhaps, my own self (51).

An ethic of care also entails more than an internal attitude. As envi- sioned by Noddings and others, an ethic of care is active. Care is dem- onstrated by concrete actions and expressions experienced by the one cared for. Specific actions of care can range from the provision of the basic physical (such as food and shelter) and emotional (such as love, compassion, and praise) necessities of life, to more subtle forms of car- ing (such as physical and spiritual presence with one in pain). In other words, to care demands an active, outward expression toward the one cared for. Both the care-giver and care-receiver are bound in a valued relationship whereby an attitude of mutual respect for the dignity, au- tonomy, and best interests of each other spur the care-giver toward seeking those things that will help the care-receiver fulfill his or her po- tential as a physical, emotional, spiritual, intellectual, and moral being.

In their evaluation of the Graham case presented earlier, the mem- bers of the study group assume the attitudes and behaviors inherent in an ethic of care, but the group never consciously explicates their con- cepts. York and Greg assume that Lena the physician failed to "care" for Doug because her behaviors on the night of Doug's death suppos- edly reflected an intent to assist Doug's desire to end his own life.

Carmen and Brittany argue that as physician and as wife, Lena extended an attitude of care toward Doug; Lena's behavior the night of Doug's death cannot be presumed to have been non-caring in and of itself. However, none of the members of the study group actually define what they mean by care and lack of care or how precisely Lena violated or did not violate her duty to care as wife and physician.

Before the group continues, they might want to research specifically how an ethic of care is perceived by a professional health care giver. Since the late 1960s and the pioneering work of Paul Ramsey on the covenant responsibilities of the physician and an ethic of care, ethicists such as Stephen Lammers and Allen Verhey, Milton Mayeroff, Thomas Shannon, Helen Holmes and Laura Purdy, Tom Beauchamp and LeRoy Walters, and others have focused on the role, function, and responsibilities of caring within the medical profession. Holding views similar to Noddings's view of care as both attitude and action, these ethicists might argue that the physician also demonstrates care by certain behaviors or developed skills. As Hauerwas points out in "Care,"[9] the physician is expected to develop and maintain a certain level of technical skill and expertise through which he or she extends a certain care through the curing or relief of pain, disease, and suffering (262-63). In "The Role of Caring in Nursing Ethics,"[10] Sara T. Fry further explores the notion, first advanced by Edmund Pellegrino, that the physician's ethic of care as technical skill is always directed toward the "good of the individual" (100) being cared for. According to Fry, to provide care that attends to the good of the individual involves three senses of good: 1) the biomedical, clinical good that an intervention offers for the treatment of the patient's illness or disease; 2) the best interests or benefits as viewed by the patient; 3) and the fulfillment of satisfactory personal goals for the individual's life (100).

In conclusion, part of the work still facing the study group involves the group's achievement of a proper understanding of an ethic of care, their ability to ascertain Lena's understanding of how an ethic of care affected her profession as a physician, and finally their facility in envisioning how this ethic affected all the dimensions of Lena and Doug's individual and married lives. In seeking an ethical resolution to the Graham case study, the study group ultimately must become aware of and then evaluate how Lena's attitude and behaviors of caring supported or failed to support Doug's need for emotional, spiritual, and intellectual—as well as physical—care.

V. A Model for Ethical Decision Making

A variety of methods have been developed to facilitate ethical decision making.[11] Often the method that a person favors is the result of a combination of experience, common sense, ease of method, and practicality. Because of the complexity of an ethical question and the need to consider a variety of factors—personal, physical, spiritual, psychological, legal, interpersonal, and moral—anyone facing an ethical dilemma will perhaps find the following ethical model useful. This model is a series of interrelated steps that not only summarize the decision-making process, but also present a practical approach that ensures that all aspects of an ethical dilemma are covered.

Ethical decision making involves the acquisition of information or content and the assimilation and handling of the content to arrive at a final decision. The ethical model[12] for decision making will be presented in five steps.

Step I requires the acquisition of information. Within Step I itself, *Step I* there is a detailed process of accumulating four major types of necessary information: A) the designation of the primary ethical problem; B) the collection of the pertinent facts; C) the determination of the motives for this particular course of action, including the prioritizing of ethical values and principles; D) the consideration of alternative courses of action, the risks and benefits for each proposed course of action, and the immediate and long-term consequences attributable to each proposed course of action.

Concurrently, as a person gathers all the pertinent information, he or *Step II* she may already have moved into Step II in the process, the seeking of advice and dialoguing with others. As Steps I and II near completion, the person is ready to move into Step III: reasoned reflection on all the acquired information and advice in light of the person's broader ethical vision of covenant relationships, quest for meaning, values, principles, and personal and social roles. As Step III is completed, the person has arrived at Step IV, the decision. Step V entails the practical implementation of this decision. The diagram, page 161, summarizes this five-step decision-making process.

The remainder of the chapter provides further details on the five steps. This section is intended to be a practical tool for decision making. The study group's continued deliberation of the Graham case will be used to illustrate the application of this model.

Step I. The Acquisition of Information
A. Naming the Primary Ethical Problem

In any given situation, there may be more than one ethical problem. After considering the situation, it is important first to list all the existing ethical problems. Then, a person must decide what is the most important ethical problem that needs addressing. Once the primary problem is located, then the other designated problems may be of less importance or urgency than initially thought. It is also possible that once the primary problem has been isolated and addressed, the secondary problems may resolve themselves.

For example, the study group must first decide whether they are evaluating Lena Graham as a physician or as a spouse who also happens to have a knowledge of medicine. After this initial decision, the study group then must state the specific ethical problem they want to handle. For example, if they decide to evaluate Lena's actions in light of her being a physician, then the study group might state their primary ethical problem this way: "As a physician, did Lena act negligently or deliberately to bring about Doug's death?" If, however, the study group were to evaluate Lena as a spouse who also has medical knowledge, then they might state their main ethical problem this way: "As a spouse, how can Lena Graham ethically justify her actions on the night of Doug's death?" After naming the primary ethical problem, the study group moves to the next step.

B. Gathering and Assessing the Facts

This step requires a gathering of a variety of facts—biological, spiritual, psychological, economical, and ethical—as they relate to the stated problem. If a problem involves professional and legal aspects, then it will be necessary to acquire information concerning the legal and ethical laws governing professional conduct. For example, the study group

A Model for Ethical Decision Making

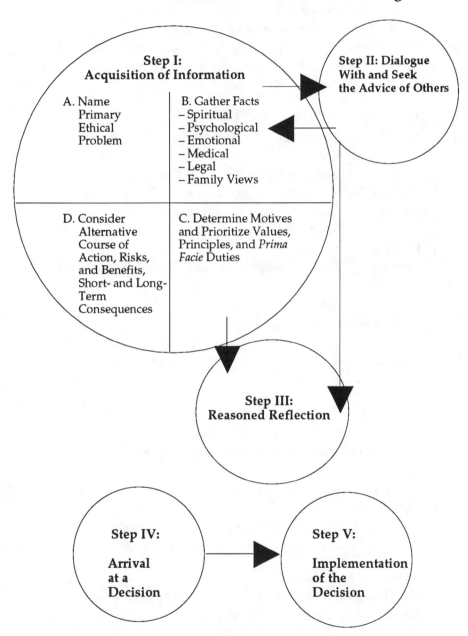

Step I:
Acquisition of Information

A. Name Primary Ethical Problem

B. Gather Facts
– Spiritual
– Psychological
– Emotional
– Medical
– Legal
– Family Views

D. Consider Alternative Course of Action, Risks, and Benefits, Short- and Long-Term Consequences

C. Determine Motives and Prioritize Values, Principles, and *Prima Facie* Duties

Step II: Dialogue With and Seek the Advice of Others

Step III:
Reasoned Reflection

Step IV:

Arrival at a Decision

Step V:

Implementation of the Decision

will have to consider Lena's professional role as a physician. They need to acquire any necessary legal facts, such as licensing rules and professional codes, that have an affect on the case.

In considering in some detail the variety of facts that must be gathered, the study group should consider the following sample questions as they gather all the pertinent information.

1. Spiritual

•In his quest for meaning, what has Doug articulated about his ultimate goals for life?

•Does Doug believe in a personal God? If so, what role does his relationship with this God have in his quest for meaning?

•Is there a particular religious or spiritual tradition that is particularly significant to Doug? What does this tradition say concerning life and death issues?

•Is there a spiritual or religious mentor with whom Doug can consult and seek guidance?

2. Psychological and Emotional

•What is Doug's current psychological and emotional status?

•Is Doug psychologically and emotionally competent to make decisions concerning his life?

3. Medical

•What is Doug's current medical diagnosis and prognosis?

•Has Lena acquired all the second medical opinions that are needed or required?

•What are the risks, benefits, and burdens to Doug of further procedures, tests, or treatment?

•What is Doug's probable life expectancy and what will his general condition be if further treatment is or is not conducted?

4. Personal Preferences

•Did Doug ever make clear statements verbally or in writing to indicate his wishes or feelings concerning treatment or non-treatment?

•If Doug has made no clear statement, is there information from anyone else regarding what he might have wanted or might reasonably be assumed to have wanted?

•Has Lena clearly shared with Doug her feelings and preferences concerning continued treatment or non-treatment?

5. Views of Family/Friends
•Do the Grahams have children or other family affected by Doug's condition and treatment decisions?

•What are their positions? Are there unresolved concerns, questions, and disagreements?

•If Lena or other family members have concerns other than medical ones, is there someone—for example, a minister, hospital chaplain, or social worker—whom it might be helpful to consult?

6. View of Significant Others
•Who else has cared for Doug—for example, specialists, nurses, chaplains, and social workers?

•What are their views? Are there any disagreements among them about continuation or cessation of any of Doug's varied treatments? Can these disagreements be resolved?

7. Legal/Other Factors
•Are there state statutes or case laws that apply to Doug's situation? That is, if Doug were competent, could he legally commit suicide?

•Are there others (in or outside the family) who should be consulted?

•Are economic issues (to Lena/family/society) a factor in the case?

•Are there objective professional standards of the American Medical Association by which a physician's conduct is judged as harmful or neglectful?

•Do the professional ethical codes of the American Medical Association prohibit Lena as a physician from supporting Doug in his decision to commit suicide?

When the study group has gathered all the facts at this level, they will move to the next area of information acquisition.

C. Determining Motives, Naming and Prioritizing
the Ethical Values and Principles

This area requires a consideration of the possible motives, values, principles, and *prima facie* obligations that underscored Lena's actions. For example, if the study group has decided to evaluate Lena in her role as a physician, then they must decide whether Lena's actions were accidental or a deliberate attempt to assist Doug in suicide. In addition, the group must also consider what ethical values, principles, and *prima facie* duties are in conflict. It would be necessary to discover how she viewed her *prima facie* obligation "to do good" (beneficence) and "to prevent harm" (nonmaleficence). The case indicates that she would not willingly help Doug commit suicide. Yet, the case does not reveal which principles and values she used in taking her anti-suicide stand.

On the other hand, if the group is considering Lena from the perspective of a spouse, then the group must determine whether Lena was so overwrought and distressed that she acted thoughtlessly but not with deliberate intent to kill or aid in suicide when she left the pills by the bedside. The case also does not reveal whether her belief in the ethical principles of respect for human dignity and integrity, autonomy, and proportionality would also prevent her from interfering with Doug's decision for suicide if he were able to make this decision.

D. Considering Alternative Courses of Action

This part of fact acquisition requires a consideration of alternate courses of action that a person facing an ethical dilemma could pursue. For each alternate course, there must also be a listing of the benefits and risks inherent in each alternative. Concurrently, the short-term and long-term consequences for each alternative course of action must be detailed and investigated.

For example, the study group will have to determine what alternative actions Lena could have taken the night of Doug's death. If Lena's actions were not intended to assist Doug in suicide, then why did she not consider either waiting for the night nurse, calling a taxi for the evening nurse, or calling a neighbor to stay with Doug? On the other hand, if Lena's actions could be construed as a deliberate assistance of suicide, the group may want to determine if Lena had presented to Doug other alternatives to suicide. Perhaps, after consultation with

Doug's primary physician, Lena could help Doug consider whether the cessation of aggressive treatments and the use of better pain control management or hospice opportunities might be the more beneficial course to pursue now. As part of their discussion, did Doug and Lena weigh the risks and benefits involved? Did they consider the short- and long-term consequences of each course of action?

Step II. Dialogue With Others/Seek Advice

Acquisition of the facts requires the continued dialogue with and advice of many others, especially those on personal and professional levels. Another area of necessary consultation for many is the moral teachings and laws of a person's religious tradition.

On one level, the study group may need to consult further with other professionals, such as an ethicist, a psychologist, a lawyer, a physician, or a religious representative, such as a rabbi, priest, or minister, to gain their unique perspectives on the various aspects of the case. They will need to understand Lena and Doug's perspectives, as well as the ethical, moral, legal, and spiritual factors that may or may not have influenced Lena's and Doug's actions.

On a second level, the individual members of the group may be experiencing personal questions and conflicts concerning various aspects of the case. They too may need to consult with personal sources to clarify their own emotional, spiritual, psychological, and ethical positions in the case.

Step III. Reasoned Reflection

The first two steps establish the necessary foundations for Step III, reasoned reflection. The person facing an ethical decision must now consider the acquired information and the advice received from the first two steps. However, as discussed in Chapter I, each person's process of assimilating and evaluating the information and advice will be affected by such factors as self-concept, attitudes and lifestyle, religion, heredity, environment, and stage of moral development. In addition, each person brings to this reasoned reflection particular ideas about covenant relationships and responsibilities, personal and social sin (Chapter II), the quest for meaning, and esteemed human values and principles (Chapter III). A person brings to this stage a conscience that has been developed and influenced by an understanding of freedom, types of and methods for using ethical knowledge, the inherent conflicts between the individual and society, and the effects of evil (Chapter IV). A person also brings a particular understanding of personal and social roles, and of the responsibilities demanded by *prima facie* duties (Chapter V).

Even with the most careful acquisition of the facts and the best knowledge of the necessary values and principles inherent in sound ethical decision making, a person will not easily resolve most ethical dilemmas. There comes a point where a person will have to pull back, assimilate, and reflect on all that has been involved in the first two steps of the process. One way to do this is to take some time for reasoned reflection, prayer, meditation, or quiet personal time at a place conducive to consideration, inspiration, and resolution.

Similarly, each person in the study group is affected consciously and unconsciously by all these factors as reasoned reflection gives way to serious consideration. For example, from the brief dialogue among the study group members, it is apparent that the individual members may not have taken time to ascertain their own personal positions on issues raised by the Graham case. Carmen, York, Greg, and Brittany, individually and as a group, need to determine the extent to which their own individual searches for meaning, visions of covenant relationships, examinations of basic human values, and particular methods of acquiring ethical knowledge are not only coloring their interpretations of the facts and advice of others, but also providing stumbling blocks to achieving a decision. Each of them may first have to take some personal time alone to consider all the factors discussed in the reasoned reflection stage before attempting another period or periods of group consideration. It is only after these times of serious individual consideration that the group is ready for the next step in the process.

Step IV. Decision

At some point each individual will have to arrive at a decision or a course of action. This is often a painful time, especially if the individual equates arriving at a sound decision with the securing of perfect certitude—that he or she has chosen absolutely the most correct choice.

Such certitude may never be realized. Rather, remaining true to self or moral integrity may be all that an individual can do while seeking a solution amid painful ethical situations. The experience of a sense of peace may be the only indicator that the person has maintained moral integrity and that a sound ethical decision has been reached.

The experiencing of peace at the end of the decision-making process does not mean, however, that a correct or sound decision will be free of emotional pain or suffering. Peace is not the same as being free of all suffering. The most correct or peaceful decision in a given situation is not necessarily the one that entails the least amount of pain. But oftentimes a person can rely on only a sense of peace amid the uncertainty and complexity of a real-life, ethical decision-making process and implementation.

In the case of the study group, once each of the individuals in the group has arrived at a personal decision about the case, then the group as a whole moves toward a sound decision best achieved through consensus. Consensus is not unanimous agreement nor the result of decision by majority rule. Rather, consensus is a process requiring mutual openness, continued dialogue, good will, and compromise, as the participants seek to understand and affirm the views of the others while striving to arrive at a common point of agreement. After much dialogue and compromise, the group may decide that although Greg and York have a persuasive argument that Lena deliberately assisted Doug in suicide, the group consensus is that her actions were accidental and ethically non-culpable.

Step V. Implementation

Once a decision has been reached, the timing and methods of implementation must also be considered. In this particular case, once the study group has agreed on a final evaluation of the Graham case, they must also devise a class presentation that will effectively present their final decision as well as their mastery of Professor Michaels's method for decision making.

Conclusion

The use of the above model for ethical decision making should enable a person, after honest and careful consideration, to arrive at a sound ethical decision that is a reflection of his or her own overall ethical vision of covenant, quest for meaning, esteemed values, and principles. Motivated by an ethic of care and guided by a well-formed conscience, it is to be hoped that the individual using this model will arrive at a decision that maintains personal integrity and social well-being.

VI. Feature: Biomedical Ethical Dilemmas[13] for Research, Reflection, and Discussion

Each of the following case studies highlights a contemporary biomedical dilemma that requires further research. Each requires an understanding of other relevant issues, such as quality of life, the rights of an incompetent minor patient, the role of a surrogate decision maker, the role of the physician and medical institution in a situation such as this, the legal, medical, and moral duty of the hospital or state to protect the interests of a minor, even if this protection goes against parental wishes, and, if the case involves euthanasia, the legal and moral status of euthanasia in the United States.

After researching the related issues surrounding each of the case studies, use the model for ethical decision making to facilitate an application of the influence of roles, *prima facie* duties, proportionate reason, and an ethic of care. Each case also requires consideration of concepts explored in these first five chapters.

1. Surrogate Decision Making

Mrs. Doe, a 28-year-old nurse, and her 30-year-old lawyer husband became the parents of a premature girl, their fourth child. Baby Doe was diagnosed as having Down Syndrome with the added complications of a cleft palate and duodenal atresia, an intestinal blockage. The intestinal blockage could be corrected surgically with minimal risk to the child; without the operation, the baby could not be fed and would die. Upon hearing the child's diagnosis, the mother refused permission for the corrective abdominal surgery, and her husband concurred. The parents said it was not fair to their normal children to raise them with a child with Down Syndrome. The hospital did not seek a court order to override the parents. The child was put in a side room and, over an eleven-day period, allowed to starve to death.

2. Organ Donation and Transplantation

Don Wentworth was a 21-year-old senior at the local university. One month prior to graduation, Don was riding his motorcycle home from the mall when he was struck by a drunk driver. After examination by medical specialists, it was determined that Don needed to be placed on life supports to maintain heart and lung function. Besides the serious and irreversible head injuries, Don had sustained some bruises but no other serious injuries. By the time the Wentworth family arrived from out of state, Don's team of physicians suspected that the brain damage had been so extensive and instantaneous that Don was now "brain dead," and that if the life supports were withdrawn, all heart and lung functions would stop. However, Don was a good candidate for major organ donation.

Dr. Levy, the staff neurosurgeon, quickly apprised Mr. and Mrs. Wentworth and their two older sons of the situation. The parents' first reaction was to see this as an opportunity to have something good come from tragedy, but their son Richard's horrified response was "What is this 'brain death?' He still looks very much alive to me. How can you do this to someone who is not dead?"

3. Allocation of Resources

A public clinic referred Maria and Jorge Garcia and their desperately ill baby, Rosa, to a regional medical center for treatment. The baby's parents, seasonal farm workers from Central America, were indigent, lacked any medical insurance, and had no family physician. After waiting in the emergency room for four hours, Rosa was finally admitted. However, Dr. Powers, the pediatrician on call, refused to treat Rosa because he did not want to provide free services. All the county pediatric facilities within a hundred mile radius were over capacity. Rosa died a few hours later.

CHAPTER VI

HUMAN SEXUALITY

Overview
The Case of Margot and Jared

I. Contemporary Changes in Human Sexuality

II. The Person and Society:
A Secular View of Human Sexuality
A. Sexuality: Sex and Gender Embodied
1. Women's Studies and Gender
2. Men's Studies and Gender
B. The Relational Context of Human Sexuality:
Differing Views of Love and Marriage
C. Sex as Distinct from Sexuality

III. Sexuality from the Perspective of Religious Traditions
A. Secular and Religious Views of Sexuality: Some Commonalities
B. A Contemporary Religious Perspective on Human Sexuality
C. Emerging Religious Trends
Trend 1: Sexuality
Trend 2: Responsible Relationality
Trend 3: Sexual Intimacy and Spirituality

IV. The Case of Margot and Jared Revisited
A. Margot and Jared's Moral Dilemma
B. Implementing the Model for Ethical Decision Making

Questions for Research, Reflection, and Discussion

Overview

As developed in Chapters I through V, the foundation of a broad-visioned covenantal ethics is a view of the person, who—as an individual and a member of a community—is constantly being bombarded with and changed by a variety of interrelated personal, social, environmental, and cultural factors. These factors can be summarized into three broad interrelated perspectives that are brought to bear in each ethical or moral decision: 1) the multidimensional person; 2) the society; and 3) the religious tradition as integrated within the self and expressed in and through each life experience.

In addition, ethical and moral decisions are shaped by each person's conscience and process of reasoned reflection. In Chapter IV the notion of reasoned reflection was explored as a way for conscience to use complex processes to arrive at sound ethical decisions and to shape identity, moral character, and basic life direction. As a way of acquiring and making use of ethical knowledge, reasoned reflection also employs a person's cognitive abilities to reason, dialogue, and reflect upon external experiences. The model for ethical decision making presented in Chapter V presumes that the individual, when faced with any ethical or moral dilemma, is able to implement the model by making use of a formed and informed conscience and a capacity for reasoned reflection.

Chapter VI focuses on the specific issue of human sexuality. Sexuality is defined as the way the multidimensional unity known as person lives in the world as a gendered being. Seen this way, sexuality is more than biology; it includes an environment affected by politics, culture, and ethical and moral values. Sexuality is distinct from and more than the physical acts (known as sex or sexual intercourse) that result in physical expression of emotions or in pregnancy. Sexuality is a lifetime discovery of the self as lovable and loved, of the ways to relate with self and members of the same and opposite sex. Sexuality is about making relational choices that simultaneously affect and are affected by a sense of embodiment, personality, intellect, emotions, social roles, stereotypes, and spiritual and moral values and principles reflective of a broader ethical world vision.

The case study of Margot and Jared illustrates some of the contemporary problems and moral dilemmas surrounding the meaning and role of human sexuality. However, as noted in previous chapters, a person's life and development are processes constantly affected by the influence and interrelationship of history, geography, culture, and society. Because human sexuality is one dimension of the total person, Chapter VI's exploration of this issue also highlights the profound influence these same factors have in the constant molding of the meaning and function of human sexuality within past and contemporary times.

Using the three broad perspectives of the multidimensional person, society, and religious tradition, Chapter VI employs reasoned reflection to discuss and to reflect upon the personal, social, and ethical dilemmas concerning human sexuality in the lives of two individuals, Margot and Jared. Although the issue specifically considered here is human sexuality, Chapter VI employs the same decision-making process presented in Chapter V, because that process can serve any ethical or moral issue.

The Case of Margot and Jared

By day, The Library was a bakery and coffee house popular with undergraduate and graduate students alike. The tables were always filled with individuals and groups who liked to adjourn for post-class discussions or study breaks. By early evening, however, The Library was transformed into a student bar and grill noted for its noisy student sociopolitical gatherings and raucous parties.

On this particular early morning, The Library was almost deserted when Serena and Margot slid onto chairs at a back table. Roommates for the past year and a half, the two young women were a study in opposites. Others were often surprised when they discovered that Serena and Margot were friends as well as roommates. Outgoing, brash, and streetwise, Serena came to the large urban campus of Brewster University from inner-city Detroit to major in dramatic arts. Margot, on the other hand, came from a small midwestern farm community to major in liberal arts; her experience of campus dorm life was the first time she had lived in a large urban area. Where Serena had an outgoing, life-of-the-party personality, Margot was more introverted, but popular with and fiercely loyal to a smaller circle of friends. Although Serena dated many boys, Margot had finally met and developed a growing eight-month relationship with Jared, an upperclassman majoring in political science. Serena had thought that an engagement might be imminent until Margot had returned to the room about midnight looking pale and distressed. Later that morning, the two girls headed for their favorite table and breakfast at The Library.

"Okay, out with it," said Serena. "What's been going on? I know you've been upset since last Saturday night. I thought you'd talk about it when you were ready. But when you came in last night, I knew things had gotten worse. So, what gives?"

Silence reigned as Margot sat with head bowed and hands nervously clasped in her lap. Finally, Margot looked up. Slowly and hesitatingly, she began to disclose the events of the past week.

"Remember the big concert the university hosted last Saturday night at the amphitheater? Well, Jared and I went to party over at one of the fraternities. The place is small; it was hot and crowded. When I asked for my usual coke, Jared made a great show about getting it for me. He told me that it was time to "broaden my horizons." He explained that he was introducing me to rum cokes. It tasted kind of funny, but I drank it anyway. We don't drink much alcohol at home. I was curious, and I've been wanting to try new things. Anyway, after my third coke, I was really lightheaded and wondered if I should stop. Jared laughed at me and said it was just the smoke and music and my being tired and all. He'd been drinking cokes too—he had two to my one. I got through about half of the fourth drink and felt really woozy and sick. I asked Jared to take me home. He didn't want to but finally agreed.

"We drove around for awhile, and the next thing I knew we were parked out by the deserted track fields. Jared said a walk around the track might help to clear my head. I felt embarrassed and wished I hadn't drunk so much. I remember apologizing over and over to Jared, and he said it was okay. He admitted he was feeling a bit drunk too. I remember feeling so glad he didn't think badly of me that the next thing I knew, I was kissing him. It felt good, and for the first time I didn't want to stop. Things were moving pretty quickly and the next thing I knew we were lying on the grass. And then it was too late.

"I must have fallen asleep afterwards, because I remember waking up later and feeling just horrible. As if the headache wasn't bad enough, I felt terribly guilty. I come from a Christian home. My parents and my church have always taught that sex outside marriage is wrong.

My parents allowed us to drink only in their presence, but alcohol always made me sick. I never really got the hang of beer.

"Jared is the first guy I have ever seriously dated. I know I'm not gorgeous or anything like the others I used to see Jared with at The Library. When we met at a disco in town, I couldn't believe at first how well we hit it off. As the months went by, Jared and I became great friends. Then Jared started bugging me lately to have sex with him. He said it was a great way to be close and a natural way to seal our relationship. I felt torn—I really think I love Jared, and yet I was always brought up to believe sex is something you save for marriage. When I told this to Jared last month, he told me that it was just an excuse; this was the late twentieth century and my refusal to seal a relationship with sex was a cover because I didn't want to make an exclusive commitment. Now I can't look Jared in the face, let alone my parents."

"What did Jared say?" inquired a sympathetic Serena.

"At the time he said nothing. He just brought me back to the dorm. Then he failed to return two of my calls and broke our standing date on Wednesday. I finally cornered him late last night outside the dorm. We walked for a long time and just talked. He told me that he hadn't started out to get me drunk. But when he noticed how alive I became as I had more to drink, he didn't try to stop me. He says he didn't realize that alcohol didn't agree with me. He swears that he never intended for it to go so far at the track field. He had never seen me so affectionate, and he expected me to put a stop to it as I usually do when I get uncomfortable. But this time I didn't, and he thought it was okay with me—that it was what I wanted. Now Jared thinks we should cool it for awhile—perhaps date other people.

"I just couldn't come home last night after that. I needed some time to think. I wanted to settle things between us but it's like Jared's too embarrassed to talk about it or to see me. I feel guilty and ashamed. I can't go to church, and I don't want to talk to my folks. What am I going to do? What about Jared and me?"

As Margot covered her face and sobbed, Serena patted her shoulder and wondered how she could best help her friend. Because Jared was also her friend, Serena was determined to get his side of the story.

Two days later, Serena was finally able to corner Jared at his favorite table at The Library.

"Okay, Jared, level with me. You know Margot is my friend too. I've gotten her side. Now I want your side of it, and don't even think of putting me off," declared a determined Serena.

"And I say it's none of your business, Serena. Sure, we used to date and we've remained friends. But this is none of your business," exclaimed a defiant Jared.

"Think again, friend. I'm making it my business. We were friends long before we even came to this place. We go different ways now, but I still count you as a friend. Margot is also my friend. I know she's hurting. The Jared I used to know would be too. But I'm not so sure now. The person I heard Margot describe sure didn't sound like the Jared I know. And if I'm right, you two are going to need some help in sorting this thing out."

Surprisingly, Jared's facade of defiance crumpled as he wearily put down his coke and began to speak hesitantly.

"I don't know what got into me or her that Saturday night. I really like and respect Margot. She's quieter and not as outgoing as the other girls I've dated. Sure, I thought she was an easy mark at first and it would be sex as usual. But as I got to really know her, things became different. I still wanted to have sex with her, but not as an easy score. Now that I think about it, I wanted it to say we were a pair, that we had an understanding. But she wouldn't give in, no matter what arguments I used.

"Then, that Saturday night after the concert, we came back to one of the fraternity parties. I got her a rum coke. When Margot asked for a second and then a third, I thought she really liked them. I know she doesn't like beer, but I thought she'd finally found something she could drink. Then, she said she was sick and wanted to go home. I thought the fresh air or a walk around the track would help. The funny thing is, she suddenly threw her arms around me and became really affectionate, petting and pawing me. I'd never seen her like this.

"I'm not sure what happened after that. Part of me wanted to take advantage of the situation—here was a new and freer Margot. Another part of me was unsure, and I really thought she would put the brakes on when things got too much out of hand. She usually does. And then I couldn't stop. This was something I really wanted to share with her. My folks have always been pretty open about sex in relationships. I'm not religious like Margot, so I really didn't think what we did was against God or a church—until Margot got so upset. You know, I used to think her refusal to consider moving in with me was prudish and just an excuse. Her actions at the track made me think I'd been duped and that it hadn't been her first time. Now I don't know what to think. I'm only sorry we had sex because Margot's so upset. I'm confused and I'm angry about the relationship. Maybe if we cooled it and dated others, things would eventually work out."

Jared paused, looked squarely at Serena, and demanded: "OK, great buddy, what would you suggest? Where do Margot and I go from here?"

Surprised, Serena sat back, contemplating how similar Jared's and Margot's questions were. But she also sensed that Margot's and Jared's questions and problems were more complex than they seemed at first.

Margot and Jared's conversations with Serena reflect their uncertainty about and confusion over the meaning and function of sexuality within relationships, the distinction between sexuality and sex, and the role of sex within varied types of relationships. In the following pages, the human sexuality issue is first presented within the context of a variety of contemporary changes. The three integral facets of the human sexuality issue—sexuality, relationships, and sex—are then discussed, first from the secular perspectives of the person and society, and then from a religious perspective. The information gathered from these discussions will then be applied to an analysis of Margot and Jared's ethical dilemma in an attempt to provide the background for a sound ethical decision.

I. Contemporary Changes in Human Sexuality

In order for one to understand the complex issues and deep emotions that Margot and Jared's ethical dilemma raises, it is important to be aware that human sexuality represents one of the most common areas of personal and societal confusion and crisis today. In fact, for centuries the meaning, role, and function of human sexuality, its relationship to sex, and the ethical and moral nature of sexual practices have been discussed and debated by individuals, societies, and religious traditions. Also, concerns about sexuality and sex practices often emerge historically in conjunction with unsettling social changes. Noting this, Albert Klassen, Colin Williams, and Eugene Levitt's *Sex and Morality in the U.S.*[1] presents a contemporary examination of age-old questions about sex and sexuality. Their work represents a current non-religious and scientific presentation of the major findings from a national survey of 3,000 adults concerning American sexual experiences and norms. In the book's opening remarks, the authors state that one of their first tasks was to determine the veracity of the notion of a "sexual revolution," a popular label used to express the seeming sexual openness that was non-existent around the 1950s but is now rampant in the United States. In defining the idea of radical changes in the sexual sphere as "revolutionary," the authors note:

> On the surface, such a label appears quite warranted. For example, never before in our society have the public representation and discussion of sexual matters been so extensive. Magazines with pictures of full frontal nudity are available at corner drug stores; movie theaters show films that depict almost every kind of sexual behavior; best selling books often include down-to-earth advice on sexual performance and relationships; and even television, which enters most homes, is gradually expanding the erotic content of both its documentary and entertainment offerings... Premarital cohabitation among the young is no longer extraordinary; jokes about sex have come out of the locker room; the revealing bathing suit has lost its shock value; "singles bars" are to be found in any city of size (3).

The authors later conclude that, although the findings from their study do not substantiate the notion that a "sexual revolution" has indeed occurred (9, 267), they do indicate that subtle but major changes "appear to have occurred or to be occurring" (9).

In *Sex and Sexuality: From Repression to Expression*,[2] Mildred Weil explicates the nature of the major changes noted by Klassen et al. She recognizes variations occurring in attitudes, in a greater tolerance of different sexual behaviors, in more permissive standards, in the changing male and female roles, and in the openness to experimenting with sex as a form of pleasure as well as a method of procreation (xi).

Similarly, from a religious perspective, the General Assembly of the Presbyterian Church in its 1991 response to its Special Committee on Human Sexuality[3] notes that

> ...we are witnessing a deep-seated crisis of sexuality in this culture...It has led to an important questioning of the meaning and place of sex and sexuality in our lives. A fundamental rethinking is going on about how to define appropriate sexual norms and expectations, as well as how to draw boundaries distinguishing acceptable from unacceptable sexual behavior (3).

As with *Sex and Morality in the U.S.*, the Presbyterian General Assembly report views this crisis of sexuality as having been caused by a variety of current social and cultural changes that have emerged in five key areas in the Western world: 1) family patterns have shifted from two-parent to single-parent homes in which the roles between men and women have become more egalitarian; 2) medical technology and advances have lengthened the average life span of men and women, and have provided a variety of forms of inexpensive contraception, legally and medically safe means for abortions, as well as new genetic and reproductive technologies, all of which have provided the means of removing the function and role of sexuality from its procreative purposes; 3) HIV, AIDS, and the dramatic increases in other sexually transmitted diseases have raised complex questions about the relationship among health, disease, and sexuality for individuals and society; 4) the increased commercialization and exploitation of sex and pornography in the media and commercial markets have dramatically increased the incidences of sexual abuse and violence; and 5) an increased awareness exists that patterns of sexual abuse and violence have permeated every socioeconomic level and have increased the personal and social costs of rape, battering, sexual harassment, and spousal and child abuse (2-3).

It is important to note that, taken together, these five vital areas of change also highlight three interrelated components of human sexuality: sexuality, relationships, and sex. In the following pages, the influence and interrelationship of each of these three components will be explored, first from the non-religious or secular perspectives of self and society, and then from a religious perspective.

II. The Person and Society:
A Secular View of Human Sexuality

A. Sexuality: Sex and Gender Embodied

As noted in Chapter I, each person is a "multidimensional unity" of many parts—the physical, spiritual, emotional, psychological, mental, and intellectual. Shaped and influenced by heredity and a variety of complex environmental factors, the unique person emerges through a gradual process of emotional, cognitive, psychological, and moral development. Sexuality is defined as the way that this multidimensional unity develops, lives, and expresses itself in the world as male or female.[4] The notion of sexuality implies the two distinct but interwoven realities of sex and gender. Each person's sexuality is experienced by the outer world through sex and gender. It is these two realities that have shaped the meaning, role, and function of sexuality in most cultural settings.

In "Do Feminist Ethics Counter Feminist Aims?" Patricia Ward Scalstas[5] notes a distinction that has been made in the feminist literature. According to her, each person has a sex or biological determination as male or female. The person also has gender, those socially and culturally constructed characteristics and roles of males and females (15). For centuries, both sex and gender have been viewed as having the same meaning and, as such, constituting the essential and unalterable differences between males and females. In this text, the two terms are seen as very distinct: sex as a biologically determined component of sexuality, and gender as a historically and culturally bound construct through which a society views the two sexes as psychologically and behaviorally different. Sparked by the feminist movement, Scalstas notes that in such fields as biology, psychology, sociology, anthropology, and ethics, serious research has been undertaken within the last thirty years that questions and reexamines the nature and role of supposed differences between the two sexes (15-16). In other words, the question that is being asked by researchers[6] is whether the biologically and genetically determined differences between males and females are significant, or if other factors, such as gender and psychological enculturation are at the source of the contemporary perceptions of male-female differences. If it is the latter, then the challenge is to understand correctly the nature and function of gender as well as the obsolete perceptions that have caused centuries-old gender inequality, oppression, and discrimination.

The following is intended to be a brief sketch of some of the recent directions taken by both women's and men's studies as they have sought to understand the historical, cultural, and social nature and causes of gender. If, as Michael Kimmel contends in "Rethinking Masculinity,"[7] the definitions of masculinity are constructed in relation to definitions of femininity, then two interrelated areas of gender study—the shifting bases for male-female relationships and a contemporary understanding of sexuality—are intimately linked to gender:

> ...Sexuality is organized around a gender axis; gender is perhaps the key organizing principle of sexuality. Gender informs sexuality, sexuality confirms gender (19).

1. Women's Studies and Gender

The feminist movement has challenged the traditional understandings of what it means to be male and female and the roles ascribed to each gender. Female studies in such fields as biology, history, sociology, psychology, and theology have undertaken the task of not only questioning the traditional economic and political status of women, but, even more fundamentally, of analyzing and reconstructing the perceived nature of the gender differences that molded and divided both women and men. With the tendency to lean more toward the examination of the historically and culturally bound constructs through which a society views men and women, female studies have examined a variety of historical and cultural influences that have joined to produce the spiritual, emotional, psychological, and behavioral distinctions that make men and women so different.

From a biological perspective, for example, feminist sociobiologist Anne Fausto-Sterling, in *Myths of Gender: Biological Theories About*

Women and Men,[8] examines certain biological myths within the scientific
world that have stressed the notion that "male and female sexuality are
so different, so at odds, that it makes sense to think of the two sexes as
separate species" (4). In scientifically examining and questioning some
commonly held myths, Fausto-Sterling finds no biological or scientific
basis for the myth that females are unable to do mathematics (53-60), or
for the myth that men are more aggressive, competitive, and risk-taking
than women (123-154). Rather, she discovers that the roots of these
myths are social constructions that favor males as superior to females
(196-204). In her conclusion, Fausto-Sterling warns her scientific colleagues as well as her readers to scrutinize the conclusions reached by
sociobiologists, as their work has often been used with far-reaching implications—for example, in employment discrimination against women
in fields of science, engineering, and corporate finance (208-212).

If the differences implied in males and females are socially constructed, then what it means to live and develop as female is a historic-
cultural phenomenon that evolves and changes. As explained in
Chapter I, the development of gender, or the socially constructed views
of what it means to be female in contemporary Western society, is itself
the subject of a complex anthropological, psychological, and sociological debate. For example, Gerda Lerner notes in *The Creation of
Patriarchy*[9] that

> ...gender is the cultural definition of behavior defined as ap-
> propriate to the sexes in a given society at a given time. Gender is
> a set of cultural roles; therefore it is a cultural product which
> changes over time...Unfortunately, the term is used both in ac-
> ademic discourse and in the media as interchangeable with "sex."
> Such usage is unfortunate, because it hides and mystifies the dif-
> ference between the biological given—sex—and the culturally
> created—gender (238).

Lerner's work attempts to trace the historical development of key
gender images, ideas, and metaphors of Western civilization that she
believes contributed to female gender inequality and discrimination
embodied in the very framework of society: its long-standing social
norms, roles, and institutions (11-13).

Similarly, Elizabeth Janeway, in *Man's World, Woman's Place: A Study in Social Mythology*,[10] and Sandra Lipsitz Bem, in *The Lenses of Gender*,[11] contend that the notion of gender itself is the creation of the Western socialization process. According to Bem, the nineteenth-century scientific adoption of the evolutionary view replaced the prevailing religious views of the meaning and role of gender. Through the decades-old conditioning of such sociocultural factors as historical time, geography, environment, heredity, and familial roles and expectations, Bem sees three beliefs about males and females slowly emerging:

That they [men and women] have fundamentally different psychological and sexual natures, that men are inherently the dominant or superior sex, and that both male-female difference and male dominance are natural...[These] hidden assumptions about sex and gender remain embedded in cultural discourses, social institutions, and individual psyches that invisibly reproduce male power in generation after generation. I call these assumptions the lenses of gender (1-2).

Bem argues that the gender distinctions that Western culture has taken for granted are not based on inherent, unalterable biological differences but on the specific cultural and historically bound enculturation process that molds and informs each person within a specific community or society (4).

Bem systematically explains how the lenses of gender, specifically defined as biological essentialism (the intrinsic biological natures of men and women as the basis for their difference) (6-38), androcentrism (male centeredness or maleness as the natural norm for life and femaleness as a deviation) (39-79), and gender polarization (the inherent male-female difference as superimposed on every aspect of sociocultural life) (80-132) have emerged, dominated, and prevailed over the past one hundred and fifty years in historical and cultural discourses. For example Bem documents how gender polarization was given scientific and medical legitimacy through the allied fields of medicine, psychiatry, psychology, and sexology. Because they held the positions of power,

...men used their positions of power to construct a social world that defined women and women's roles in relation to men and men's roles...Men in power androcentrically defined science, morality, mental health, work, politics and every other institution in society as well...They unconsciously built into those institutions whatever fundamental assumptions about reality that they came to have by virtue of their particular position in the social structure (Bem 132).

According to Bem and Janeway, the result has been a systematization and institutionalization of gender inequality that has been pervasive in Western socialization processes for centuries. It is this culturally determined gender inequality that has been the impetus behind the current charges of oppression and discrimination by the feminist and black movements.

2. Men's Studies and Gender

Pioneer writers in the area of men's studies, such as Harry Brod, Sam Keen, and Joseph Pleck, have acknowledged the impetus and influence of the women's studies movement upon the recently developing field of male studies. In attempting to delineate the similarities and differences between women's and men's studies, Harry Brod acknowledges in "A Case for Men's Studies"[12] that men's studies goes beyond the traditionally male-biased scholarship; like women's studies it attempts to weaken the "patriarchal ideology's masquerade as knowledge" (264). Brod contends that the subject matter of men's studies is the study of "masculinities and male experiences in their own right as specific and varying social, cultural and historical formations" (264).

Men's studies concern themselves with discovering what constitutes the essence of masculinity and understanding some of the historical, cultural, and social forces that traditionally and recently have shaped what a society deems the ideal expressions of masculinity. In *Fire in The Belly*, Sam Keen[13] sketches a traditional stereotypical picture of masculinity and the "ideal" male:

...In the accepted mythology of our time, men are independent, women dependent, men dominate and women yield; men make history and women provide emotional support. Folklore...has it that men are phobic about intimacy, are tongue-tied about emotions, and generally keep an antiseptic distance between themselves and females of their species...Real men don't depend on women. We stand tall and alone (14).

When, how, and why did such a portrait arise and come to be so widely accepted in contemporary society?

In his research on males and their roles, Joseph Pleck's historical work "American Fathering in Historical Perspective"[14] investigates how "contradictory images of fatherhood from the past have left their mark on contemporary attitudes" (84). Beginning with the eighteenth-century image of the father as integrally involved with the family and as the moral overseer who instructed the children in "what God as well as the world required of them" (84), Pleck traces the shifting economic, psychological, and cultural patterns caused by increased industrialization, immigration, and urbanization in the United States that resulted in another image change in the mid-nineteenth to mid-twentieth centuries: the absentee, breadwinning father whose place in the home had been usurped by the dominating feminine influence of the mother (86-89). Moving through the events of two World Wars and the post-war depiction of American men as absent and passive, Pleck contends that in the 1950s a new theory about gender development articulated a more significant role for men: the sex role (92). According to the theory, "too much mothering and inadequate fathering" led to problems in male identity. In placing the father as the center of healthy sex role development, the new theory not only increased paternal involvement, but contributed to the already prevailing view of distinct maternal and paternal roles in child rearing (92-93). Pleck's conclusion is that changing historical, psychological, and economic forces have contributed and continue to contribute to the cultural images of masculinity that dominate a particular historical period.

Another direction, taken by Robert Moore and Douglas Gillette[15] is to discover the meaning of masculinity and its role in sexuality, relationships, and sex as conveyed through the images and stories contained in anthropology, religion, psychology, and literature. In *The*

Magician Within, Moore and Gillette use Carl Jung's writings about archetypal myths and explore the implications of these myths for understanding male sexuality. As they explain it, located deep within the psyche of each individual are "archetypal action patterns" which, as Jung saw it, are "equivalent to the instincts of other animals" (36) and are "the accumulated collective memory of the entire human race" (37). Both life enhancing and destructive, these archetypal structures within the psyche serve as "conduits for great charges of primal psychological energy...or life force that expresses itself through imaginal...spiritual and sexual impulses" (37-38).

Moore and Gillette's research envisions that the key to understanding the essence of masculinity, and the forging of a sound, contemporary male sexuality, involves unlocking the symbols and archetypal messages contained in the world's myths. As they explain it,

> ...myths are true stories that describe the ways of the psyche and the means by which our psychological energies interact. Myths project our inner dynamics onto the outer world and allow us to experience it through the filter of how we think and feel (32).

Moore and Gillette's work concentrates on unmasking and understanding the four basic archetypes—the King, the Warrior, the Magician, and The Lover—as well as their antithetical or shadow dimensions, that continually recur in the myths of most civilizations. Each is a part of a psychically whole self, and all complement one another (55).

Throughout history, these archetypes have merged and diverged in a variety of complex configurations, but their basic intent is to shed light on the "opposite points of view, opposite impulses, emotions and imaginal realms" of the archetypes as reflected in the human psyche (75). For example, the Magician, a male archetype in its whole, healthy reflection, expresses wisdom, insight, and imagination. He is an emotionally attuned quester, "the locator, consecrator, container and steward of sacred space and time" (232). If distorted, however, the male psyche exhibits characteristics of the Magician's Shadow side with its opposing poles of the Trickster on the one hand and the Innocent on the other. These Shadow or antithetical poles of the Magician are expressed in contemporary times in cultural and social patterns of extreme individualism or in dysfunctional behaviors, such as threats of nuclear destruction, ecological devastation, and mass human extinctions (103).

Another writer finding rich meaning in ancient stories and legends is Robert Bly. In *Iron John*[16] Bly explores the symbolic and psychological meanings behind the Grimm fairy tale, "Iron John or the Wild Man." He uses this tale to unearth seven long-forgotten characters or images of masculinity that are keys to understanding the male psyche and sound masculinity: the King, Warrior, the Lover, the Trickster, the Mythologist, the Grief Man, and the Wild Man. Although the much-forgotten dimension of the Wild Man is the central focus of *Iron John*, Bly contends that if contemporary men are ever to learn the real meaning of masculinity, then they must work to be in touch with all seven dimensions of the male psyche.

In Chapter One of *Iron John*, for example, Bly explains that the quest to understand the Wild Man hidden deep within each male psyche begins when a young boy finally separates from his mother and joins the male world of father and other male adults in work and companionship. Contemporary technological cultures, however, often lack the much-needed experiences and community rituals related to birth and death, initiations into adulthood, and rituals of conflict, marriage, and celebrations. In ancient civilizations, community rituals not only marked important periods of a man's growth to maturity but also left him with enduring symbols and memories of the essence of masculinity.

Through experiences with the father or a male mentor and these initiatory rights of passage, each young man is encouraged and supported in his individual challenge to unlock the mysteries of his soul or, as symbolized by Bly, to know the "Wild Man." To do this, each boy must move through stages of growth, which Bly explains through such symbolic phrases as

...taking the first wound, doing kitchen work and ashes work, creating a garden, bringing wild flowers to the Holy Woman, experiencing the warrior, riding the red, the white and the black horses, learning to create art, and receiving the second heart (225).

Ultimately, if he perseveres through these necessary stages of growth, the boy might possess the ability to be in touch with the Wild Man. It is in the capturing and integrating of the Wild Man's qualities that the boy is transformed into the mature man who possesses the important qualities that characterize masculinity: love of spontaneity, association with nature and wilderness, and an emotional capacity for grief, ecstasy, and spirit (222-227).

There are two common threads that seem to run through these pioneering works in men's studies. The first is the willingness to use a variety of methods to plumb the real meaning and sources of male sexuality that lie behind contemporary stereotypes of masculinity. The second thread is the importance of the relational to the healthy development of male sexuality. Despite the contemporary and popular mystique that stresses male independence and individualism, the works of these writers reflect a lost male sense of being part of a larger community that shapes and is being shaped by the individual. What continually emerges from the myths and stories are instances of male bonding with the father, of the guiding influence of the community elders, and of the traditional rites of passage and initiation, all of which challenge the young boy to incorporate within his developing sense of self a similar feeling for the meaning and importance of communal relationships. In contradistinction to contemporary belief, men's studies stress that a sound male sexuality is doomed to distortion or failure if the individual and communal learning processes are not interwoven. As Michael Meade contends in *Men and the Water of Life*,[17]

...[if] the fires that innately burn in youths are not intentionally and lovingly added to the hearth of community, they will burn down the structures of culture just to feel the warmth. Each generation is a fire of individual and collective heat that only learns its purpose by burning...The individual life is "made" in those initiatory moments when the individual sees both ways into the soul. The validity of that vision can only be verified by a return to community. A man cannot look back accurately enough or look forward long enough if he is standing alone and isolated...Unless enough men can gather together and hold the genuine threads of their lives so that the pattern of community and of the elders can be seen, even temporarily, there is no promise of healing waters ahead (19).

In summary, from the perspectives of women's and men's studies, a contemporary understanding of human sexuality is incomplete unless there is an awareness of the distinction between the terms "sex" and "gender," the former a mostly unalterable biological determinant and the latter a changeable social phenomenon. As demonstrated by both women's and men's studies, one of the implications of this distinction is experienced in gender formation, the social enculturation process whereby females and males learn the meaning and roles of what it means to be a woman and a man in their society. As expressed earlier in Chapter IV, this gender formation in turn affects how females and males acquire, interpret, and implement the knowledge of head and knowledge of the heart needed in ethical decision making.

B. The Relational Context of Human Sexuality:
Differing Views of Love and Marriage

As noted earlier, in the Report of the Presbyterian General Assembly (see page 179), the common thread that runs through the five areas of contemporary cultural and societal change is that of relationships. Whether it be the medical threat of AIDS or the marked increase in the publicity about sexual exploitation and abuse, these areas bespeak tumultuous changes in the ways modern cultures and societies view the meaning and function of relationships.

As we saw in Chapter II, one of the enduring facts of human life is that persons are both individuals and communal beings. From a non-religious or secular perspective, the relational bond is expressed and experienced in the challenge of each individual to develop the potential of the unique self while also learning how to channel that potential toward the group through the assumption of socially accepted roles, whether it be in a small neighborhood community or the larger society of the world. In other words, there seems to be a continued tension between strains of individualism and relationalism within Western culture. Because each of the five areas of change highlighted by the Presbyterian General Assembly represents an emphasis on the individual and a decline of sound, loving, moral relational bonds, a potential threat has emerged to the establishment or maintenance of healthy, communal relationships.

Furthermore, each of the five changes highlights the historical and social struggle between two competing images of human sexuality. On the one hand, there is the image of sexuality whose goals for personal fulfillment are based on increased sexual individuality and expression. On the other hand, another image of human sexuality exists that has as its goals relational interdependence, mutual self-development, and intimacy.

Francesca M. Cancian traces the roots of this cyclical redefining of human sexuality according to individualistic or relational lines in her historical study *Love in America*.[18] Her research unearthed patterns that tie differing views of human sexuality to periodic sociohistorical changes that in turn reflect transformations in the meaning and function of love and marriage in the United States during the past three centuries.

In Colonial America, for example, love, like sex and economic roles, was not separated along male and female lines (16). Materially and economically dependent upon each other, husbands and wives were also jointly involved in the care and nurturing of the children.

By the middle of the nineteenth century, however, there had emerged an ideology of the separate spheres of the home and the workplace; of two different sets of role expectations for women and men (the nurturing, emotional woman versus the brave, tough, bread-winning male); of two different sets of personality traits, the feminine and the masculine (16-20). In what Cancian calls the "feminization of love" (23), human sexuality in the nineteenth century was epitomized by marital and family relationships that were portrayed by separate spheres of the independent, virile, self-made man and of the dependent, loving woman.

Later, the "Family Duty blueprint," as Cancian labels it, evolved in which the ideal family was depicted as the harmonious, nuclear family supported by an economically successful father (22); in this blueprint the cultural images of the ideal woman tended to emphasize tenderness, expression of emotion, and weakness. Concepts of marital love also shifted: Love became a private feeling shared only between the couple in the privacy of the bedroom and was disassociated from the public life of economic production and practical action to help others (23-24).

By the end of the nineteenth century the Family Duty blueprint of love and marriage had led to a lack of intimacy, companionship, and affection in the married relationship on the one hand (29), and an intense, emotional tie between mothers and children on the other (31). By this time, according to Cancian, the Family Duty blueprint was already in tension with individualism, another relational model. Marked by what Cancian discovered and Robert Bellah et al. labeled in *Habits of the Heart*[19] as "expressive individualism," the dynamics of this model are conveyed by an "expansive and deeply feeling self...along with the freedom to express oneself" that became the mark of a successful life (Bellah 34).

In sharp contrast to these relational models is the love and marriage concept labeled by Cancian as the Androgynous Love blueprint of the 1960s-1970s. This relational model contains two different strains: One strain emphasizes individual independence and self-development, and the other stresses relational interdependence, mutual self-development, and commitment. Spurred on by historic social changes, notions stressing the freedom, independence, and development of the individual competed with the traditional notion of family ties and relational commitments amid evidence of a rising divorce rate, an increase in the number of couples engaging in premarital sex or living together without being married, and the emergence of the two-career family and expanded economic opportunities for women (38). What finally emerged ⅄ is a relational model characterized by what Cancian calls "self-fulfillment, flexible roles and intimacy and open communication," (39) and by partners who develop a fulfilled and independent self. Gone is the expectation that one partner sacrifices the self for the other. Family and gender roles are more flexible while relationships are centered on open communication of needs, confrontation, and negotiation of problems (39-41).

The work of Cancian and Bellah et al. is important in that it highlights another important relational trend in Western culture's view of human sexuality. The traditional view of marriage, as the ideal, committed relationship whereby one multidimensional self can work with another self to fulfill individual potential, now contends with the modern notion that the healthy development of human sexuality and relationships does not necessarily include marriage (Cancian 70, Weil 72-

78, Janeway 200). As Cancian notes in her historical studies, sex, an act traditionally and socially sanctioned only for marriage, has now increasingly moved outside marriage (38-39). Cancian and Weil have concluded that there is a current tendency to view sex as a socially acceptable, premarital physical act expressing a positive level of feelings of love or affection without a concomitant level of dedication to and endurance of the relationship (Weil 63-103, Cancian 149-154). According to them, personal and relational growth can be experienced as well by any two people, whether heterosexual or homosexual, who have expressed a degree of commitment to each other. As Cancian remarks, such contemporary blueprints for love and relationships

> do not legitimate predetermined roles or sexual division of labor; they are blueprints for "relationships, not marriages. Both partners are expected to work on the relationship, communicate openly and develop themselves...Love is no longer part of a woman's special sphere" (40).

Similarly, Bellah et al. have noted that the ways people think about love is central to the way they define the meaning of human sexuality and communal relationships. These authors concur with Cancian that the traditional concepts of love, intimacy, and marriage that used to define committed, marital relationships are today "increasingly a source of insecurity, confusion, and uncertainty" (108). According to Bellah et al., the deeply ingrained individualism seemingly inherent in United States culture has affirmed each person's need to develop a sound human sexuality that finds mutual fulfillment in lasting relationships. This same individualism, however, has also transformed the notion of intimate, lasting relationships into one in which such a relationship is possible only so long as the relationship meets the needs of the individuals involved (108). As Bellah et al. see it, such a view reduces love to no more than an exchange with no rules except an obligation to open communication. Should such a trend continue, these authors fear, the continued deterioration of traditional moral and cultural traditions concerning human sexuality, love, and marriage will result in a lack of relationships bound by ideals of genuine attachment to the other, mutual sacrifice, and the willingness to risk loss or hurt in the relationship (110).

The natural need for individuals to experience and express their sexuality in close relationships also reflects the contemporary tendency to reduce and to equate human sexuality and intimacy to the physical act called sex. As Weil notes, there is a difference between sexuality as a form of honest communication and sexuality as a debilitating obsession; the former enables persons to deal with their sexuality creatively and honestly while the latter reduces sexuality to physical performance. In United States society over the past three decades, the increasing tendency to reduce sexuality to a physical performance or to a materialistic system of gratification and rewards (Weil 8-9) is slowly being replaced by what Weil calls the "new sexuality"—"part of a new system which is based upon the search for a means of combining an individual's identity, feelings, mind and body" (10).

C. Sex as Distinct from Sexuality

As previously discussed, the term "sex" refers to a person's biological determination as male or female. However, both in the written word and in popular speech, a second usage is evident for the term "sex," namely the physical act of intercourse or coitus. Klassen et al., in their evaluation and interpretations of the data on premarital sex, noted the following contemporary usages and meanings for the term sex: an expression of affection, intimacy, deep love, social status; an indication of a degree of appeal and attraction to the opposite sex; a means of gratification, punishment, and reward; and a source of violence and exploitation of another (160-64).

There is also a popular tendency to equate the word "sexuality" with genital sex. Besides increasing popular confusion, this tendency creates another problem: By equating sexuality with sex, the many and varied dimensions that constitute and delineate the person are reduced to just one aspect, that of the physical dimension and the physical act of intercourse. Idealized and obsessed by contemporary media, sex has seemingly become the only and ultimate expression of two integral aspects of the committed relationship: love and intimacy.

Within the field of human sexuality, the works of such authors as Rita Nakashima Brock, Michael S. Kimmel, Jordan et al., and Mildred Weil[20] distinguish between "sexuality"—multidimensional person in relationship—and "sex"—one physical expression of the person. They also explore the proper interplay of these two facets within a relationship. Weil remarks that

> ...Sex as pleasure should not be confused with the idea that genital sex is the same as human sexuality. It is not. Sexuality refers to a total relationship not only to sex as coitus. This means that it is necessary to integrate sex into personality and human relationships, as sexuality requires personal meaning and personal and sociocultural referents (8).

As Weil's comments indicate, sex, as one expression of the physical dimension of a person, has its meaning only in reference to personal and social contexts. Fundamentally social, human beings have developed the capacity for relationships based on varied degrees of emotion, from interest to affection to love. In her definition of love in the contemporary United States, Cancian includes physical affection, acceptance, commitment, and empathy (69-70). In addition to these, Weil adds interpersonal competence, intelligence, trust, and creativity (73-76). However, Weil, Cancian, and Janeway[21] also include one other important facet of love: the need for intimacy or closeness. Abraham Maslow[22] notes that among the important psychological needs that a person must fulfill in order to be fully developed, intimacy—closeness to a few significant people—is essential. In "The Development of Women's Sense of Self," Jean Baker Miller[23] notes that recent gender development studies have discovered that although both genders experience this need for intimacy, cultural and social factors cause males and females to experience and express relational intimacy differently. Miller describes relational intimacy as

> ...wanting to be in relationship with others, to really comprehend the other; wanting to contribute to the other;...wanting the nature of the relationship to be one in which the other person(s) is engaged in this way (22).

Intimacy connotes relational levels that have moved beyond the acquaintance stage. It implies that those in the relationship have begun the intricate and complex move toward a relationship that has many meanings. The most basic stage is friendship. Intimacy within this stage is expressed in physical and non-physical ways. For example, a meaningful look, a touch of the hand, a warmly spoken word: all can imply a developing sense of closeness. According to Weil, intimacy within a non-sexual context is the expression of one's innermost thoughts and feelings with another:

> ...Sharing implies mutuality in experiencing personal thoughts, feelings and experiences between the pair. Thus, for a person to be intimate with another means to have knowledge of the innermost being of another (10).

Zick Rubin and E.B. McNeil, in *The Psychology of Being Human*,[24] and Elizabeth Janeway reiterate Weil's concept of relational intimacy. Janeway remarks that intimacy within a relationship implies both risk and courage; intimacy means to "...deliver oneself into the hands of just one other person"; it "means that one reveals oneself a great deal more fully than by giving a bit of oneself here and another bit there: one gives oneself away" (200-201).

Weil and Janeway both imply that intimacy involves a high degree of sharing on many levels: emotional, intellectual, spiritual, and psychological. Also included as one other aspect of intimacy is physical sharing connoted by the act of intercourse or sex. As noted earlier, Janeway, Weil, and others maintain that sex, no longer the earmark of marriage, is considered by increasing segments in contemporary society to be an acceptable practice within any relationship between two adults who have formed a committed or exclusive relationship characterized by friendship and love, emotional attachment and affection, and mutual interdependence; when linked to any committed, exclusive relationship, sex becomes the ultimate expression of relational intimacy.

Within contemporary times, however, a problem has arisen when "sex" takes on another connotation. What had once been one of many ways to express intimacy has become elevated in contemporary society to being *the* only and most significant indicator of relational appeal and intimacy. Nowhere is this more pronounced than in modern media advertisements. In products from automobiles, beer, and personal hygiene items to clothes and sporting events, the sexual appeal of beautiful women is featured and visually packaged because Madison Avenue has created the mystique that sex is what sells. Although Laura Mulvey's "Visual Pleasure and Narrative Cinema"[25] mainly pertains to the Hollywood portrayal of women on film, her comments about the underlying message are also indicative of what has happened in television and newsprint advertisements:

> ...Women are simultaneously looked at and displayed, with their appearance coded for visual and erotic impact so that they can be said to connote to-be-looked-at-ness. Woman displayed as sexual object is the leit-motif of erotic spectacle:...she holds the look, plays to and signifies male desire...(348-49).

The degree of female physical attractiveness and sex appeal have come to define men and women and, in so doing, have commercialized and distorted sex or physical closeness. Without sex appeal and sexual activity, relationships are, according to the media messages, evaluated as less than successful, and intimacy as less fulfilling. In elevating sex— seeing the sexual expression of intimacy as the ultimate barometer of relational success—the contemporary media have not only demeaned the real meaning of sex as a physical expression of intimacy, but have also removed the sexual from its place as only one of the many dimensions of the person expressed through sexuality.

In conclusion, the secular perspective of sexuality, with its interrelated components of relationships and sex, reflects a variety of contemporary personal and social trends and messages. Jared and Margot, the case study characters from the beginning of the chapter, reflect some of these social trends and messages. However, their experience also reveals another important influence that is affecting their ideas about sexuality: the religious perspective.

III. Sexuality from the Perspective of Religious Traditions

Historically, religion in general and religious perspectives of human sexuality, relationships, and sex in particular have had a significant influence on world cultures and institutions. Because religion is an important creator of values, attitudes, and ethics within a society, religion, according to Klassen et al. and Weil,[26] has traditionally been and continues to be influential in the development of individual and social attitudes and behaviors surrounding human sexuality. Just as there is a contemporary concern in secular circles to establish sound attitudes, behaviors, and norms concerning issues of human sexuality, so too religious traditions are grappling with a centuries-old dilemma of how to establish a relationship that, as the Presbyterian General Assembly Report notes, "interacts with others as loving, responsible, and compassionate persons, expressing sexuality with confidence, joy and moral integrity" (3).

Beginning from points of commonality between secular and religious notions on human sexuality, the following pages explore in broad strokes some of the traditional religious notions that have governed the development of human sexuality in Judaism, Roman Catholicism, and mainstream Protestantism. Emerging religious trends in sexuality are then discussed in light of their impact on the three integral components: sexuality, relationships, and sex. Together, the secular and religious perspectives on sexuality provide important background information concerning how the person, society, and religious traditions view this particular issue. The background data is crucial to the attempts Margot and Jared will make to resolve their moral dilemmas.

A. Secular and Religious Views of Sexuality: Some Commonalities

Although seemingly at two different ends of the moral spectrum, the sexual ethics and moral theology of the religious traditions do share many points in common with secular views and trends. First, the religious and secular views of sexuality have traditionally tended to share four perspectives:[27] 1) both usually have equated sexuality with sex or a person's genital and affective expressions; 2) they have perpetuated social and economic systems that view male gender and roles as superior to that of women; 3) they have generally placed the proper expression of sexuality/genital expressions of the person within the context of the marriage relationship and have considered other types of expression, such as premarital sex and homosexuality, as being taboo;

4) both have in the past stressed the purpose of genital sex as primarily procreative rather than unitive or mutually developmental.

Second, the views that secular and religious traditions have shared about the meanings, functions, and roles of human sexuality have been challenged within the last thirty years by the emergence of such movements as feminism, black theology, and liberation theology.[28] In addition, traditional moral codes about sexuality also have been questioned by new world changes and conditions. These changes include 1) advances in the behavioral and social sciences that have provided new insights into the purpose and meaning of sexuality; 2) developments in biblical and historical theology leading to a more person-oriented and holistic approach to morality, 3) an increased sense of personal responsibility and freedom of choice in determining one's life that rejects uncritical conformity to authority; 4) a deeper appreciation for the dignity and freedom of each person, and women's refusal to be considered inferior; 5) relationships grounded in mutual respect and dignity; and 6) experiences of intimacy that are non-exploitive and non-abusive.

As these changes have been experienced by members of religious traditions, there has emerged an increasing awareness of the growing gap between official church teachings and the sexual practices of church members who have judged conventional sexual moral codes as outdated and inadequate. As a result, many religious traditions have attempted to reexamine and articulate a view of sexuality more informed by contemporary research in such areas as anthropology, sociology, theology, psychology, and ethics.[29] As the 1991 Presbyterians and Human Sexuality document acknowledges,

> ...there is an almost deafening cry, a deep yearning expressed in many quarters for a new order of righteousness, a different pattern of sexual and social relations. The yearning looks for a renewed understanding of personhood and community, for a more holistic ethic of sexual relating, and for a theology reuniting sexuality and spirituality in life-enhancing ways (4).

Another area of commonality between the secular and religious worlds is that the topic of sexuality in general and its related components of sex, gender, and relationships in particular have been a continual source of concern, discussion, debate, and conflict for centuries, especially during the latter part of this century. In an attempt to explain the struggle that Judaism and Christianity have faced concerning issues of sexuality, James B. Nelson's work, *Between Two Gardens*, maintains that the traditional religious treatment of sexuality has been narrowly focused on a one-way question (74): What does the Bible, a religious tradition, or Christian theology say about human sexuality? As Jack Dominian notes in *Dynamics of Marriage*,[30] historically, the response to that question has been a poor one in the Christian tradition (68). Religious teachings on sexuality, and its related topics—the role of women, marriage, divorce, homosexuality, premarital and extramarital activities, masturbation, and birth control and abortion—reflect the religious tradition's major focus upon issues of sexuality. The teachings themselves are also a testimony to the complex, controversial, and interrelated historical, sociocultural, economic, theological, and ethical forces being shaped by and, in turn, shaping each religious tradition's view of human sexuality.

For example, the Jewish and early Christian tradition share the same biblical roots of the creation stories of Genesis, which affirm that "God created humankind in his image, in the image of God he created them; male and female he created them" (Genesis 1:27). In *Sexual Morality: A Catholic Perspective*, Philip Keane maintains that the creation accounts of Genesis establish a fundamental, positive theological anthropological fact for both Judaism and Christianity: "Human sexuality is a profound good, a great good given by God to human persons as part of creation" (3-4). However, as noted in the historical surveys of Keane, Nelson, Dominian, and Kosnik et al.,[31] once Christianity began to extend into the Roman and Hellenistic worlds, profound changes occurred that affected the Christian understanding of the meaning and role of human sexuality. For example, Keane notes that the influence of various strains of Gnosticism resulted at times in a dualism, or body/spirit split, that taught that good resides in the spiritual realities, including the human soul, and evil resides in material realities, including the body. According to Gnosticism, the body and all things related to it, such as sexual intercourse with its procreative potential, are basically evil and enemies of the spirit (6).

Similarly, various opinions and writings of individual Greek and

Latin leaders of the church's Patristic Era (second-fifth centuries) tend to perpetuate this gnostic or dualistic split. According to Kosnik et al., St. Augustine of Hippo (354-430 C.E.), one of the most influential early Christian writers and leaders, had a profound effect on future Christian views of sexuality. Influenced by the gnostic movement of Manicheism, Augustine's view of sexual intercourse was bleak, holding that even within marriage it was slightly sinful and to be condoned only for its procreative purposes. According to Augustine the good that was marriage resided in three realities: procreation, mutual faithfulness, and indissolubility (36-37). The results were that sexuality became equated with genital sex and biology rather than with a personal and relational growth and commitment based on mutual love and fulfillment. Furthermore, the purposes of marriage and intercourse were linked solely to procreation (70). Kosnik et al. remark that by the end of the fifth century,

> ...the Christian attitude toward human sexuality was generally pessimistic. Although sexuality of itself was recognized as good because of its procreative function, the pleasure attached to sex was viewed as a consequence of original sin. The experience of sexual pleasure, therefore, even indeliberate, and even within marriage for the purpose of procreation, was regarded somehow as tainted with sin (37).

By the close of the late Middle Ages, the influence of the work of Thomas Aquinas on natural law and reason was reflected in a sexual ethics governed by natural law knowable through human reason. If the natural end or primary reason for sexual intercourse is procreation, then actions like masturbation, homosexuality, and artificial birth control violate the natural law of sexuality. According to this view, because the sperm is considered the active principle in procreation, in the focus of sexual laws, women are valueless except as "receptacles for the seed-gardens, as it were, for human reproduction" (Kosnik 41). With the advent of the "moral manuals" for training confessors in the fifteenth century, the procreation criteria dominated Christian sexual ethics and led to

> ...the division between sexual sins "in accordance with nature"

and those "contrary to nature" (unnatural). The former (fornication, adultery, incest, rape) preserve the procreative possibility and are consequently regarded...as a lesser violation of the moral order. The latter (masturbation, sodomy and homosexuality) violate this procreative purpose and therefore are looked upon as the moral radical abuse of human sexuality (Kosnik 43).

By the end of the nineteenth century, Roman Catholic Christianity had developed a highly negative, juridical, and act-centered morality based on moral absolutes. According to Keane and Nelson,[32] such a morality not only focuses disproportionately on genital sexuality but also reduces sexuality to "the physical contours of actions rather than their relational meanings to a person" (Nelson 60).

Because of its roots in Judeo-Christian traditions, mainstream Protestant religions' views of sexuality contain some similarities to the views of Roman Catholicism. Like Catholicism, Protestantism tends to equate sexuality with sex, to view sexuality as a good gift from God, and to accept the concept of the body/spirit split as well as a patriarchal dualism that affirms, in Nelson's words, that "men assumed the superior part (spirit, male) so as to lead and discipline the inferior part (body, female)" (60). This sentiment was never more evident than in the late nineteenth-century Victorian views of sexuality characterized by

...a strong suspicion of sexuality, including marital sexual excess, horror over masturbation and homosexuality...and a strong tendency towards "spiritual femininity"—the placing of women (especially of the middle and upper classes) on a pedestal, characterizing them as delicate and above the animality of sex (71).

There are also differences between the Protestant and Roman Catholic views on sexuality. Nelson and Brock argue that Protestantism, in contrast to Catholicism, believes that sexuality, like all aspects of human life, was irrevocably marred and distorted by "the Fall" or the original sin of Adam and Eve.[33] The resulting alienation from self, God, and others is experienced sexually as well as in all the other dimensions of human life. Protestantism, unlike Catholicism, also moved rather early away from the notion of procreation as the primary purpose of marriage and sexual expression. As Nelson notes, mainline Protestantism had begun to move by the mid-twentieth century from a negative, act-orientated sexuality toward a more interpersonal focus on sexual expressions, and from a view of procreation as the primary focus of marriage and sexual expression to one of mutual love and fulfillment (66-67). Finally, according to Nelson, Protestantism, unlike Catholicism, has seemed more responsive to the contemporary voices that reflect a call for openness to

> ...new empirical knowledge about sexuality, the historically and culturally relative nature of sexual norms, and feminist consciousness concerning the pervasive conditioning by male sexism of the church's understandings (67).

In summary, the traditional Christian religious views on sexuality have historically tended to equate sexuality with sex or genital intercourse. Reduced to the single dimension of the physical, human sexuality in turn was defined by how each religious tradition interpreted the meaning and function of the primary relational context of marriage. Accordingly, within religious traditions like Catholicism, the related sexuality issues—that of a couple's mutual personal and social development, intimacy, love, gender roles and expectations—all become subservient to the primary marital goals of procreation and family continuity. By the mid-twentieth century, however, the calls for reform within Christian traditions were already moving the churches toward different directions about human sexuality.

B. A Contemporary Religious Perspective on Human Sexuality

With the emergence of feminist, black, and liberation theologies, new directions have emerged in the religious traditions' treatment of human sexuality. In *Between Two Gardens*, James Nelson summarizes the contemporary direction that human sexuality seems to be taking when he maintains that

> ...for sexuality, the concern becomes two-directional, dialogical

and not monological. In addition to the still-important question of what our religious tradition says about human sexuality is another question: What does our experience as sexual human beings say about the ways in which we experience God, interpret our religious tradition, and attempt to live the life of faith? (74)

The immediate implication behind this question is that the focus shifts from a genital-act oriented view of sexuality to one in which, as Keane characterizes it, the person's "responsibility in relationship is...the operative concept in a system of Christian sexual morality" (14). As both the person and religious tradition grapple with specific sexual issues, they need to be guided by the fundamental task of exploring the best possible ways a person as an individual and as a member of a religious tradition relates most responsibly as a sexual being in covenant with God, self, and others. When issues about sexuality are framed in terms of responsible relationality, Keane maintains that

...the answers we shall give to specific questions of sexual morality will be, in general, fairly similar to those given in the Christian tradition of the past. But the whole spirit behind the answers will be different, for we shall be focusing on the essential goodness of sexuality and its application to all of human life. This should enable people to live happier and healthier sexual lives...(14).

The far-reaching implications behind the contemporary religious response to Nelson's and Keane's questions are found in three emerging religious trends that correspond to the three integral parts of the human sexuality issue discussed above: sexuality, relationships, and sex. These three aspects are, according to Nelson, Keane, and Kosnik et al.,[34] the result of an evolution of interdisciplinary thought that has emerged and influenced Christianity in the United States over the last sixty years. Within Protestantism, Kosnik et al. note that, as early as 1930, the Anglican bishops' meeting at the Lambeth Conference approved a historic resolution that favored for the first time a view of marriage that separated the traditional procreative and unitive (relational) goals (45).

Nelson also notes a tendency in mainstream Protestantism, beginning in the middle of the twentieth century, to move away from a

sexual ethics predominantly concerned with abstract rules and categories of actions. Convinced that ethics must be more oriented toward
the person and relationships, Protestantism has experienced a greater
openness to the clinical and social sciences and to a focus more on the
motivations and concrete situations underlying specific sexual issues
(73).

Within Roman Catholic tradition, Kosnik et al. note that a similar
consciousness regarding the relational purposes of marriage did not
really emerge in official church documents until the declaration of
Vatican Council II's *Constitution on the Church in the Modern World*
(*Gaudium et Spes*) in December 1965 (48). In this document,[35] the church
declares a fundamental stand, based on the belief that

> the intimate partnership of married life and love has been es-
> tablished by the Creator and qualified by his laws. It is treated in
> the conjugal covenant of irrevocable personal consent...This love
> is an eminently human one since it is directed from one person to
> another through an affection of the will. (This love) involves the
> good of the whole person. Therefore it can enrich the expressions
> of the body and mind with a unique dignity, ...This love the Lord
> has judged worthy of special gifts, healing, perfecting and ex-
> alting gifts of grace and of charity (48, 49).

Kosnik et al. argue that this document marks a significant turning
point in the Catholic treatment of sexuality and marriage for two reasons: 1) it moves away from the hierarchical ordering of the goals of
marriage as primarily procreative and secondarily relational, and 2) it
recognizes the development and fulfillment of personal and interpersonal values as an integral part of human sexuality and as a viable
goal within the context of marriage (49-50). Although, in the eyes of the
Catholic church, the marital relation and the family continue to be emphasized as the only context in which sexuality and sex reach their ultimate fulfillment, post-Vatican II papal documents do restate the
importance of the development of a sound human sexuality for its own
sake. For example, in 1984 Pope John Paul II[36] reiterated that

...the human body is not merely an organism of sexual reactions, but it is, at the same time, the means of expressing the entire person, which reveals itself by means of the "language of the body." This "language" has an important interpersonal meaning, especially in the mutual relationships between man and woman...In the "language of the body," man and woman mutually express themselves in the fullest and most profound way possible to them...Man and woman express themselves in the measure of the whole truth of the human person.

In conclusion, religious traditions have begun to view human sexuality as a positive means through which the person and community experience covenant with self, others, and God. The value of human sexuality transcends the traditional emphasis placed solely on marriage and the family and becomes integral to the healthy development of human life and ethical decision making.

C. Emerging Religious Trends

Although similar to current secular views, the emerging religious trends in human sexuality do contain some differences. The root of the differences lies with the common Jewish-Christian heritage that colors the religious view of human sexuality. This heritage is grounded in the fundamental notion that the attainment of a sound human sexuality is just one more reflection of covenant relationship and the broad ethical vision needed for ethical living and decision making.

Each of the three trends discussed below addresses one of the corresponding integral parts: sexuality, relationships, and sex. Yet, because of its religious context, each trend is transformed into one more pattern that is added to the overall tapestry marking each person's broad ethical vision.

Trend 1: Sexuality

Similar to movements in secular circles, the first religious trend in human sexuality is a growing personal and social awareness that sexuality is distinct from and more than genital sexual expression; instead, it is seen as only one dimension of the holistic, multidimensional unity that is the person. As Nelson characterizes it in *Embodiment*, sexuality is

...our self understanding and the way of being in the world as male and female. It includes our appropriation of attitudes and characteristics which have been culturally defined as masculine and feminine. It involves our affective orientation toward those of the opposite and/or same sex. It is our attitudes toward ourselves and others as *body*-selves. It is our capacity for sensuousness. It is all of this (18).

Although similar to current secular views, this religious trend is different in that the Christian traditions look to models such as Jesus Christ to illumine the ways that a sense of covenant relationship shapes a person's sexuality. In *Models of God* Sallie McFague[37] reflects the struggle within some Christian circles to articulate in new metaphors and language the ways that Jesus' sexuality revealed not only the fullness of human potential but also that of the divine. In exploring new metaphors of God as parent, lover, and friend, and their resulting implications of creation, nurturing, passionate concern, attraction, respect, cooperation, and mutuality, McFague's work highlights these characteristics of the divine. If, as McFague contends, Jesus "is genuinely revelatory of God"(60), then the divine characteristics of parent, lover, and friend that Jesus manifested in his life and ministry are also significant indicators of a sound human sexuality that each of Jesus' followers are called to emulate in and through covenant relationship with self, God, and others.

Trend 2: Responsible Relationality

A second contemporary religious trend maintains that sexuality and genital sexual expressions can only be viewed from within a context of responsible personal and social relationships. From a personalist perspective, sexuality and genital sexual expressions are defined and evaluated not from an act-oriented, static legalistic standpoint, but from one of responsible relationality in which the persons involved develop and share in experiences of mutual love, intimacy, and fulfillment. In *Journeys by Heart*, Rita Brock further characterizes relational responsibility as fundamentally motivated by *eros*, a Greek term for love that has been inaccurately equated through the centuries with lust or sex. As Brock describes it, *eros* unites love with power, the psychological and the political, the personal and social dimensions of life. The result is a primal interrelatedness that

> ...creates and connects hearts, involves the whole person in re-
> lationships of self-awareness, vulnerability, openness and car-
> ing...Eros encompasses the "life force," the unique human energy
> which springs from desire for existence with meaning, for a con-
> sciousness informed by feeling, for experience that integrates the
> sensual and the rational, the spiritual and the political (25-26).

Unlike the similar secular trend toward relationality, the responsible relationality aspect of sexuality also involves a social or communal dimension: The moral convictions about the sacredness and dignity of human sexuality must be translated into effective social policy. In "Sexuality and Social Policy," Beverly Wildung Harrison[38] articulates and explores some of the moral questions of social policy as it relates to human sexuality. Echoing Brock, Harrison sees many of the contemporary problems in sexuality and social policy as failures to recognize the morally inappropriate power relations between people or as a distortion of the erotic capacity of individuals to develop mutually satisfying relationships (112). Harrison judges morally evil behaviors that are frequently classified as sex offenses—molestation, pornography, rape, and incest—as wrong because they "express a need for control and a disordered incapacity for relationship over an appropriate capacity for interdependence" (112). She calls for a social policy that is based on a relational view of sexuality that is grounded in the right to bodily integrity and individual consent between adults. As Harrison explains it,

> ...Our body selves, the zone of body-space we possess by virtue of
> being embodied persons, deserve explicit protection from ar-
> bitrary interference and unjustified coercion. "Consent" at this
> level is a condition of having a moral relationship. From a moral
> point of view, embracing "consent" as a criterion is not to deny a
> norm or to be merely "permissive." In our most intimate, inter-
> personal relations, consent or self-direction is a critical condition
> of human well-being. Space in which it can be expressed is a so-
> cial good (113).

Trend 3: Sexual Intimacy and Spirituality

As discussed above, sex is understood in the secular view as a means of achieving the ultimate in relational intimacy or communion with another human being. A third religious trend affirms an intimate link between sexuality and spirituality, which Nelson characterizes as a mystery and a symbol of humankind's need to communicate and to experience communion with God and others:

> ...The mystery of sexuality is the mystery of the human need to reach out for the physical and spiritual embrace of others...Sexuality always involves more than what we do with our genitals. More fundamentally, it is who we are as body-selves who experience the emotional, cognitive, physical, and spiritual need for intimate communion, both creaturely and divine (6).

In an attempt to construct new metaphors or images to describe in contemporary terms the intimate relationship between God and humankind, Sallie McFague, in *Models of God*, grounds the God-human relationship in images based on the three traditional Greek words *philos*, *eros*, and *agape*, which represent three different aspects of the same phenomenon known as love. McFague contends that as sexual beings, human beings are called by God to a divine and interpersonal relationship that is characterized by *eros* (128-29). Like Brock, McFague's explanation of eros implies that,

> ...the crux of being in love is not lust, sex, or desire...the crux is value. It is finding someone else valuable and being found valuable...Lovers...find each other valuable just because the other person is who he or she is. Being found valuable in this way is the most complete affirmation possible. It says, I love you just because you are you...you are precious beyond all saying to me (128).

For McFague, *eros* characterizes sound sexuality and relational responsibility because it illuminates the core values linking sexual human beings with the divine: "interdependence, mutuality, and an empowering sensibility of care and responsibility toward all life" (60).

Using the metaphor of the universe as God's "body," God's palpable presence in all space and time, McFague contends that to express toward self, others, and the universe the loving, valuing, and healing that epitomizes *eros* is also to love God (130-31).

In summary, these three contemporary trends have emerged slowly as the religious traditions have begun to articulate new directions concerning their views of human sexuality. What is evident from the emerging religious trends is that a contemporary religious view of human sexuality and sexual ethics demands an attitude that binds the human and divine relationships with something more than rules and standards. A sound human sexuality and sexual ethic must arise out of an ongoing awareness that sexuality, relationships, and sex are interrelated and multidimensional experiences that not only define personal identity and social relatedness but also symbolize in unique ways the fundamental relationship between Creator and creation.

IV. The Case of Margot and Jared Revisited

A. Margot and Jared's Moral Dilemma

As discussed throughout this text, ethical living and decision making are fundamentally about relationships and the decisions that nurture or destroy them. As a multidimensional unity, each person is challenged daily to make decisions that will help develop not only all the aspects of self but those of others as well. Bound by covenant and a broad ethical vision, each person must weigh and balance a number of factors so as to maintain meaningful relationships with self, others, and God (a greater power). Values and principles common to humankind and those that religious traditions specifically ascribe to are established to guide individuals and societies in their quest for meaningful and sound relational decisions.

Sexuality and the ethical values and principles that guide the meaning and expression of sexuality are but one more significant piece of the overall challenge to live and decide as ethical beings in covenant. Woven throughout the pattern of each person's understanding of the meaning and role of sexuality are the learned teachings, values, and principles of a particular culture and, for many, of a religious tradition.

Even if a person does not consciously subscribe to a religious tradition, religion continues to exert subtle but significant influence upon secular institutions, views, values, and principles. Because ethics is about sound decision making, and relationships and sexuality are central to relationships, ethical decisions will affect and be affected by sexuality.

The interrelationship among sexuality, relationships, and ethics is precisely the situation confronting Margot and Jared. The ethical or moral dilemma they both face is whether they consider the continued inclusion of genital expressions as ethically or morally appropriate for their relationship. Because their experience of intercourse after the fraternity party cannot be undone, they must take two important steps—both individually and as a couple (if they choose to continue their growing relationship).

First, each of them must come to grips—spiritually, emotionally, and psychologically—with the events that occurred after the Saturday night concert. Margot has already expressed feelings of guilt and shame concerning the alcohol and intercourse and what these events mean to her in terms of her relationship with self, others, and God. Her past experiences of familial and religious training have informed her that what she did that Saturday night was not morally appropriate. Unless Margot is able to seek consultation with a trusted advisor (e.g., a counselor or religious representative) to sort out the varied meanings that the events have for her and to arrive at a sense of inner peace and forgiveness, her relationships with self, God, family, and others, especially Jared, may be permanently scarred or destroyed. Although Jared does not seem to be bothered by strong religious convictions about alcohol and premarital sex, he does experience confusion and anger over the events in terms of the meaning and role of sexuality and sex in his continued relationship with Margot.

Second, Margot and Jared will have to discuss and decide, individually and as a couple, the exact nature of a future relationship. If they decide to continue their relationship, they must also decide 1) whether it will be as exclusive or committed as Jared seems to have wanted initially, 2) the ways that their sexuality contributes to their individual and combined growth within the relationship, and 3) the role sex will have in a continued relationship. In bringing their own personal views and experiences to the discussion, Margot and Jared will also reflect integrated views, values, and principles from cultural and religious backgrounds. Their ultimate decision concerning their moral dilemma will reflect the secular and religious perspectives of sexuality, relationships, and sex, as well as those concerning covenant, quest for meaning, and moral and ethical codes. Ultimately, at least for Margot, the religious perspective will weigh heavily not only in whether she and Jared will continue their relationship as a couple but also in how ethically appropriate she will view the role of premarital sex.

Chapter V presented a practical method for ethical decision making based on a five-step model. In the following pages, we will use this model to explore Margot and Jared's moral dilemma. The following case analysis is made on the presumption that Margot and Jared each have moved satisfactorily toward resolving the post-concert events. With the help of a campus minister who is also a licensed counselor, they are ready to explore the potential for a future relationship together. In each of the five steps, questions and concerns are listed that Margot and Jared should consider individually and as a couple as they seek resolution to the moral dilemma of the moral appropriateness of premarital sex within their continued relationship.

B. Implementing the Model for Ethical Decision Making
Step 1: The Acquisition of Information
A. Name the Primary Ethical Problem

Do Margot and Jared, as individuals and as a couple, consider the continued inclusion of genital expressions as ethically or morally appropriate for their relationship?

B. Gather and Assess the Facts
1. Spiritual

•In their individual quest for meaning, what have Margot and Jared determined as ultimate personal and relational goals for life?

•Do Margot and Jared believe in a personal God, and what role does this relationship have in their quest for meaning?

•Is there a particular religious or spiritual tradition that is particularly significant to Margot and to Jared? How do these traditions view the interdependence of sexuality, relationships, and sex as well as related topics such as marriage and premarital sex?

•What would the spiritual impact on Jared and Margot be should they decide to continue to engage in premarital sex?

•What spiritual and moral needs, concerns, and expectations do they have concerning a nonmarital committed relationship in general and the inclusion of premarital sex in particular?

2. Psychological and Emotional

•What is the current psychological and emotional status of Margot and Jared?

•What psychological and emotional needs, concerns, and expectations do they have concerning a nonmarital committed relationship in general and the inclusion of premarital sex in particular?

•What psychological and emotional problems can they anticipate?

•Are Margot and Jared reasonably psychologically and emotionally aware of the personal, familial, and social consequences of their including sex in a nonmarital relationship?

3. Medical

•What are the risks and benefits to Margot and Jared because of the inclusion of sex in their relationship?

•Do they have economic resources and medical insurance to support sexual activity and any possible consequences in their relationship?

4. Personal Preferences

•Have Margot and Jared clearly shared with each other their feelings and preferences concerning such topics as to how they see a nonmarital sexual relationship nurturing their sexuality, their personal needs and expectations, and their hopes about marriage?

5. Views of Family

•How will their relationships with family and relatives be affected by a decision to enter a nonmarital relationship that includes sex?

•Are there unresolved family concerns, questions, and disagreements that will personally and jointly affect Margot and Jared?

6. Views of Non-Family

•How will their relationships with their friends be affected by a decision to enter into an exclusive or committed relationship that includes sex?

7. Legal/Other Factors

•Are there any legal issues that apply to this situation?

•Are economic issues a factor for Margot/Jared/family/society?

C. Determine Motives, Name and Prioritize the Ethical Values and Principles

•What are the individual and joint motives for continuing their relationship and for engaging in premarital sex?

•What ethical values, principles, and *prima facie* duties are in conflict for Margot and Jared in this case?

D. Consideration of Alternative Courses of Action

•What alternate courses of action can Margot and Jared pursue?

•What are the benefits and risks inherent to each alternative?

•What are the short-term and long-term consequences for each alternative course of action?

Step II. Dialogue with Others/Seek Advice

•Are there other professionals, such as a trusted faculty member, a physician, or a religious representative (a rabbi, priest, or minister) that Margot and Jared can continue to consult independently and jointly to acquire their unique perspectives on the various aspects of the case?

•In light of any personal questions and conflicts concerning various aspects of the case, are there personal sources that each can consult independently so as to clarify their own emotional, spiritual, psychological, and ethical positions in the case?

Step III. Reasoned Reflection

It is at this point that Margot and Jared must individually consider the acquired information and the advice received from Steps One and Two of the process. Reasoned reflection can occur during times of personal reflection, prayer, and meditation.

Steps IV and V. Decision and Implementation

At some point, Margot and Jared, as individuals and as a couple, will have to arrive at and implement a decision or a course of action. This may be a painful time, and remaining true to self or moral integrity may be all that each can do while seeking a solution in this ethical dilemma. The experience of a sense of peace may be the only indicator that either one has maintained moral integrity and that a sound ethical decision has been reached.

Questions for Research, Reflection, and Discussion

1. Research for comparison purposes another culture's and another religious tradition's perspectives of sexuality, relationships, and sex. How might another culture and religious tradition view the moral dilemma facing Margot and Jared?

2. Research, compare, and contrast the ways secular and religious views together affect the contemporary treatment of an issue of sexuality such as homosexuality, abortion, birth control, or premarital sex.

3. Research the creative efforts that a particular secular or religious community has experimented with in their efforts to educate and promote their particular perspectives on human sexuality.

4. Research the ways that the media present, enhance, or distort the various aspects of human sexuality. What economic and political factors contribute to the media's positive or negative treatment of human sexuality?

5. Research contemporary works that have studied the linkage of sexuality with violence and brutality in contemporary society. What grassroots, multicultural, or multiracial movements have emerged, and how successful have they been in counteracting the exploitation of sexuality through such means as pornography, violent films, rape, child abuse, and sexual harassment?

CHAPTER VII

ENVISIONING THE FUTURE
OF ETHICS

Overview
The Tale of the Unfinished Tapestry—Continued

I. Ethical Visions Revisited

II. Ethics for the Twenty-First Century
A. The Global Context of Ethics:
Toward Moral and Social Solidarity
B. Harmonious Tension Between the Individual
and the Common Good
C. The Interdependence of Fields of Human Knowledge
D. The Individual Conscience versus the Common Good
E. Models of Ethical Decision Making

III. Specific Ethical Issues
A. Environmental Ethics
B. Business Ethics
C. Social Ethics
D. Biomedical Ethics
E. Sexual Ethics

Two roads diverged in a wood, and I—
I took the one less traveled by,
And that has made all the difference.

Robert Frost (1874-1963)[1]

Overview

Chapter II of this text began with the visions of an old Native American weaver. It is fitting to conclude the text by revisiting The Tale of the Unfinished Tapestry…

The unfinished tapestry itself had not been touched for decades, as both desire and skill were lacking for adding to the original ancient weaver's art. Now, however, young Coyote Swift, a descendant of the ancient weaver, stood ready to add to the ancient pattern. Years away at college and graduate school studying a variety of subjects—literature, ethics, anthropology, and sociology—had not dimmed the feelings of sacredness and awe she had always felt when standing before the ancient tapestry hanging on its loom.

Coyote had taken it upon herself at a young age to learn the almost forgotten art of tribal tapestry weaving, and over the years her skill had been honed to perfection. She had files filled with the stories of tribal members and events that she and her mother had been collecting for years. And now the tribal council had finally given her permission to add to the sacred tapestry.

As she stood in the early morning light that first day, the words that had been recounted about that ancient weaver whispered in her mind: "They see only an old rug. I see the lines and patterns of a tapestry that marks the larger story of the joys, struggles, failures, and victories of our people. The different patterns represent the many people and events that have shaped and been shaped by the fabric of our tribal life. Each thread of the pattern represents the unique gifts that each person has been to us." As Coyote's young fingers reverently picked up the threads to begin the laborious task of interweaving new threads with old ones, her hand stopped in mid-air.

As she studied the tapestry she suddenly realized that although each thread and pattern represented the gift of the persons and events that had shaped the total life of the tribe, the tapestry itself symbolized so much more: It signified the very moral fabric of the tribal life. The decades-old tapestry had unwittingly captured the individual paths taken as a result of many moral choices made by each of the members as well as the tribal community as a whole.

And yet, there suddenly came to Coyote another startling realization, one captured by the words of Robert Frost's immortal poem "The Road Not Taken." As she pondered this poem, what struck Coyote was the idea that for every woven thread and pattern that bespoke the individual and moral choices of the tribe, there were countless other choices and decisions not followed and consequently not represented in the tapestry, for if they had been, the threads and resulting overall patterns would have produced a different tapestry.

Slowly and reverently, Coyote began to intertwine the new threads into the fragile fabric. Though young in years, Coyote brought to her task the hallowed wisdom of the ancient weaver who too had imbued her patterns with the realization that each person's individual journey and those of the entire tribe stood in mute testimony to all the less-traveled roads taken.

I. Ethical Visions Revisited

The Tale of the Unfinished Tapestry symbolizes the main tenets that underscore this text's vision of sound ethical living and decision making. First, each person is a multidimensional unity that lives in the world as a gendered individual who is also shaped by a multitude of complex, interrelated factors that affect all who reside in the universe. Throughout a lifelong process of growth and development, each person is challenged to grow psychosocially, spiritually, physically, emotionally, sexually, and ethically. The environment within which this growth and development occur is always subject to the changing variances of history, geography, culture, and society.

Second, just as a person's growth and development as an individual is a process spanning the length of a human life, so too the challenge for each person is to nurture, develop, and maintain an equally complex, interrelated network of social relationships. These relationships are grounded in and facilitated by individual and communal broad ethical visions, quests for meaning, values, and principles that subsequently form the basis for secular and religious wisdom, codes, and teachings. All of these, in turn, inform each person's and each society's understanding of and socialization in ethical and moral living and decision making, which is essentially all about making sound decisions and choices about what will nurture and maintain the networks of relationships so necessary for human survival.

Third, sound ethical living and decision making also entail the realization that the individual, as well as society, lives in constant tension as religious ethical visions, values, and principles compete with secular ones to shape a sense of civil and moral responsibilities, personal and social sin, and individual, institutional, and societal evils. Living ethically and healthily with the tension between secular and religious worlds places each person continually at divergent roads, and each person must choose which road to take. Often the two roads are equally good. However, to choose one road, one must reject, for a multitude of reasons, the other road. And in so choosing, to use the analogy of the unfinished tapestry, each person continually adds certain threads to the fabric of his or her life while rejecting and leaving out others. These threads represent differences in the kinds of experiences that each person will know because of the choices he or she has made. These choices, in turn, will affect the overall finished tapestry.

A fourth tenet of the text is that the human conscience uniquely equips each person for ethical living and decision making. However, just as a variety of complex factors shape the growth and development of the human conscience, so too do a variety of interrelated and multifaceted components affect the formation and development of personal and social consciences. As each person faces countless diverging paths, the freedom to choose also entails complex levels of capacity and responsibility as well as the acquisition of a balance between knowledge of the head and knowledge of the heart. Whether the person finally selects the road less or more often traveled, the ultimate path will also be affected by an ethical or moral choice that is also shaped by a conscience that can use reasoned reflection to weigh impinging factors such as role obligations, *prima facie* duties, and the underlying relevance of an ethic of love and care.

In the end, each person, like Coyote, must realize that life's journey is a constant selecting between diverging paths of ethical or moral choices. Although each path may represent equally good and exciting possibilities, only one can be undertaken at any given time. In so choosing, each person narrows the range of future choices. With each subsequent selection, a pattern is forged and a life is shaped, just as it is also shaped by the interwoven patterns and lives of others. At life's end, each person must look back over the tapestry of his or her life and decide, like Frost, if the roads traveled have truly resulted in the best choices for sound ethical living and decision making.

II. Ethics for the Twenty-First Century

Attempting to predict the shape and texture of the tapestry of ethical living and decision making for the twenty-first century can result in a tapestry quite different from that which actually unfolds. Yet, if one examines closely the existing threads and patterns that have been woven into the meaning and role of ethics in this text, the future of ethics might not be as difficult to discern. While providing a past and present context to the discussion, each chapter has attempted to interject the threads of a continuing conversation among the many disciplines that are affecting the emerging patterns in modern ethics. The following section provides a brief, general overview of some of the present ethical and moral threads that will continue to influence the emerging picture of twenty-first century ethical living and decision making.

A. The Global Context of Ethics: Toward Moral and Social Solidarity

In "Tradition and the Traditions in Health/Medicine and Religion," Protestant ethicist and theologian Martin E. Marty[2] comments that tradition in general and religious traditions in particular have exerted and continue to wield great influence on ethical living and decision making:

> People do not live by alphabets or chronology alone. They really do live in traditions, *all* of them do, even those who inhabit the tradition of those who rebel and reject tradition, for tradition derives from the *traditum*, that which is "handed down." Thus every

intelligible word all people use is "handed down" from the
speech of people who have gone before in a tradition. Religious
people share a common story, a divine law or an announcement
of good news. They together respond to visions and symbols...There are certain things that religious people know are "not
done," or others that must be done. They know of inherited taboos or prescriptions, ways of life or behavior patterns. These are
all part of tradition and are grasped in traditions of faith (4).

Marty's article is important to the ethical visions of this text for two
reasons. First, while exploring the distinctiveness of particular religious
traditions and the persistent attempt by many religious traditions to remain separate from others, Marty also discusses a rising trend toward
more ecumenical cooperation and collaboration, especially in the fields
of ethics, medicine, and health (22-23). A closer examination of the expanding global role of religious traditions reveals that although there is
an awareness of the distinct values, principles, and teachings of each religion, there is also an increasing awareness of the need for greater toleration of the ways that each tradition affects the lives and moral
decision making of its members. The traditional tendency to stress that
a particular tradition is the only and best way to achieve spiritual salva-
tion and ethical rightness is slowly being tempered by an emerging realization that the primary goal of right and sound relationships with
God or a higher power, self, and others has many divergent paths.
Respect for and cooperation with these many emerging paths, as represented by the expansion of world religious traditions, is a first step toward that primary relational goal.

A global ethics for the twenty-first century, however, calls for more
than toleration of and mutual respect for the differing ethical values,
principles, and theological teachings of various religious traditions. A
second ethical pattern is emerging that involves an increasing sense of
the active, expanding role of the world's religious traditions in promoting such shared global values as respect for the life, liberty, and justice for all who inhabit the earth. For example, in 1986 the United States
Catholic bishops issued "Economic Justice for All: A Pastoral Letter on
Catholic Social Teaching and the U.S. Economy."[3] Although aimed at
Roman Catholics in the United States, the document represents a sim-

ilar trend in other religious traditions to energize not only their members but also nations toward viewing issues like poverty, economic injustices, and political oppression as moral imperatives involving the whole global community:

> ...We regret that no political entity now exists with the responsibility and power to promote the global common good, and we urge the United States to support UN efforts to move in that direction...We must expand our understanding of the moral responsibility of citizens to serve the common good of the entire planet. Cooperation is not limited to the local, regional or national level...The fact that the "social question has become worldwide" challenges us to broaden our horizons and enhance our collaboration and sense of solidarity on the global level (#261, p. 637; #322, p. 652).

No longer are world problems the moral and sociopolitical responsibility of one religious tradition or one nation. What affects one affects all, and the ethical decisions and moral obligations articulated by one religious tradition are also envisioned by others as ethical imperatives for right relationships between a higher power, self, and others. Such is the case, for example, of the view of liberal politics and civil religion in the United States. As Robert Wuthnow comments in *The Restructuring of American Religion*,[4] the liberal view of the United States and its mainstream religions expresses itself more in terms of human rights, common life-death problems, and the special obligation the United States should accept in working for human rights, international security, or economic justice (250). Global interdependence and human solidarity become the impetus behind civil and religious involvement, with religious faith playing "a role chiefly as a motivating element, supplying strength to keep going against what often appear as insuperable odds"(251).

B. Harmonious Tension Between the Individual and the Common Good

The history of right living and decision making (ethics and morality) has always involved a tension between the individual and the community as a whole. From primitive times, human beings have learned that basic survival needs can only be met when people band together in shared efforts. Secular laws and ethical codes evolved in order to regulate relationships as emerging individual and social needs for growth and development often came into conflict. Concurrently, secular and religious disciplines have always sought, on the one hand, to affirm the dignity and rights of the human being while, on the other hand, reminding the individual of his or her place as a member of larger social groups. Although at times history reflects periods in which individualism and independence seem to have replaced a sense of communal interdependence and solidarity, the truth is that both are not only necessary for, but also integral to, sound human growth and development. As symbolized by *The Book of Discipline of the United Methodist Church* (1992),[5] it is the human community, secular and religious, that is charged with nurturing human life, whether it be that of the individual or of society as a whole:

> ...The community provides the potential for nurturing human beings into the fullness of their humanity. We believe we have a responsibility to innovate, sponsor, and evaluate new forms of community that will encourage development of the fullest potential in individuals. Primary for us is the gospel understanding that all persons are important—because they are human beings created by God and loved through and by Jesus Christ and not because they have merited significance. We therefore support social climates in which human communities are maintained and strengthened for the sake of all persons and their growth (paragraph 71, p. 70).

The need for a harmonious balance between the ever-present threads of individualism and communal interdependence will continue to pervade ethics in the twenty-first century. There is also, however, an emerging sense that individualism and interdependence must also take on a more universal context. Understandings of community must expand not only to other human peoples but also to non-human forms of life. Just as the need for the individual to reach full potential always exists in tension with the interrelated needs of a society to grow and develop, so too, there must exist the awareness of the interdependence and solidarity of all life forms on the planet. This can only be done when human beings take the moral values that have sought to universalize respect and reverence for human life and establish a broader ethical system whose fundamental principle of morality is, in the words of Albert Schweitzer,[6]

> ...not a matter only of arranging and deepening current views of good and evil, but also of expanding and extending these. A man is really ethical only when he obeys the constraint laid on him to help all life which he is able to succor, and when he goes out of his way to avoid injuring anything living....To him life as such is sacred. He shatters no ice crystal that sparkles in the sun, tears no leaf from its tree, breaks off no flower...But the time is coming when people will be amazed that the human race was so long before it recognized that thoughtless injury to life is incompatible with real ethics. Ethics is in its unqualified form extended responsibility with regard to everything that has life (66).

No longer will the broad ethical visions of the twenty-first century tolerate the traditional andropocentrism that has dominated traditional concepts of ethics. The emerging pattern of a global awareness is one that reverences all forms of life and respects varied moral and ethical traditions.

C. The Interdependence of Fields of Human Knowledge

As the explosion of new information and telecommunication resources and technologies increase in the twenty-first century, they will shape and be shaped by a more global interdisciplinary approach to all fields of human learning. For example, throughout this text there are continual references to the influences such diverse fields as anthropology, psychology, sociology, theology, and morality have upon the challenge to understand and relativize ethical and moral living and decision making. These influences will expand as many secular and religious fields experience an increased cooperation and collaborative effort as they seek to innovate, sponsor, and evaluate all new information in terms of nurturing a broad, global vision of ethics. As traditional disciplines like theology, philosophy, history, literature, and ethics struggle to understand and shape new paradigms for ethical living on this planet, they too are shaping and continually being shaped by contributions from fields such as medicine, ecology, and female and male studies.

D. The Individual Conscience versus the Common Good

Just as a global ethic in the twenty-first century must answer the challenge of continually harmonizing the tension between the individual and the community, so too will a twenty-first century ethic have to harmonize the tension between paths chosen by an informed, reasoned conscience and a conscience motivated by blind obedience to secular and religious ethical systems. Traditionally, secular and religious sources of wisdom have been presented as certain repositories for all correct living. Within an ethical or moral context, this became translated as following unquestioningly the written or preached rules for moral living and decision making. The result was to see ethics and morality as a faithful, unquestioning response to a situation viewed in black (evil) or white (good) terms. For example, the civil and religious prohibition against the taking of innocent life through assisted suicide was fairly straightforward before the advent of the new biomedical advances of the mid-latter twentieth century. After the introduction of mechanical life supports, new antibiotic protocols, and genetic research, the issues are more gray and answers less easily discernable or certain.

The result has been an increasing tendency toward decisions based on individual preference or criteria with, in increasing cases, little or no adherence to traditional civil or religious values. This may be partly due to the complexity of contemporary life and decision making in which individuals perceive traditional sources of ethical wisdom as too inadequate, insensitive, or simplistic to provide relevant answers to complex and important life questions. As noted above, the continual tension between individualism and the common good is now reenacted on a personal level as individuals struggle to attend to both an informed conscience and the vast array of religious and civil sources of wisdom.

In order to keep a sound balance between the individual and society, twenty-first century secular and religious systems of education must become more expert at imbuing and nurturing a better integrated individual and social conscience. As a multidimensional unity in relationship, each person is challenged to see freedom never as license but as responsibility for and toward self, a higher power, and others. Every decision is an invitation to understand and accept the complex and interdependent influences that impinge on presenting alternatives and exercising prudent judgment in arriving at a decision that, in turn, will have known and unknown consequences upon oneself and society as a whole.

The development of an integrated individual and social conscience involves arriving at a consensus concerning an expanded view of anthropology within a global context, the universal values and principles to be taught, methods for the development of a sound conscience that uses both knowledge of head and knowledge of heart, and ways to integrate more harmoniously the sacred and secular into ethical living and decision making. Blind obedience to authoritative or traditional sources of secular and religious wisdom will be replaced by a healthy and informed conscience that responsibly questions, investigates, and analyzes all aspects of an ethical dilemma while at the same time seeking a resolution that balances the person's growth and development against the needs and concerns of society. Integral to this entire process will be the exposure to, learning about, and adoption of a specific method of ethical decision making.

E. Models of Ethical Decision Making

Chapter V of this text presented one model for ethical decision making. Known as the Covenantal Model, this ethical system flows from the relationality of all persons created as equals and bound in patterns of individual and social responsibility to self, a higher power, and others.

The Covenantal Model[7] is only one of many that have been articulated in various fields over a number of years. For example, within the field of clinical ethics, Gerald McKenney and Jonathan Sande have explored in *Theological Analyses of the Clinical Encounter*[8] a variety of types of clinical models distinguished not only by method but also by content. James Childress and Tom Beauchamp's *Principles of Biomedical Ethics*[9] represents a Principles Model of ethics that uses a descriptive, analogical reasoning approach to ethical decision making. The works of Stanley Hauerwas, Karen Lebacqz, Susan Sherwin, and Richard Zaner[10] represent yet another model, the Contextual Model, which understands ethical decision making as a process focusing on discerning all the dynamics of the involved persons and relationships as affected by such factors as power, control, and political and social organizations.

These and other models represent divergent paths toward the same goal: sound ethical and moral decision making. As experiences multiply and ethical visions continue to expand, newer models will emerge in the twenty-first century. The newer models will need to articulate more in content and method the varied emerging threads alluded to in the previous sections. The important point, however, is not that there be one agreed upon model used by a majority of people. Rather, as the complexity of ethical decision making increases and evolves, it will be absolutely necessary that people be informed and educated about the variety of models so as to choose ultimately the model that most closely identifies with their informed views about ethical living and decision making.

Just as there is a need for increased respect and tolerance for the expanding presence and role of religious traditions, so too will there have to be an increased understanding and respect for individual and social models for ethical decision making. The challenge of the twenty-first century models will not only be to articulate representative methods and content for decision making, but also to be, to use popular terminology, "user friendly and technologically compatible." Future ethical models will have to be able to provide workable bridges between differing individual and social views about ethical issues. Ethical decision making in the twenty-first century will increasingly be about consensus and compromise, both of which will be impossible if the multitude of voices cannot use ethical models that are understandable and acceptable to all involved.

III. Specific Ethical Issues

Each of the chapters in this text contains a case presentation that briefly illustrates one of the many ethical dilemmas faced by a particular ethical discipline. The case studies or vignettes are in no way intended to encompass the breadth and depth of ethical concerns. Rather, they are microstudies that give the reader a flavor of the complexity and the interdependence of issues involved in but a few of the many disciplines within the fields of ethics and morality. For example, Chapter II highlights the issues of sexual harassment, urban poverty and violence, and legal justice for minority peoples—all concerns of social ethics. The vignettes in Chapter III center around ethical practices in business ethics, while Chapter V highlights one of the many complex dilemmas involved in contemporary biomedical ethics. In Chapter VI the issue of premarital sex and its relational, medical, spiritual, and psychosocial consequences represents only one of varied and interrelated problems facing the field of sexual ethics.

As the varied types of disciplines within ethics move toward the twenty-first century, specific issues are emerging whose solutions will entail a more global cooperation and collaboration among secular and religious groups. As rapid advances in telecommunication and information networking shrink the actual time and distances between the event and disbursement of information about an event, there is a corresponding expansion of personal and social awareness concerning the interrelatedness of ethical issues and the need to find more international solutions for ethical issues. For example, although the issues of violence, unemployment, poverty, and economic oppression concern social ethics nationally and internationally, these same issues impact corresponding dilemmas in environmental, biomedical, and business ethics.

The following is a brief glance at some of the many complex types of ethical problems and the specific dilemmas each ethical discipline will deal with in the twenty-first century.

A. Environmental Ethics

In the future, a more biocentric and ecocentric ethic will form the basis of an environmental ethics that seeks to inculcate in the world a reverence for and awareness of the fundamental interdependence of all forms of life on the planet. Eastern and Western perspectives on environmental ethics will become more integrated and collaborative in seeking solutions to the ecological crises and problems of the twentieth century. Some of these problems are the preservation of animal and plant species, the protection of animal rights, the safe disposal of hazardous wastes, the harnessing of alternative forms of energy, and the reduction of overpopulation with its strain on limited food, air, and water resources. One of the primary goals of environmental ethics in the twenty-first century will be to maintain a sense of global responsibility to ensure the health and well-being of present and future life forms.

Just as ethical decision making in general moves to a greater global awareness in the twenty-first century, so too will ethical decision making in particular ethical disciplines become more sensitive to the ways it affects and is affected by correlating concerns within the other ethical disciplines. Take for example the environmental ethical issue of just allocation of limited resources of air, water, land, and food. Unless greater international collaboration emerges and seriously addresses this issue, then limited resources and related problems of overpopulation and poverty will have a ripple effect, creating further social ethical problems centered around such issues as continued social, political, and economic imperialism, oppression, and discrimination.

B. Business Ethics

The concurrence of ethical concerns within the field of environmental ethics also has wider implications within business ethics. Increasingly, a global shift is occurring whereby business ethical decisions are no longer based solely on what any one individual community or nation decides to do to increase economic growth and production. Rather, the need for increased social responsibility within business and economics is resulting in an expanded international effort to monitor, patrol, and eliminate, when possible, traditional business practices that flagrantly disregard the environment, circumvent employee and consumer protection policies, distort labeling and packaging laws, and undermine native health and welfare through unrestricted advertising and marketing practices. No longer will large conglomerates be able to invade with impunity lesser developed countries, undermine native manufacturing and economic structures in the name of modernism, deplete and strip the natural and personal resources of the country, and then move on when more profitable markets open up in other countries. Business ethics of the future will seek to establish more stringent international policies for ethical and profitable business practices. They also will be guided by a different set of fundamental questions. For example, no longer will a primary question be the degree of possible individual or corporate material economic wealth and development. The more important question will be the depth to which any economic development or practice will bring about more environmental, social economic, and psychosocial good than harm.

C. Social Ethics

The first task of social ethics of the twenty-first century will be to nurture and broaden existing twentieth-century international collaborative efforts toward a global ethics that esteems international moral and social responsibility for the problems that face the planet. It therefore becomes an international moral imperative to maintain cooperatively the integrity and security of existing national borders, to ensure world peace, to respect all life forms, and to squash imperialist and terrorist movements.

Social ethics of the future faces a second major task. In order to attend properly to these environmental, economic, and social ethical concerns, secular and religious groups will need to increase international collaboration and support to the point that the plurality of cultures and beliefs will be seen more as a positive resource for achieving global solidarity, and less as a negative source of nationalism, racism, and prejudice. The degree to which global solidarity can be achieved will support world efforts to minimize drastically the outbreaks of war, genocide, nuclear armament, and military and political terrorism. Similarly, related social ethical questions regarding the best ways to provide for the educational, occupational, medical, and psychological needs of all peoples in the face of limited resources also implies two parallel actions: 1) global attempts to ensure the inclusion of the minority, the physically and emotionally disadvantaged, and the immigrant members of society and 2) international ethical policies that seek to root out all forms of religious, sexual, and social discrimination, oppression, and injustice.

D. Biomedical Ethics

Biomedical ethics in the twenty-first century will face the burgeoning medical, theological, philosophical, and spiritual dilemmas created by the advances in biomedical research and technology. For example, advances in the research areas of fetal tissue and organ donation, DNA mapping, and genetic therapy and coding all raise fundamental questions concerning the exact nature of what it means to be a unique human being. These advances also raise issues regarding the beginning and the end of human life, the meaning and role of parenting, and the right of human beings to alter artificially or to interfere in the creation and maintenance of life for present and future generations.

The environmental and social ethical concerns regarding the just allocation of limited resources also have implications for the future of biomedical ethics. If efforts to forge international collaboration and cooperation in resolving mutual problems have also kept pace in biomedical ethics, then a more global, interdisciplinary, and intercultural perspective will color both the content and clinical approach of biomedical decisions. Such a perspective will bring to bear a broader understanding of and potential solutions for the complex theological, philosophical, spiritual, sociopolitical, and economical aspects underlying most biomedical dilemmas.

International sensitivity to the limits of resources and the need for a more prudent use of what is available, balanced by the awareness of the high cost of health care and medical insurance, will affect the availability and suitability of certain procedures, such as organ transplants. Finding a solution to these complex problems will necessitate more theological, philosophical, and religious collaboration not only on such issues as the primary meaning and goals of life but also regarding a more informed view of death, the individual's ability or right to decide whether to live or to die, and whether a person or medical institution can be morally justified in refusing a life-ensuring organ transplant.

Similarly, how these questions are perceived and addressed by individuals, nations, and international bodies will in turn impact the global institutions and policies established to allocate and disburse limited resources for other groups of people, such as the elderly and families on welfare who face multiple medical, social, and economic limitations, as well as those considered less competent to engage in such medical determinations: for example, the mentally or emotionally disabled or disadvantaged, hydrocephalic babies, and persons in a persistent vegetative state who do not demonstrate overt human characteristics and behaviors.

E. Sexual Ethics

Because the field of ethics is basically about establishing and maintaining sound ethical relationships, the emerging patterns in one discipline in ethics will affect and be affected by the threads and patterns of other ethical disciplines. For example, the environmental, social, and biomedical ethical concerns regarding reverencing all life forms, determining the meaning of life and death, and maintaining a quality of life over the human life span are also important to the field of sexual ethics. Within this field, the nurture and maintenance of relationships in general and committed adult relationships in particular also form the basis for the resolution of a host of questions and problems surrounding the meaning and role of marriage, family, human sexuality, homosexuality, divorce, and premarital and extramarital sexual activities.

Sexual ethics of the future may come to view as primary the person's focusing less on sex and more on the interrelationship between the meaning and role of sexuality and relationships. A broader view of marriage may emerge in which the heterosexuality or homosexuality of the couple is less important than the couple's commitment to fostering healthy relationships based on psychosocial, sexual, and spiritual growth and development for the couple and any future children. The implications of such a view of marriage would have a ripple effect upon the theological, philosophical, psychosocial, and legal understanding of family and will foster many possibilities for the creation and nurture of society's younger members and the cherishing and affirmation of older members.

Each one of these topics in turn raises other related questions. For example, how individuals and societies of the twenty-first century define marriage and family will also impact the ways they interpret and legislate medical, social, and economic resources for parenting, abortion, contraception, and surrogacy, as well as the social and legal guidelines concerning relational infidelity, physical and sexual harassment and abuse. Also affected will be the related medical concerns regarding responsible sexual practices; the transference of sexually transmitted diseases, especially HIV; the fair and just availability of sound medical and sexual education; the affordability of basic medical insurance; and the provision of treatments for less financially sound populations.

In conclusion, each ethical discipline faces many divergent roads as it seeks greater interdisciplinary and international cooperation and collaboration to resolve complex, interrelated issues. Contemporary choices between divergent roads challenge both individuals and nations to reconsider choosing newer and less-traveled paths towards resolutions appropriate for the next century. As Kierkegaard once remarked, "Life can only be understood backwards: but it must be lived forwards." Only time and the perspective of hindsight will reveal whether the roads chosen now truly made the most positive differences in helping to fashion patterns that reflect the best overall ethical tapestry for life and decision making in the twenty-first century.

FOR FURTHER READING

Chapter I: The Emerging Psychosocial and Ethical Individual

Erikson, Erik. *Childhood and Society*. New York: W.W. Norton & Co., Inc., 1963.

Gilligan, Carol. *In a Different Voice: Psychological Theory and Women's Development*. Cambridge, MA: Harvard University Press, 1982.

Jordan, Judith, Alexandra Kaplan, Jean Baker Miller et al. *Women's Growth in Connection*. New York: Guilford Press, 1991.

Maddi, Salvatore L. *Personality Theories: A Comparative Analysis*. 5th ed. Pacific Grove, CA: Brooks/Cole Publishing Company, 1989.

Maslow, Abraham. *Toward a Psychology of Being*. 2nd ed. New York: Van Nostrand Reinhold Company, 1968.

McGuire, Meredith. *Religion: The Social Context*. 3rd ed. Belmont, CA: Wadsworth Publishing Co., 1992.

Wilson, Bryan. *The Social Dimensions of Sectarianism: Sects & New Religious Movements in Contemporary Society*. Oxford: Clarendon Press, 1992.

Wuthnow, Robert. *The Restructuring of American Religion*. Princeton, NJ: Princeton University Press, 1988.

Chapter II: The Emerging Social Self

Allen, Joseph. *Love and Conflict: A Covenantal Model of Christian Ethics*. Nashville: Abingdon Press, 1984.

Arrien, Angeles. *The Four-Fold Way: Walking the Paths of the Warrior, Teacher, Healer, and Visionary*. San Francisco: HarperSanFrancisco, 1993.

Lebacqz, Karen. *Six Theories of Justice: Perspectives From Philosophical and Theological Ethics*. Minneapolis: Augsburg Publishing House, 1986.

_____. *Justice in an Unjust World: Foundations for a Christian Approach to Justice*. Minneapolis: Augsburg Publishing House, 1987.

McFague, Sallie. *The Body of God: An Ecological Theology*. Minneapolis: Augsburg Fortress Press, 1993.

Merchant, Carolyn. *Radical Ecology: The Search for a Livable World*. New York: Routledge, Chapman & Hall, Inc., 1992.

_____. *The Death of Nature: Women, Ecology and the Scientific Revolution*. San Francisco: Harper & Row, 1980.

Ramsay, Paul. *The Patient as Person*. New Haven: Yale University Press, 1970.

Robb, Carol S., ed. *Beverly Wildung Harrison, Making the Connections: Essays in Feminist Social Ethics*. Boston: Beacon Press, 1985.

Tong, Rosemarie. *Feminist Thought: A Comprehensive Introduction*. San Francisco: Westview Press, 1989.

Chapter III: A Quest for Meaning and
the Development of Values and Principles

Armstrong, Karen. *A History of God: The 4000-Year Quest of Judaism, Christianity and Islam*. New York: Ballantine Books, 1993.

Beauchamp, Tom L., and James F. Childress. *Principles of Biomedical Ethics*. Fourth Edition. New York: Oxford University Press, 1994.

Callahan, Sidney. *In Good Conscience: Reason and Emotion in Moral Decision Making*. San Francisco: HarperSanFrancisco, 1991.

Cannon, Katie G. *Black Womanist Ethics*. Atlanta: Scholars Press, 1988.

Fowler, James W. *Stages of Faith: The Psychology of Human Development and the Quest for Meaning*. San Francisco: HarperSanFrancisco, 1981.

Frankena, William. *Ethics*. Englewood Cliffs, NJ: Prentice Hall, Inc., 1963.

Frankl, Viktor E. *Man's Search For Meaning: An Introduction to Logotherapy*. New York: Washington Square Press, Inc., 1963.

Gula, Richard. *Reason Informed By Faith: Foundations of Catholic Morality*. New York: Paulist Press, 1989.

MacIntyre, Alasdair. *A Short History of Ethics*. New York: Collier Books, 1966.

McFague, Sallie. *Models of God: Theology for an Ecological, Nuclear Age*. Philadelphia: Fortress Press, 1987.

Chapter IV: The Role of Conscience and Ethical Decision Making

Abraham, K.C., ed. *Third World Theologies: Commonalities and Divergences*. Maryknoll, NY: Orbis Books, 1990.

Bender, David L., and Bruno Leone, Series Editors. *The Third World: Opposing Viewpoints*. San Diego: Greenhaven Press, Inc., 1989.

Brown, Robert McAfee. *Gustavo Gutiérrez: An Introduction to Liberation Theology*. Maryknoll, NY: Orbis Books, 1990.

Goldberg, Michael. *Theology & Narrative: A Critical Introduction*. Nashville: Abingdon Press, 1982.

Gutiérrez, Gustavo. *A Theology of Liberation*. Maryknoll, NY: Orbis Books, 1973.

Hauerwas, Stanley. *Naming the Silences: God, Medicine and the Problem of Suffering*. Grand Rapids, MI: Wm. B. Eerdmans Publishing Company, 1990.

Kammer, Fred. *Doing Faithjustice: An Introduction to Catholic Social Thought*. New York: Paulist Press, 1991.

O'Brien, David J., and Thomas A. Shannon, eds. *Catholic Social Thought: The Documentary Heritage*. Maryknoll, NY: Orbis Books, 1992.

Chapter V: A Practical Method for Ethical Decision Making

Brock, Rita Nakashima. *Journeys by Heart*. New York: Crossroads, 1994.

Chodorow, Nancy. *The Reproduction of Mothering*. Berkeley: University of California Press, 1978.

Holmes, Helen, and Laura Purdy, eds. *Feminist Perspectives in Medical Ethics*. Bloomington: Indiana University Press, 1992.

Hoopes, Margaret, and James Harper. *Birth Order Role & Sibling Patterns in Individual & Family Therapy*. Rockville, MD: Aspen Publishers, Inc., 1987.

May, William F. *The Physician's Covenant: Images of the Healer in Medical Ethics*. Philadelphia: Westminster Press, 1983.

McCarthy, Jeremiah J., and Judith A. Caron, *Medical Ethics: A Catholic Guide to Healthcare Decisions*. Liguori, MO: Liguori Publications, 1990.

Moore, Thomas. *Care of the Soul*. New York: HarperSanFrancisco, 1992.

Noddings, Nel. *Caring: A Feminine Approach to Ethics & Moral Education*. Berkeley: University of California Press, 1984.

Chapter VI: Human Sexuality

Bellah, Robert et al. *Habits of the Heart.* New York: Harper & Row Publishers, 1985.

Cancian, Francesca. *Love in America.* New York: Cambridge University Press, 1987.

Keen, Sam. *Fire in the Belly: On Being a Man.* New York: Bantam Books, 1991.

Kimmel, Michael, ed. *Changing Men: New Directions in Research on Men and Masculinity.* Newbury Park, CA: Sage Publications, 1987.

Lipsitz Bem, Sandra. *The Lenses of Gender.* New Haven: Yale University Press, 1993.

Meade, Michael. *Men and the Water of Life: Initiation and the Tempering of Men.* New York: HarperCollins Publishers, 1993.

Nelson, James B. *Between Two Gardens: Reflections on Sexuality and Religious Experience.* New York: The Pilgrim Press, 1983.

The 203rd General Assembly (1991). *Presbyterians and Human Sexuality.* Louisville: Office of General Assembly Presbyterian Church (U.S.A.), 1991.

Weil, Mildred. *Sex and Sexuality: From Repression to Expression.* Lanham, MD: University Press of America, Inc., 1990.

Chapter VII: Envisioning the Future of Ethics

Cobb, John, Jr. *Matters of Life and Death.* Louisville: Westminster Press, 1991.

Gustafson, James. *Ethics from a Theocentric Perspective.* Chicago: University of Chicago Press, 1991.

Lebacqz, Karen. *Professional Ethics: Power and Paradox.* Nashville: Abingdon Press, 1985.

Marty, Martin E., and Kenneth L. Vaux, eds. *Health/Medicine and the Faith Traditions.* Philadelphia: Fortress Press, 1982.

McKenney, Gerald, and Jonathan Sande, eds. *Theological Analyses of the Clinical Encounter.* Dordrecht, the Netherlands: Kluwer Academic Publishers, 1994.

O'Brien, David J., and Thomas A. Shannon, eds. *Catholic Social Thought: The Documentary Heritage.* Maryknoll, NY: Orbis Books, 1992.

Pojman, Louis J., ed. *Environmental Ethics: Readings in Theory and Application.* Boston: Jones & Bartlett Publishers, 1994.

Sherwin, Susan. *No Longer Patient: Feminist Ethics & Health Care.* Philadelphia: Temple University Press, 1992.

NOTES

Introduction
1. Robert Bellah et al., *Habits of the Heart* (New York: Harper & Row Publishers, 1985).

Chapter I: The Emerging Psychosocial and Ethical Individual
1. Paul Tillich, "The Meaning of Health," in S. Lammers & A. Verhey, eds., *On Moral Medicine: Theological Perspectives in Medical Ethics* (Grand Rapids, MI: Wm. B. Eerdmans Publishing Company, 1987), 161-165.

2. Erik Erikson, *Childhood and Society* (New York: W.W. Norton & Co., Inc., 1963).

3. Salvatore L. Maddi, *Personality Theories: A Comparative Analysis*, 5th ed. (Pacific Grove, CA: Brooks/Cole Publishing Company, 1989). William C. Crain, *Theories of Development: Concepts and Applications* (Englewood Cliffs, NJ: Prentice Hall, Inc., 1980).

4. Sigmund Freud, "The Ego and The Id," (1923) as found in John Rickman, M.D., ed., *A General Selection from The Works of Sigmund Freud* (New York: Liveright Publishing Corp., 1957), 210-235. Erikson, *Childhood and Society*.

5. Abraham Maslow, *Toward a Psychology of Being*, 2nd ed. (New York: Van Nostrand Reinhold Company, 1968).

6. Milton Rokeach, *Beliefs, Attitudes and Values: A Theory of Organization and Change* (San Francisco: Jossey-Bass, Inc., 1969).

7. David Brink, *Moral Realism and the Foundation of Ethics* (Cambridge: Cambridge University Press, 1989).

8. William Frankena, *Ethics* (Englewood Cliffs, NJ: Prentice Hall, Inc., 1963). William Kurtines, Margarita Azmitia, and Jacob L. Gewirtz, eds., *The Role of Values in Psychology and Human Development* (New York: John Wiley & Sons, Inc., 1992).

9. Meredith McGuire, *Religion: The Social Context*, 3rd ed. (Belmont, CA: Wadsworth Publishing Co., 1992). Robert Wuthnow, *The Restructuring of American Religion* (Princeton, NJ: Princeton University Press, 1988). Wade Clark Roof and Wm. McKinney, *American Mainline Religion: Its Changing Shape and Future* (New Brunswick, NJ: Rutgers University Press, 1987).

10. Bryan Wilson, *The Social Dimensions of Sectarianism: Sects & New Religious Movements in Contemporary Society* (Oxford; Clarendon Press, 1992). Rodney Stark and William S. Bainbridge, *The Future of Religion: Secularization, Revival and Cult Formation* (Berkeley, CA: University of California Press, 1985).

11. Abd al-Rahman Azzam, *The Eternal Message of Muhammad* (Cambridge: The Islamic Texts Society, 1993), 82-83.

12. Lawrence Kohlberg, "Moral and Religious Education and the Public Schools: A Developmental View," in Theodore Sizer, *Religion and Public Education* (New York: Houghton Mifflin Company, 1967), 164-183.

13. Carol Gilligan, *In a Different Voice: Psychological Theory and Women's Development* (Cambridge, MA: Harvard University Press, 1982). Nancy Chodorow, "Family Structure and Feminine Personality," in M.Z. Rosaldo and L. Lamphere, eds., *Woman, Culture and Society* (Stanford: Stanford University Press, 1974). Janet Lever, "Sex Differences in the Games Children Play," *Social Problems* 23 (1976), 478-87. Barrie Thorne, *Gender Play: Girls and Boys in School* (New Brunswick, NJ: Rutgers University Press, 1993).

236

14. Jean Piaget, "The Rules of The Game," in *Moral Judgment of the Child*, translated by Marjorie Gabain, as found in Howard Gruber and J. Jacques Voneche, eds., *The Essential Piaget* (New York: Basic Books, Inc., 1977), 157-193. Janet Lever, "Sex Differences in the Complexity of Children's Play and Games," *American Sociological Review* 43 (1978), 471-83.

15. Ward J. Fellows, *Religions East and West* (New York: Holt, Rinehart and Winston, 1979).

16. Hans Wolfgang Schumann, *Buddhism* (Wheaton, Il: The Theosophical Publishing House, 1973), 39, 55, 65, 69-79.

17. Ahmed Ali, *Al-Quran: A Contemporary Translation* (Princeton, NJ: Princeton University Press, 1984).

18. Andrea Stone, "There Is No One Kind of Muslim" in *USA Today*, 27 January 1994, Sec. A, p.1-2.

Chapter II: The Emerging Social Self

1. Lawrence Boadt, *Reading the Old Testament* (New York: Paulist Press, 1984), 174-181.

2. Raymond E. Brown, Joseph A. Fitzmeyer, Roland E. Murphy, eds., "Samaritan as a Term of Opprobrium," *The New Jerome Biblical Commentary*, 61:124 (Englewood Cliffs, NJ: Prentice Hall, Inc., 1990), 967.

3. Boadt (1984), 356-358.

4. Raymond E. Brown et al. (1990), "Covenant," 77:74-98, 1297-1301; Joseph Allen, *Love and Conflict: A Covenantal Model of Christian Ethics* (Nashville, TN: Abingdon Press, 1984).

5. Angeles Arrien, *The Four-Fold Way: Walking the Paths of the Warrior, Teacher, Healer, and Visionary* (San Francisco: HarperSanFrancisco Publishers, 1993).

6. Carolyn Merchant, *Radical Ecology: The Search for a Livable World* (New York: Routledge, Chapman & Hall, Inc., 1992), *The Death of Nature: Women, Ecology and the Scientific Revolution* (San Francisco: Harper & Row, Publishers, 1980).

7. Sallie McFague, *The Body of God: An Ecological Theology* (Minneapolis: Augsburg Fortress Press, 1993).

8. Carol S. Robb, ed., *Beverly Wildung Harrison, Making the Connections: Essays in Feminist Social Ethics* (Boston: Beacon Press, 1985); Rosemarie Tong, *Feminist Thought: A Comprehensive Introduction* (San Francisco: Westview Press, 1989).

9. "The Power of Anger in the Work of Love," in Robb (1985), 3-21; see also Harrison's "Theological Reflection in the Struggle for Liberation," in Robb (1985), 235-263.

10. David Hollenbach, *Claims in Conflict: Retrieving and Renewing the Catholic Human Rights Tradition* (New York: Paulist Press, 1979); David J. O'Brien and Thomas Shannon, eds., *Renewing the Earth: Catholic Documents on Peace, Justice and Liberation* (Garden City, NY: Image Books, 1977).

11. Karen Lebacqz, *Six Theories of Justice: Perspectives From Philosophical and Theological Ethics* (Minneapolis: Augsburg Publishing House, 1986).

12. Walter M. Abbott, general editor, *Gaudium et Spes, The Documents of Vatican II* (New York: The America Press, 1966), 199-308.

13. Campaign for Human Development, *Sourcebook on Poverty, Development and Justice* (Washington, DC: U.S. Catholic Conference, 1973).

14. Dennis M. Doyle, *The Church Emerging From Vatican II* (Mystic, CT: Twenty-Third Publications, 1992).

15. Walter M. Abbott, (1966), "Declaration on Religious Freedom," 678-696.

16. Raymond E. Brown et al. (1990), "Biblical Concept of Sin" *The New Jerome Biblical Commentary*, 77:125, 1305.

17. Karen Lebacqz, *Justice in an Unjust World: Foundations for a Christian Approach to Justice* (Minneapolis: Augsburg Publishing House, 1987).

18. Dennis Doyle, *The Church Emerging*, 278-86.

19. Lebacqz (1987).

20. Paul Ramsey, *The Patient as Person* (New Haven: Yale University Press, 1970).

**Chapter III: A Quest for Meaning
and the Development of Values and Principles**

1. Viktor E. Frankl, *Man's Search for Meaning: An Introduction to Logotherapy* (New York: Washington Square Press, Inc., 1963).

2. James W. Fowler, "Faith and the Structuring of Meaning," in Craig Dykstra and Sharon Parks, eds., *Faith Development and Fowler* (Birmingham, AL: Religious Education Press, 1986), 15-42.

3. Richard M. Gula, *Reason Informed by Faith: Foundations of Catholic Morality* (New York: Paulist Press, 1989).

4. Sidney Callahan, *In Good Conscience: Reason and Emotion in Moral Decision Making* (San Francisco: HarperSanFrancisco 1991).

5. James W. Fowler, *Stages of Faith: The Psychology of Human Development and the Quest for Meaning* (San Francisco: HarperSanFrancisco, 1981).

6. Brennan R. Hill, Paul Knitter, and William Madges, *Faith, Religion & Theology: A Contemporary Introduction* (Mystic, CT: Twenty-Third Publications, 1990).

7. Angeles Arrien, *The Four-Fold Way* (San Francisco: HarperSanFrancisco Publishers, 1993).

8. Donald Walhout, *The Good and the Realm of Values* (Notre Dame, IN: University of Notre Dame Press, 1978).

9. William Frankena, *Ethics* (Englewood Cliffs, NJ: Prentice Hall, Inc., 1963).

10. Timothy E. O'Connell, *Principles for a Catholic Morality: Revised Edition* (San Francisco: HarperSanFrancisco, 1990).

11. Michael Walzer, *Spheres of Justice: A Defense of Pluralism and Equality* (New York: Basic Books, Inc., 1983).

12. Alasdair MacIntyre, *A Short History of Ethics* (New York: Collier Books, 1966).

13. United Nations General Assembly, "Universal Declaration of Human Rights" (1948) as copied from *The New Encyclopedia Britannica*, 15th Edition, 12 (1991), 163-164.

14. Albert C. Outler, "The Beginnings of Personhood: Theological Considerations," in Stephen E. Lammers and Allen Verhey, eds., *On Moral Medicine: Theological Perspectives in Medical Ethics* (Grand Rapids, MI: Wm. B. Eerdmans Publishing Company, 1987), 391-396. James M. Gustafson, "The Transcendence of God and the Value of Human Life," in Stephen E. Lammers and Allen Verhey, eds., *On Moral Medicine: Theological Perspectives in Medical Ethics* (Grand Rapids, MI: Wm. B. Eerdmans Publishing Company, 1987), 121-126.

15. United Nations General Assembly, "Universal Declaration of Human Rights" (1948), 163.

16. J.M. Rodwell, *The Koran* (London: J.M. Dent, Orion Publishing Group, 1944), 418.

17. Louis Janssens, "Norms and Priorities in a Love Ethics," *Louvain Studies* 4 (Spring, 1977), 207-238.

Chapter IV: The Role of Conscience in Ethical Decision Making

1. Desmond Doig, *Mother Teresa: Her People and Her Work* (Great Britain: Fount Paperbacks, 1978).

2. Gula, *Reason Informed by Faith*, 130-135; Timothy E. O'Connell, *Principles for a Catholic Morality*, Revised Edition, 1990, 109-114.

3. Michael Goldberg, *Theology & Narrative: A Critical Introduction* (Nashville: Abingdon Press, 1982); James Wm. McClendon, Jr., *Biography as Theology: How Life Stories Can Remake Today's Theologies* (Nashville: Abingdon Press, 1974); Stanley Hauerwas, *Naming the Silences: God, Medicine and the Problem of Suffering* (Grand Rapids, MI: Wm. B. Eerdmans Publishing Company, 1990); Sidney Callahan, "Nurturing Conscience" in *In Good Conscience*, 1991, 206-208.

4. Joseph Allen, *Love & Conflict: A Covenantal Model of Christian Ethics* (Nashville: Abingdon Press, 1984); Reinhold Niebuhr, *Moral Man and Immoral Society* (New York: Charles Scribner's Sons, 1932), 40-41.

5. Katie G. Cannon, *Black Womanist Ethics* (Atlanta, GA: Scholars Press), 1988.

6. Callahan, *In Good Conscience*, 1991.

7. Tom L. Beauchamp and James F. Childress, *Principles of Biomedical Ethics*, 3rd ed. (New York: Oxford University Press, 1989).

8. David L. Bender and Bruno Leone, Series Editors, *The Third World: Opposing Viewpoints* (San Diego: Greenhaven Press, Inc., 1989).

9. John Grisham, *The Client* (New York: Bantam Doubleday Dell Publishing Group, Inc., 1993).

10. Stephen David Ross, *The Nature of Moral Responsibility* (Detroit: Wayne State University Press, 1973).

11. Vernon J. Bourke, *Will in Western Thought: An Historico-Critical Survey* (New York: Sheed & Ward, Inc., 1964), 79-80.

12. B. Jewett, translator, *The Republic and Other Works by Plato* (New York: Anchor Books, Doubleday, 1989).

13. Aristotle, "Nicomachean Ethics," as found in Reginald E. Allen, ed., *Greek Philosophy: Thales to Aristotle*, Edition II (New York: The Free Press, 1985), 384-412.

14. John Locke, "The Second Treatise of Government" as found in Peter Laslett, *John Locke: Two Treatises of Government* (Cambridge: Cambridge University Press, 1989) 265-428.

15. Roger Burggraeve, "Responsibility Precedes Freedom: In Search of a Biblical-Philosophical Foundation of a Personalistic Love Ethic," in Joseph A. Selling, ed., *Personalist Morals* (Leuven, Belgium: Leuven University Press, 1988), 109-132.

16. Albert R. Jonsen, *Responsibility in Modern Religious Ethics* (Washington, DC: Corpus Books, 1968), 153-171.

17. Erik Erikson, "Eight Ages of Man," in Salvatore R. Maddi, *Perspectives on Personality: A Comparative Approach* (Boston: Little, Brown and Company, 1971), 96-114.

18. Paul Schotsmans, "Responsible Involvement and Conscientious Freedom: A Relational Approach to Medical Ethics," in Selling, *Personalist Morals*, 167-184.

19. Howard Harrod, *The Human Center: Moral Agency in the Social World* (Philadelphia: Fortress Press, 1981).

20. Frederick Copleston, *A History of Philosophy: Book I* Vol. II (New York: Bantam Doubleday Dell Publishing Group, 1985) 398-411; Gula, *Reason Informed by Faith*, 220-249; Timothy E. O'Connell, *Principles for a Catholic Morality*, Revised Edition, 1990, 149-173; Dolores L. Christie, *Adequately Considered: An American Perspective on Louis Janssens' Personalist Morals* (Louvain, Belgium: Peeters Press, 1990), 106-119.

21. Timothy McDermott, ed., *St. Thomas Aquinas: Summa Theologiae, A Concise Translation* (Westminster, MD: Christian Classics, 1989).

22. O'Connell, *Principles for a Catholic Morality*, Revised Edition, 1990, 72-74.

23. Eric Mount, Jr., *Conscience and Responsibility* (Richmond, VA: John Knox Press, 1969).

24. Erich Fromm, "Human Nature and Character," in Maddi, *Perspectives on Personality*, 329-351.

25. Christie, *Adequately Considered*, 1990, 68-69; Callahan, 202-204.

26. Lawrence Kohlberg, "Moral and Religious Education and the Public Schools: A Developmental View," in Theodore Sizer, *Religion and Public Education* (New York: Houghton Mifflin Company, 1967), 164-183.

27. Meredith McGuire, *Religion: The Social Context*, 3rd ed. (Belmont, CA: Wadsworth Publishing Co., 1992).

28. Daniel Stevich, *Civil Disobedience and the Christian* (New York: The Seabury Press, 1969), 102-113; Richard McCormick, S.J., *Notes on Moral Theology: 1965 through 1980* (Washington, DC: University Press of America, Inc., 1981), 206-208.

29. Etty Hillesum, *An Interrupted Life: The Diaries of Etty Hillesum, 1941-1943* (New York: Pantheon Books, 1983).

30. United Nations General Assembly, "Universal Declaration of Human Rights" (1948) as copied from *The New Encyclopedia Britannica*, 15th Edition, 12 (1991), 163-164.

31. Gustavo Gutiérrez, *A Theology of Liberation* (Maryknoll, NY: Orbis Books, 1973).

32. Robert McAfee Brown, *Gustavo Gutiérrez: An Introduction to Liberation Theology* (Maryknoll, NY: Orbis Books, 1990).

33. Walter M. Abbott, general editor, *Gaudium et Spes, The Documents of Vatican II* (New York: The America Press, 1966), 199-308.

34. Campaign for Human Development, *Sourcebook on Poverty, Development and Justice* (Washington, DC: U.S. Catholic Conference, 1973), 70-73.

35. Gustavo Gutiérrez, *A Theology of Liberation* (Maryknoll, NY: Orbis Books, 1973); Leonardo Boff, *Way of the Cross—Way of Justice* (Maryknoll, NY: Orbis Books, 1980); Juan Luis Segundo, *The Liberation of Theology* (Maryknoll, NY: Orbis Books, 1976); José Míguez Bonino, *Toward a Christian Political Ethics* (Philadelphia: Fortress Press, 1983).

36. K. C. Abraham, ed., *Third World Theologies: Commonalities and Divergences* (Maryknoll, NY: Orbis Books, 1990), 62-64; Brown, *Gustavo Gutiérrez*, 1990, 13, 73-74.

37. National Conference of Catholic Bishops, "Economic Justice for All: A Pastoral Letter on Catholic Social Teaching and the U.S. Economy," 1986, in David J. O'Brien and Thomas A. Shannon, eds., *Catholic Social Thought: The Documentary Social Heritage* (Maryknoll, NY: Orbis Books, 1992) 572-680; Fred Kammer, *Doing Faithjustice: An Introduction to Catholic Social Thought* (New York: Paulist Press, 1991).

Chapter V: A Practical Method for Ethical Decision Making

1. Timothy O'Connell, *Principles for a Catholic Morality*, Revised Edition, 196-201; Richard Gula, *Reason Informed by Faith*, 265-268; Louis Janssens, "Norms and Principles in a Love Ethics," *Louvain Studies* 3 (1977), 231-235; Richard McCormick, *Notes on Moral Theology: 1965 through 1980*, 529-535.

2. O'Connell, *Principles for a Catholic Morality*, Revised Edition, 211-213; McCormick, *Notes on Moral Theology: 1965 through 1980*, 536.

3. Margaret Hoopes and James Harper, *Birth Order Role & Sibling Patterns in Individual & Family Therapy* (Rockville, MD: Aspen Publishers, Inc., 1987).

4. William F. May, *The Physician's Covenant: Images Of The Healer In Medical Ethics* (Philadelphia: Westminster Press, 1983).

5. W. D. Ross, *The Right and The Good* (Oxford: Clarendon Press, 1930), 16-47.

6. Tom L. Beauchamp and James F. Childress, *Principles of Biomedical Ethics*, 3rd ed. (New York: Oxford University Press, 1989).

7. Alastair V. Campbell, "Caring and Being Cared For," in Stephen Lammers and Allen Verhey, eds., *On Moral Medicine: Theological Perspectives in Medical Ethics* (Grand Rapids: Wm. B. Eerdmans Publishing Company, 1987), 266-272.

8. Nel Noddings, *Caring: A Feminine Approach to Ethics & Moral Education* (Berkeley, CA: University of California Press, 1984).

9. Stanley Hauerwas, "Care," in Lammers and Verhey, *On Moral Medicine*, 262-266.

10. Sara T. Fry, "The Role of Caring in a Theory of Nursing Ethics," in Helen Holmes and Laura Purdy, eds., *Feminist Perspectives in Medical Ethics* (Bloomington: Indiana University Press, 1992), 93-106.

11. This approach was originally presented in Jeremiah J. McCarthy and Judith A. Caron, *Medical Ethics: A Catholic Guide to Healthcare Decisions* (Liguori, MO: Liguori Publications, 1990).

12. The author is grateful for insights from the work of Judith Wilson Ross with S. Corrine Bayley, Vicki Michel, and Deborah Pugh, *Handbook for Hospital Ethics Committees* (Chicago: American Hospital Publications, Inc., 1986), 25-27, in "A Process for Approaching A Bioethical Dilemma" prepared in 1985 by the Center for Bioethics, St. Joseph Health System, Orange, CA, and in other sources.

13. Basic writings on these key biomedical dilemmas, the issues that surround them, and other case studies can be found in Paul Ramsey, *Ethics at the Edges of Life: Medical and Legal Intersections* (New Haven: Yale University Press, 1980); Thomas Shannon, *Bioethics*, Revised, (Ramsey, NJ: Paulist Press, 1981); Robert M. Veatch, *Case Studies in Medical Ethics* (Cambridge: Harvard University Press, 1977).

Chapter VI: Human Sexuality

1. Albert Klassen, Colin Williams, and Eugene Levitt, *Sex and Morality in the U.S.* (Middletown, CT: Wesleyan University Press, 1989).

2. Mildred Weil, *Sex and Sexuality: From Repression to Expression* (Lanham, MD: University Press of America, Inc., 1990); Patricia Beattie Jung and Ralph F. Smith, *Heterosexism: An Ethical Challenge* (Albany, NY: State University of New York Press, 1993).

3. The 203rd General Assembly (1991), *Presbyterians and Human Sexuality* (Louisville, KY: Office of General Assembly Presbyterian Church [U.S.A.], 1991).

4. See also James B. Nelson, *Between Two Gardens: Reflections on Sexuality and Religious Experience* (New York: The Pilgrim Press, 1983), 5-6.

5. Patricia Ward Scalstas, "Do Feminist Ethics Counter Feminist Aims?" in Eve Browning Cole and Susan Coultrap McQuin, *Explorations in Feminist Ethics: Theory and Practice* (Bloomington, IN: Indiana University Press, 1992), 15.

6. Philip Turner, ed., *Men and Women: Sexual Ethics in Turbulent Times* (Cambridge, MA: Cowley Publications, 1989); Mary Vetterling-Braggin, ed., *"Femininity," "Masculinity," and "Androgyny"* (Totowa, NJ: Littlefield, Adams & Co., 1982); Ruth T. Barnhouse and Urban T. Holmes, III (eds.), *Male and Female: Christian Approaches to Sexuality* (New York: Seabury Press, 1976).

7. Michael Kimmel, "Rethinking 'Masculinity': New Directions in Research," as found in Michael Kimmel, ed., *Changing Men: New Directions in Research on Men and Masculinity* (Newbury Park, CA: Sage Publications, 1987), 9-24.

8. Anne Fausto-Sterling, *Myths of Gender: Biological Theories and Women and Men* (New York: Basic Books, Inc., 1985), 80-81.

9. Gerda Lerner, *The Creation of Patriarchy* (New York: Oxford University Press, 1986).

10. Elizabeth Janeway, *Man's World, Woman's Place: A Study in Social Mythology* (New York: William Morrow and Co., Inc., 1971).

11. Sandra Lipsitz Bem, *The Lenses of Gender* (New Haven: Yale University Press, 1993), 2-3, 133-175.

12. Harry Brod, "A Case for Men's Studies," in Kimmel, *Changing Men: New Directions in Research on Men and Masculinity*, 263-277.

13. Sam Keen, *Fire in the Belly: On Being a Man* (New York: Bantam Books, 1991).

14. Joseph H. Pleck, "American Fathering in Historical Perspective," as found in Kimmel, ed., *Changing Men: New Directions in Research on Men and Masculinity*, 83-97.

15. Robert Moore and Douglas Gillette, *The Magician Within* (New York: Avon Books, 1993).

16. Robert Bly, *Iron John: A Book About Men* (New York: Vintage Books, 1990).

17. Michael Meade, *Men and the Water of Life: Initiation and the Tempering of Men* (New York: HarperCollins Publishers, 1993).

18. Francesca Cancian, *Love in America* (New York: Cambridge University Press, 1987).

19. Robert Bellah, et al., *Habits of the Heart* (New York: Harper & Row Publishers, 1985).

20. Rita Nakashima Brock, *Journeys By Heart* (New York: Crossroad, 1994); Michael S. Kimmel, "Rethinking 'Masculinity'" in *Changing Men*; Judith Jordan, Alexandra Kaplan, Jean Baker Miller et al., *Women's Growth in Connection* (New York: Guilford Press, 1991); Weil, *Sex and Sexuality* (1990.

21. Weil, 8-14; Cancian, 39-46; Janeway, 200-202.

22. Abraham H. Maslow, " Growth and Self Actualization Psychology," in Salvatore R. Maddi, *Perspectives on Personality: A Comparative Approach* (Boston: Little, Brown and Company, 1971), 216-219.

23. Jean Baker Miller, "The Development of Women's Sense of Self," in Jordan et al., *Women's Growth in Connection*, 11-26.

24. Zick Rubin and E.B. McNeil, *The Psychology of Being Human* (New York: Harper & Row Publishers, 1981).

25. Laura Mulvey, "Visual Pleasure and Narrative Cinema," in Maggie Humm, ed., *Modern Feminisms: Political, Literary, Cultural* (New York: Columbia University Press, 1992), 348-53.

26. Klassen et al., 267-71; Weil, 65.

27. Philip S. Keane, *Sexual Morality: A Catholic Perspective* (New York: Paulist Press, 1977), 3-19; James B. Nelson, *Between Two Gardens: Reflections on Sexuality and Religious Experience,* 56-95.

28. James B. Nelson, *Embodiment: An Approach to Sexuality and Christian Theology* (Minneapolis, MN: Augsburg Publishing House, 1978), 14-15, 37-69; James B. Nelson, *Between Two Gardens: Reflections on Sexuality and Religious Experience,* 72-74; Rita Brock, *Journeys by Heart,* 4-17; Rita Manning, *Speaking From the Heart: A Feminist Perspective on Ethics* (Lanham, MD: Rowman & Littlefield Publishers, Inc., 1992).

29. Vincent J. Genovesi, *In Pursuit of Love: Catholic Morality and Human Sexuality* (Collegeville, MN: The Liturgical Press, 1987); Ruth T. Barnhouse and Urban T. Holmes, III, eds., *Male and Female: Christian Approaches to Sexuality* (New York: Seabury Press, 1976); Katie G. Cannon, *Black Womanist Ethics* (Atlanta: Scholars Press, 1988); Anthony Kosnik et al., *Human Sexuality: New Directions in American Catholic Thought* (New York: Paulist Press, 1977); Eve Browning Cole and Susan Coultrap McQuin, *Explorations in Feminist Ethics: Theory and Practice* (Bloomington, IN: Indiana University Press, 1992).

30. Jack Dominian, *Dynamics of Marriage: Love, Sex and Growth from a Christian Perspective* (Mystic, CT: Twenty-Third Publications, 1993).

31. Keane, 4-13; Nelson, *Between Two Gardens,* 56-84; Dominian, 68-71; Kosnik et al., 33-52.

32. Keane, 8-10; Nelson, *Between Two Gardens,* 59-64.

33. Brock, 3-24.

34. Nelson, *Between Two Gardens,* 60-64, 71-85; Keane, 20-56; Kosnik et al., 44-88.

35. Walter M. Abbott, general editor, "Constitution on the Church in the Modern World," *The Documents of Vatican II* (New York: The America Press, 1966), #49-51, 252-256.

36. Pope John Paul II, "The Transmission of Life" (Aug. 22, 1984), *The Pope Speaks,* 29: no. 4, 1984, 349-51 as found in Kevin O'Rourke, O.P. and Philip Boyle, *Medical Ethics: Sources of Catholic Teachings,* 2nd ed. (Washington, D.C.: Georgetown University Press, 1993), 76-77.

37. Sallie McFague, *Models of God: Theology for an Ecological, Nuclear Age* (Philadelphia: Fortress Press, 1987).

38. Beverly Wildung Harrison, "Sexuality and Social Policy," in Carol S. Robb, ed., *Beverly Wildung Harrison, Making The Connections: Essays in Feminist Social Ethics* (Boston: Beacon Press, 1985), 83-114.

Chapter VII: Envisioning the Future of Ethics

1. Robert Frost, "The Road Not Taken," as found in Laurence Perrine, *Sound and Sense: An Introduction to Poetry,* 7th ed. (San Diego: Harcourt Brace Jovanovich, Publishers, 1987), 78.

2. Martin E. Marty, "Tradition and the Traditions in Health/Medicine and Religion," as found in Martin E. Marty and Kenneth L. Vaux, eds., *Health/Medicine and The Faith Traditions* (Philadelphia: Fortress Press, 1982), 3-26.

3. United States Catholic Bishops, "Economic Justice for All: A Pastoral Letter on Catholic Social Teaching and the U.S. Economy" (1986), as found in David J. O'Brien and Thomas A. Shannon, eds., *Catholic Social Thought: The Documentary Heritage* (Maryknoll, NY: Orbis Books, 1992), 572-680.

4. Robert Wuthnow, *The Restructuring of American Religion: Society & Faith Since World War II* (Princeton, NJ: Princeton University Press, 1988).

5. *The Book of Discipline of the United Methodist Church (1992),* (Nashville: The

United Methodist Publishing House, 1992), 90-91.

6. Albert Schweitzer, "Reverence for Life," as found in Louis J. Pojman, ed., *Environmental Ethics: Readings in Theory and Application* (Boston: Jones & Bartlett Publishers, 1994), 65-71.

7. The Covenantal Model is also found in John Cobb, Jr., *Matters of Life and Death* (Louisville: Westminster Press, 1991); James Gustafson, *Ethics from a Theocentric Perspective* (Chicago: University of Chicago Press, 1991).

8. Gerald McKenney and Jonathan Sande, eds., *Theological Analyses of the Clinical Encounter* (Dordrecht, the Netherlands: Kluwer Academic Publishers, 1994).

9. Tom Beauchamp and James Childress, *Principles of Biomedical Ethics*, 3rd ed. (New York: Oxford University Press, 1988).

10. The Contextual Model is found in Stanley Hauerwas, *Naming the Silences: God, Medicine and the Problem of Suffering* (Grand Rapids, MI: Wm. B. Eerdmans Publishing Company, 1990); Karen Lebacqz, *Professional Ethics: Power and Paradox* (Nashville: Abingdon Press, 1985); Susan Sherwin, *No Longer Patient: Feminist Ethics & Health Care* (Philadelphia: Temple University Press, 1992); Richard Zaner, "Voices and Time: The Venture of Clinical Ethics," in *The Journal of Medicine and Philosophy*,18, #1 (1993), 9-31.

Index

245